Latin America

Regional Studies Series

The Regional Studies Series

Africa
China
Europe

The Subcontinent of India
Japan and Korea
Latin America
The Middle East and North Africa
Russia and the Commonwealth

Latin America

Regional Studies Series

Consultant
Lois Athey

GLOBE BOOK COMPANY
A Division of Simon & Schuster
Paramus, New Jersey

Lois Athey

Lois Athey earned her B.A. at Smith College and her M.A. in political science at Columbia University. Her Ph.D. in political science, with specialization in Latin America, is also from Columbia University. Lois Athey has lived and worked in Latin America for a number of years, including six years in Chile working at an urban research institute and teaching political science. She has published studies on Latin American political and housing issues and has worked as a research analyst at the Library of Congress.

Area Specialist: Daniel J. Mugan, president, Association of Teachers of Latin American Studies

Reviewers: Steven Wolfson, Assistant Principal: Supervision, Social Studies, Fort Hamilton High School, Brooklyn, New York, and Angelo Cabeza, social studies teacher, John Dewey High School, New York, New York

Cover Image: The picture on the cover shows a railroad station in Buenos Aires, Argentina.
Maps: Mapping Specialists, Ltd.
Graphs, Diagrams, and Charts: Keithley & Associates

Photograph acknowlegments are on page 252.

ISBN 835-90415-6

Printed in the United States of America   5 6 7 8 9 10 96

CONTENTS

Graphs, Charts, and Diagrams

The America of Moctezuma and Atahualpa,
the aromatic America of Columbus, . . . our America,
trembling with hurricanes, trembling with Love: . . .
Our America lives. And dreams. And loves.
And it is the daughter of the Sun. . . .

—Rubén Darío

Latin America

UNITED STATES

ATLANTIC
OCEAN

Rio Grande

Tropic of
Cancer

Bermuda (U.K.)

Gulf of
Mexico

Nassau
★ BAHAMAS

Turks & Caicos Islands (U.K.)
Santo Domingo **DOMINICAN REPUBLIC**
Puerto Rico (U.S.)

Havana
CUBA

MEXICO

Mexico
City ★

Belmopan
BELIZE

Port-au-Prince **HAITI**
Kingston
JAMAICA

Virgin Islands (U.S.) and **British Virgin Islands** (U.K.)
Basseterre **SAINT KITTS & NEVIS**
Anguilla (U.K.)
Saint John's **ANTIGUA & BARBUDA**
Guadeloupe (Fr.)
Roseau **DOMINICA**
Castries **SAINT LUCIA**
Bridgetown **BARBADOS**
Kingstown **SAINT VINCENT & THE GRENADINES**
Saint George's **GRENADA**
Port-of-Spain **TRINIDAD & TOBAGO**

Guatemala City
GUATEMALA

Caribbean Sea

Montserrat (U.K.)
Martinique (Fr.)

San Salvador
EL SALVADOR

Tegucigalpa
HONDURAS

Aruba (Neth.)

Netherland
Antilles
(Neth.)

Managua
NICARAGUA

Caracas

**PACIFIC
OCEAN**

San José
COSTA RICA

Panama City
PANAMA

Bogotá
★

VENEZUELA

GUYANA

Georgetown

Paramaribo **SURINAME**

French Guiana (Fr.)

Galápagos Islands
(Ecuador)

COLOMBIA

Equator

N

Quito
★
ECUADOR

Amazon River

PERU

Lima

B R A Z I L

Brasília

**PACIFIC
OCEAN**

BOLIVIA
★ La Paz
Sucre
★

PARAGUAY

Tropic of
Capricorn

CHILE

Asunción

ATLANTIC
OCEAN

A R G E N T I N A

Santiago
★

URUGUAY

Buenos
Aires ★

★ Montevideo

Río de la Plata

0   1000 MILES
0   1000 KILOMETERS

★ Capital city

Falkland Islands (U.K.,
claimed by Argentina;
called **Islas Malvinas**)

Cape Horn

1 *The Land*

Latin America is the vast area located south and southeast of the United States. It extends from the northern border of Mexico, southward to the tip of South America, and includes the islands of the West Indies.

WHAT AND WHERE IS LATIN AMERICA?

The name "Latin America" was given to the area because it was settled mainly by people from Spain and Portugal. Most of the people of the region speak Spanish or Portuguese. These languages derive from Latin, the language of the ancient Roman Empire. In addition, in most of the area, the laws are based on ancient Roman law and on the Napoleonic Code of France, another Latin nation. As in Spain and Portugal, Roman Catholicism is the official religion of most of the region. The architecture of many Latin American cities and towns shows the influence of Roman, Portuguese, and Spanish styles. It is important to remember, however, that "Latin America," while a convenient term, is not entirely accurate. There are many sections of the region where the dominant culture is not Latin at all, but Indian or African, or in a few cases, English or Dutch.

The Countries of Latin America. Latin America includes 33 independent nations and about a dozen semi-independent or dependent islands or other areas. Latin America can be divided into four main geographical areas: South America, Central America, Mexico, and Caribbean America. The chart on page 2 lists the countries and territories of these areas. An "I" indicates that the country is independent.

1

Countries and Territories of Latin America

AREA	COUNTRY OR TERRITORY
South America	Argentina (I), Bolivia (I), Brazil (I), Chile (I), Colombia (I), Ecuador (I), Falkland Islands (United Kingdom; claimed by Argentina, which calls them the Malvinas), French Guiana (France), Guyana (I), Paraguay (I), Peru (I), Suriname (I), Uruguay (I), Venezuela (I)
Central America	Belize (I), Costa Rica (I), El Salvador (I), Guatemala (I), Honduras (I), Nicaragua (I), Panama (I)
Mexico	Mexico (I)
Caribbean America	Greater Antilles: Cuba (I), Dominican Republic (I), Haiti (I), Jamaica (I), Puerto Rico (U.S.)
	Lesser Antilles: *Windward Islands:* Barbados (I), Grenada (I), Martinique (France), Saint Lucia (I) Saint Vincent and the Grenadines (I) *Leeward Islands:* Anguilla (United Kingdom), Antigua and Barbuda (I), British Virgin Islands (United Kingdom), Dominica (I), Guadeloupe (France), Montserrat (United Kingdom), Netherlands Antilles (Netherlands), St. Christopher and Nevis (I), Virgin Islands (U.S.), Aruba (Neth.), Trinidad and Tobago(I)
	Others: Bahamas (I) and Bermuda (United Kingdom) in the Atlantic Ocean, not the Caribbean Sea; Cayman Islands (United Kingdom), Turks and Caicos Islands (United Kingdom)

Location and Size. Latin America occupies the southern portion of the continent of North America and the entire continent of South America. Look closely at the map facing page 1 and you will note that Latin America lies south and *east* of the United States. See where the meridian 80° west longitude cuts Latin America.

Latin America is bordered on the north by the United States, on the west by the Pacific Ocean, and on the east by the Atlantic Ocean. In the south, it is separated from Antarctica by a wide body of water called the Drake Passage, which connects the Atlantic and Pacific oceans.

Latin America extends from 33° north latitude to 56° south latitude, the greatest latitudinal range of any world region. As a consequence, it has a highly diverse climate and geography. A large part of Latin America lies between the Tropic of Cancer and the Tropic of Capricorn, a region generally known as the **tropics**.

Much of Latin America is very far away from the United States. For example, the city of Recife, in Brazil, is almost the same distance from Miami, Florida, as it is from Madrid. The northeastern coast of Brazil near Recife is closer to Europe than to any part of the United States. The airline distance between New York and Buenos Aires, Argentina, is 5,300 miles.

Larger than the United States and Canada combined, Latin America has an area of 8.7 million square miles. From north to south, the land stretches more than 6,000 miles, from the northern border of Mexico to the southern tip of Chile. Its greatest width, from eastern Brazil to northwestern Peru, is 3,100 miles. The nations of Latin America vary greatly in size—from Brazil, almost as large as the entire United States, to some of the island republics in the West Indies, which are smaller than New York City.

Latin America is a physically varied region. All four of the world's major landforms—mountains, hills, plateaus, and plains—are found here. The major rivers of the region are found in South America. Latin America as a whole has relatively few large or important lakes.

PHYSICAL FEATURES

Mountains. A major feature of Latin America's geography is the chain of mountains that extends through Mexico into Central America and then continues along the entire west coast of South America. These mountains are a continuation of the Rocky Mountains of the United States and Canada.

3

A view of Mt. Illimani, one of the highest peaks in the Andean mountain range. The city of La Paz, Bolivia, is in the foreground.

In Mexico the mountains separate into two chains. These are the Sierra Madre Occidental, or Western Sierra Madre, and the Sierra Madre Oriental, or Eastern Sierra Madre. Between these two mountain chains lies the Central Plateau, Mexico's largest and most important region. In Central America, the eastern chain continues into the Caribbean Sea. Some of the mountaintops rise above the water to form the islands of the Greater Antilles. The western chain continues southward through Central America before it levels out in Panama.

In South America, the mountains are called the Andes. The "backbone" of South America, the Andes are the longest mountain range in the world and the highest mountains in the Western Hemisphere. Forty-eight peaks in the Andes are over 20,000 feet, with the highest, Aconcagua (ak-uhn-KAHG-wuh), in Argentina, reaching 22,834 feet. Only several Asian mountain chains, including the Himalayas, are higher.

The Andes vary in width from about 200 miles in Ecuador to about 400 miles in Bolivia. Travel through them from east to west is extremely difficult. Some of the gaps between the peaks are choked by tropical rain forest. Others—even at the equator—are closed by snow for much of the year. Because they are so rugged, these mountains have played a major role in Latin America's history. They have hindered travel, trade, and communication and prevented exploration and development.

Rivers. The principal rivers of Latin America are the Amazon, the Río de la Plata, the Orinoco, and the São Francisco. They are all located in South America. (See map on page 6.)

The *Amazon*, the longest river in Latin America, is the second longest river in the world. It flows for 4,080 miles. Most of its waters are in Brazil, but some of its more than 200 tributaries reach into Peru, Bolivia, Ecuador, Colombia, and Venezuela. Several of the tributaries of the Amazon are major rivers in their own right, over 1,500 miles long.

The source of the Amazon is in the Peruvian Andes, only 100 miles from the Pacific Ocean on the west coast of the continent. The river generally travels from west to east, before emptying into the Atlantic Ocean at Belém, Brazil. Oceangoing ships can navigate the Amazon for more than 2,300 miles, up to the inland port city of Iquitos, in Peru. A wide variety of reptiles, birds, and fish can be found in and along the Amazon. One of the most fascinating species is the piranha, a small fish that often attacks and dangerously wounds humans and large animals that come into its waters.

The Amazon carries 20 percent of the total fresh water in the world. Its **estuary,** or partially enclosed body of water connected with the open sea and affected by its tides, is 207 miles wide. The river discharges more than 12 times the volume of water as does the Mississippi River. Marajó (meh-reh-ZHOH) Island, located in the estuary, is as large as southern New England. Many of the people who live along the Amazon or its tributaries have to build their houses on stilts to protect them from flooding.

The second largest river system in South America and its most important commercial waterway is the *Río de la Plata* (REE-oh-duh-la PLAHT-uh), or "river of silver." The Río de la Plata is an estuary formed by the Paraná and Uruguay rivers and is 150 miles across at its mouth. It serves three countries: Argentina, Uruguay, and Paraguay. Argentina and Uruguay are often called the countries of the Plata.

The Río de la Plata drains an area of 1.2 million square miles in Argentina, Bolivia, Brazil, Uruguay, and Paraguay. It is relatively shallow, ranging from eight to eighteen feet, and its shores are lined with mud flats. However, during the flood season, ocean ships can travel up it for more than 1,000 miles to Asunción, the capital of Paraguay. There are over 200 ports along this lengthy river system. However, the two most highly developed, Buenos Aires (BWAY-nehs EHR-eez) in Argentina and Montevideo (mahn-tuh-vuh-DAY-oh) in Uruguay, dominate the region. Buenos Aires is one of the world's major seaports. It is second only to New

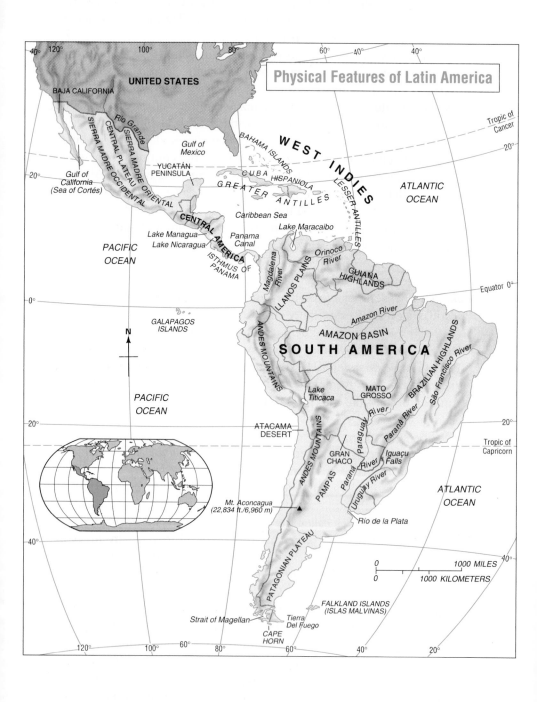

Physical Features of Latin America

UNITED STATES

BAJA CALIFORNIA

Rio Grande

SIERRA MADRE OCCIDENTAL

CENTRAL PLATEAU

SIERRA MADRE ORIENTAL

Gulf of Mexico

YUCATÁN PENINSULA

Gulf of California (Sea of Cortés)

BAHAMA ISLANDS

WEST INDIES

CUBA

HISPANIOLA

GREATER ANTILLES

LESSER ANTILLES

ATLANTIC OCEAN

Tropic of Cancer

20°

CENTRAL AMERICA

Caribbean Sea

Lake Managua

Lake Nicaragua

Panama Canal

ISTHMUS OF PANAMA

Lake Maracaibo

Orinoco River

GUIANA HIGHLANDS

Magdalena River

LLANOS PLAINS

PACIFIC OCEAN

GALAPAGOS ISLANDS

N

Amazon River

AMAZON BASIN

SOUTH AMERICA

Equator 0°

ANDES MOUNTAINS

BRAZILIAN HIGHLANDS

São Francisco River

Lake Titicaca

MATO GROSSO

PACIFIC OCEAN

20°

ATACAMA DESERT

Paraguay River

Paraná River

Tropic of Capricorn

20°

ANDES MOUNTAINS

GRAN CHACO

Paraná River

Iguaçu Falls

Uruguay River

PAMPAS

ATLANTIC OCEAN

Mt. Aconcagua (22,834 ft./6,960 m)

Rio de la Plata

40°

PATAGONIAN PLATEAU

0   1000 MILES

0   1000 KILOMETERS

40°

FALKLAND ISLANDS (ISLAS MALVINAS)

Strait of Magellan

Tierra Del Fuego

CAPE HORN

120°   100°   80°   60°   40°   20°

York in the volume of its trade. The principal exports are meat and grain.

The *Orinoco* (oh-ruh-NOH-koh), is Latin America's third largest river system. It rises in the Andes Mountains and snakes for 1,600 miles through Venezuela before emptying into the Atlantic Ocean. The Orinoco drains an area of 450,000 square miles, including most of Venezuela and about one-quarter of Colombia. Ciudad Bolivár (see-YOO-dahd boh-LEE-vahr), in Venezuela, is the most important city on the Orinoco. It is a seaport, even though it is 270 miles from the river's swampy mouth.

In the Brazilian Highlands, the São Francisco (sow fruhn-sis-koh) rises and flows northward for 1,730 miles. Then it twists around to the southeast and empties into the Atlantic. The river has a number of rapids, and the 262-foot-high Paulo Afonso Falls, located at the bend of the river, are an obstacle to navigation. Nevertheless, Brazilians have used the São Francisco to penetrate the interior since colonial times.

Lakes. There are few large lakes in Latin America. Perhaps the best known is Lake Titicaca (tit-i-KAHK-uh), which has an area of 3,100 square miles. Located 12,497 feet above sea level on the border between Bolivia and Peru, it is the highest navigable lake in the world. Other South American lakes are Lake Maracaibo (mahr-uh-KEYE-boh), in Venezuela's oil fields, and Lake Poopó (poh-oh-POH), in Bolivia. These lakes are all economically important.

The largest lake in Central America is Lake Nicaragua, located on the border between Nicaragua and Costa Rica. It has an area of 2,170 square miles. It is fed from the smaller Lake Managua, on which the Nicaraguan capital of Managua is located. The San Juan River connects these lakes with the Caribbean Sea, and the river and lakes serve as important highways into the interior.

In addition, Mexico and Guatemala have several sizable mountain lakes of considerable beauty. Fish from these lakes are important sources of food for the local populations. There are also a number of beautiful mountain lakes in Chile and Argentina.

Physical Geography and Communications. An area's physical geography has an important effect upon its people and their way of life. In Latin America, vast mountains, long unnavigable rivers, and dense tropical forests have isolated the people from each other as well as from the rest of the world.

In recent times, however, modern technology has enabled Latin

Americans to overcome many of these obstacles of nature. Against all odds and under the most difficult circumstances, effective systems of transportation and communication have gradually been developed.

One major engineering achievement was the construction in the nineteenth century of a railroad linking the sea-level city of Lima, Peru, with copper mines in Cerro de Pasco (SEHR-roh thay PAHS-koh), one of the highest cities in the world. This railroad took 23 years to complete. It climbs through a series of spiral tunnels inside mountains, moving backward and forward until it reaches the 13,973-foot altitude at which Cerro de Pasco is located.

Another major feat was the construction of the Panama Canal, connecting the Atlantic and Pacific oceans, in the early twentieth century. Working to clear mosquito-infested swamps, over 35,000 men toiled for years—and many lost their lives—to complete this project.

A particularly effective way to deal with Latin America's geographic problems is through air travel. With the development of the airplane, many Latin American countries built local airports to make it easier to transport goods and people. In Colombia, Brazil, Chile, and Bolivia, many towns can be reached only by air or by sea.

Latin Americans have made much progress in conquering their environment. However, many challenges still remain. For example, a vast network of roads has been built from Mexico in the north to Chile in the south. But this highway, known as the Pan American highway system, remained unfinished in the early 1990s. A swampy jungle in southern Panama has defeated all efforts to build a bridge across it.

Although modern transportation and communications facilities do exist, the people of Latin America are generally poor, and cannot afford to use them. Throughout Latin America, women are seen carrying baskets, packages, and firewood on their heads. In the high Andes of Bolivia and Peru, the Indians rely on camel-like animals called llamas to carry their burdens. These animals are slow and stubborn. When they feel tired or overloaded, llamas simply lie down and refuse to move.

SOUTH AMERICA

Because of its size and vast extent, South America has great geographic variety. Almost every type of landform, climate, vegetation, and resource is found in some area of South America. One important fact to remember about the climate: Much of the land of South America lies south of the equator, in the Southern Hemisphere. Seasons are the reverse of those in the Northern Hemisphere. This means that in June, July, and August, when it is summer in the United States, it is winter in Brazil. And in December, January, and February, when it is winter in the United States, it is summer in Brazil.

Most of South America enjoys a tropical or warm climate. However, contrary to what many people think, this does not mean that South American countries are very hot. For example, the average maximum temperature in Rio de Janeiro is 79°F. The relative humidity, on the other hand, is very high, averaging 78 percent.

All of the countries of South America except Chile have jungles. There are also many miles of desert. Severe winters, as we know them in the United States, are absent from South America. This is because of the influence of the ocean and the fact that most of South America is in the low latitudes.

South America, the largest area of Latin America, can be divided into ten major regions. These are the Patagonian Plateau, the pampas, the Gran Chaco, the Brazilian Highlands, the Mato Grosso, the Amazon Basin, the llanos, the Guiana Highlands, the Andes, and the southern Pacific coast.

The Patagonian Plateau.   At the southern tip of South America, the Patagonian Plateau includes a small portion of Chile and one quarter of Argentina. Visiting the area in 1520, the Portuguese explorer Ferdinand Magellan (muh-JEL-uhn) and his crew noted that the Indians of the region had big feet—*patagones* in Spanish. Ever since, the region has been called Patagonia, the "land of the big feet."

Patagonia is bleak and forlorn and almost unpopulated. It is an area of sharp contrasts and desolate beauty. In Chilean Patagonia, glaciers and mountains rise steeply from the sea. Many fiords cut into the coast. Storms blow in from the Pacific Ocean, and the region is cold and humid.

Argentine Patagonia is also a land of rugged coasts and deep canyons. However, oceans moderate the climate somewhat, and sheep graze on the grasses that grow here. Wool and meat from the sheep and oil and natural gas are the only commercial products of the region.

The Pampas.   Directly north of Patagonia, in central Argentina and extending into Uruguay, lie the **pampas**. *Pampas* is an old Quechua Indian word meaning land mass or space, and the pampas are a vast grassy, treeless plain that stretches from the Andes Mountains to the Atlantic Ocean. They are similar to the prairies of North America.

Northwestern Patagonia in Argentina has large sheep ranches that require very few workers except at shearing time.

The climate of the pampas varies according to distance from the Andes Mountains. In the west, the pampas are dry and almost barren. This area, which is close to the Andes, is in a **rain shadow**. The winds in this area normally blow from the Pacific, in the west. These winds drop most of their rain on the western side of the Andes, before they reach the pampas. As a result, the western pampas may get as little as 12 inches of rain per year.

In the eastern pampas, however, rain is plentiful, usually 30 or 40 inches per year—as much as 60 inches per year in Uruguay. The areas nearer the Andes have higher elevations and, as a result, cooler temperatures. The humid lowlands in the east have higher temperatures.

The eastern pampas have some of the richest soils in the world and are one of Latin America's most prosperous agricultural regions. Cattle graze on the grassy plains, and grains such as wheat and corn grow in abundance. Meat, wool, hides, and grain are the region's major exports, and important deposits of oil, natural gas, and uranium have been found. The major city of the pampas is Buenos Aires, the capital of Argentina.

The Gran Chaco. North of the pampas is a region called the Gran Chaco. This extensive lowland plain covers 280,000 square miles in Argentina, Paraguay, Bolivia, and Brazil. Most of the Gran Chaco is arid land, dotted with swamps during the rainy season and dense stretches of impenetrable jungle. It is extremely hot throughout the year. Because of its extreme climate, remote location, and obstructions to navigation and communication, most of the Gran Chaco is thinly settled and undeveloped, even today. However, tannin, a substance used to finish leather, is extracted from the abundant quebracho trees of the area's forests. An interesting sight on the Gran Chaco is the *palo borracho,* or drunken-branch, tree, so called because of the precarious angle at which it grows. This strange tree has a thorn-studded trunk and produces huge pods shaped like avocados.

The only habitable portion of the Gran Chaco is in the east, in Paraguay. This area, which has a pleasant, subtropical climate, produces commercial timber and a wide variety of crops, particularly the bitter tea known as **yerba maté**. Workers strip the maté leaves off the trees and then dry the leaves over small fires. The dried leaves are loaded onto mules and shipped to the nearest railroad. The leaves are then ground and dried further. To drink maté one pours the maté leaves and boiling water into a hollowed-out gourd. The hot tea is sipped through a metal straw.

The Brazilian Highlands. To the north and east of the Gran Chaco lie the Brazilian Highlands, a vast upland plateau ranging in elevation from 1,000 to 9,500 feet above sea level. The Brazilian Highlands cover almost all of eastern Brazil and form 2,000 miles of that country's Atlantic coastline. Most of Brazil's richest farmlands, important mineral reserves, and major population centers, including São Paulo and Belo Horizonte, are located in the Highlands.

Because of their great extent, the Brazilian Highlands stretch through several climate and vegetation zones. In the southwest, where Brazil meets Argentina, lie the breathtaking Iguaçú Falls. About 2.5 miles wide, these waters tumble down from a height of 230 feet (higher than Niagara Falls). Their beauty is enhanced by the orchids, ferns, birds, and butterflies commonly found around them. Just west of the Iguaçú Falls is the 643-foot-high Itaipú (ee-tah-eh-POO) Dam, part of the world's largest hydroelectric project.

Farther north is an area of grasslands. The climate in this area is warm and rainfall is abundant—as much as 80 inches per year. Brazil's famous coffee-growing plantations are located here, on mountain slopes 3,000 to 7,000 feet above sea level. Coffee is harvested almost all year round. It is not unusual to see flowers, buds, and berries all on the same tree. Men, women, and children pick the ripe berries, which are then taken to a warehouse to be washed. The washed berries are spread out in the sun to dry for several days, or even weeks. When dried, the berries

Climates of Latin America

40° 120° 100° 80° 60° 40° 40°

Tropic of Cancer
20°

Gulf of Mexico

ATLANTIC OCEAN

20°

★Mexico City

Caribbean Sea

Caracas★

N

★Bogotá

Equator 0°

PACIFIC OCEAN

0°

Manaus•

•Recife

Lima★

Belo Horizonte•
20°

Rio de Janeiro•
São Paulo•

Tropic of Capricorn

Buenos Aires★

ATLANTIC OCEAN

0   1000 MILES
0   1000 KILOMETERS

40°

Legend:

- Rain forest *(hot/rainy)*
- Savanna *(hot/very wet and very dry seasons)*
- Steppe *(hot summers; cold winters/ light rainfall)*
- Desert *(hot/dry)*
- Mediterranean *(mild, moist winters/ dry, warm summers)*
- Humid subtropical *(long, humid summers/ short, mild winters)*
- Marine *(cool/rainy)*
- Vertical *(temperature and rainfall vary with altitude)*

120° 100° 80° 60° 40° 20°

are put into a machine that removes the outer husks. The beans are then bagged according to size and shipped to markets throughout the world.

A narrow coastal strip in the eastern Highlands has a warm, humid climate moderated by sea breezes. This coastal region has been the center of Brazil's sugar industry since colonial times. It contains the important port cities of Santos, Rio de Janeiro (REE-oh duh zhuh-NAYR-oh), and Salvador.

Inland from the coastal strip, the northeastern Brazilian Highlands are an arid clay desert. The region frequently suffers from an almost total lack of rainfall. Some grazing is practiced, but the region is very poor, and drought has been an ongoing problem for much of the last 20 years.

The Mato Grosso.   West of the Brazilian Highlands, stretching across southwestern Brazil to Bolivia and Paraguay, is the Mato Grosso. A sparsely inhabited, underdeveloped region, this is generally regarded as Brazil's last frontier. *Mato Grosso* means "thick forests" in Portuguese, and this is an area of woodlands and wooded grasslands. The region receives over 60 inches of rain each year; however, very little rain falls from May to October. The Mato Grosso has excellent cattle grazing lands, but the soil is poor for farming. Once gold was mined in the area, but today the mines are exhausted.

The Amazon Basin.   The Amazon Basin, covering 2.7 million square miles, is the largest lowland area of South America. It occupies all the land drained by the Amazon River and its tributaries and includes almost all of northern Brazil, as well as parts of Venezuela, Colombia, Ecuador, Peru, and Bolivia.

Most of the Amazon Basin lies on or near the equator. Rain falls almost every day, and the nights are hot and humid, with no change of seasons.

Everywhere the Amazon Basin is covered by tropical rain forest. The heavy rain and constant heat encourage rapid and dense plant growth. Many of the trees grow as high as 100 feet, entwined by vines as thick as a human body. The tree leaves form a dense canopy that blocks out all sunlight; less than 1 percent of the sun's rays reach the forest floor, and few small plants are able to survive.

The Amazon abounds in exotic wildlife, including monkeys and brilliantly colored parrots. Less appealing are the many insects: in one ten-mile area, an American scientist counted 150 species of mosquitoes! The capybara, the world's largest rodent, lives in these tropical forests.

Rain forest vegetation. Many different types of trees and plants grow in the rain forest. The tall, slender trees on the left are bamboo.

The combined heat, rain, and insect life make the Amazon Basin an unattractive place to live. However, a number of Indian nations make their home in the area, burning sections of the forest to make clearings for planting manioc (an edible root) and bananas. Fruits are plentiful throughout the region. Brazilians eat more fruit per person than the people of any other country in the world. In the late eighteenth and early nineteenth centuries, the harvesting of latex from the area's rubber trees was an important industry. **Latex** is the sap, or liquid, from which rubber is made. However, with the introduction of commercial production in other countries and the invention of synthetic, or artificial, rubber, the market for Amazon rubber disappeared.

Today, the products of the Amazon include a number of hardwoods, such as rosewood, ebony, and mahogany, used for making fine furniture; the bark of the cinchona (sin-KOH-nuh) tree, used for making quinine to treat malaria victims; and cacao beans, from which chocolate is extracted. A paper-making plant has recently been constructed in the region. The two principal cities of the Amazon Basin are Manaus (mah-NOWS), in Brazil, and Iquitos (ih-KEE-tohs), in Peru.

The Llanos.   The llanos are tropical savannas, or grasslands, located north of the rain forests of the Amazon, in Venezuela and eastern Colombia. **Llanos** is a Spanish word for "plains."

The llanos have a wet and a dry season. During the rainy months, much of the land is under water; the people build their villages on high ground. During the dry season, the grass turns brown and the earth is parched. The principal industry of the llanos is cattle raising. Ciudad Bolívar, Venezuela's inland seaport, is the export center for beef and hides.

People who live on these plains are called **llaneros.** They are descendants of Spanish colonists and Indians, and are skilled horseback riders. Recently, oil has been discovered in the llanos, and many other Latin Americans have begun to migrate to the area.

A llanero, *or cowboy of the* llanos, *grasslands of South America.*

The Guianas.   The Guianas lie east of the llanos and northeast of the Amazon Basin. They consist of the Guiana Highlands and a narrow coastal plain.

The Guiana Highlands is a vast plateau with an average altitude of about 2,500 feet. It is separated from the Amazon Basin by low mountains, and is largely a continuation of the Amazon rain forest. It is drained by a number of large rivers, some of which are navigable for up to 150 miles from their mouths. The area is noted for gold, diamond, and bauxite mines.

The coastal plain occupies only 10 percent of the Guianas, but has 90 percent of the population. The climate of the coastal plain is warm and humid, but the nights are cool. The most important crops are sugar, rice, citrus fruits, and bananas. Cattle are raised, and fish and frozen shrimp are exported.

The Andean Highlands.   The Andean Highlands are located in Venezuela, Colombia, Ecuador, Peru, and Bolivia. This region has a **vertical climate**: the higher the altitude, the lower the temperature.

The Andean Highlands have distinct bands of climate and vegetation at different elevations. The lower altitudes are hot and are covered by tropical rain forests. The highest altitudes are forbiddingly cold and the land is barren. In the lower tropical altitudes, bananas and sugar cane can be grown. In the warm highlands, coffee and cocoa are produced and cattle and sheep are raised.

Most of the population of the Andean Highlands lives in high mountain valleys, where the weather is cool and pleasant. The **altiplano** (ahl-tih-PLAHN-oh), a plateau with an average elevation of 12,000 to 14,000 feet, is the most densely populated part of Bolivia and Peru. At this high altitude, many people have trouble breathing. In Peru, *soroche*, or mountain sickness, is common, producing dizziness and nausea. Although dry and generally treeless, the altiplano is excellent for growing potatoes, the mainstay of the local Indian population.

In contrast, the High Andes of Venezuela, Colombia, and Ecuador are cool and damp. Abundant rainfall, distributed throughout the year, produces fine grazing land. Llamas and alpacas, another camel-like animal, are raised here. These animals supply wool from which beautifully woven sweaters and ponchos are made. The Indians also eat llama meat and use the dried dung for fuel.

In the 1980s a climatic catastrophe hit the Andean Highlands. This disaster was caused by *El Niño*, "the child." *El Niño* is the equatorial Pacific warm water current. The trade winds were upset, especially in

16

the South Pacific. Thus, the warm currents disrupted the cold Humboldt current off the southern Chilean coast. As a result, areas of drought received rain for the first time in decades while fertile farming areas were completely dry. One-quarter of Bolivia's population was in danger of famine.

Several major cities, including La Paz in Bolivia, Quito (KEE-toh) in Ecuador, and Bogotá (boh-guh-TAH) in Bolivia, are located high up in the Andes Mountains. Houses in these cities are built along the sides of mountains. Other cities, such as Lima (LEE-muh), Peru, and Guayaquil (gwy-uh-KEEL), Ecuador, are located at sea level. The area is rich in minerals, including gold, silver, and copper. Colombia is also known for its emeralds, which it exports. Because of their common cultural traditions and geographic location, Chile, Bolivia, Ecuador, Peru, and Colombia are grouped together as the Andean countries.

The Southern Pacific Coast.   The southern Pacific coast of South America is long and narrow. In the north, stretching 2,200 miles from Ecuador through Peru and much of Chile, is one of the longest deserts in the world. The greatest wasteland, the Atacama Desert in Chile, is rich in copper and sodium nitrate. The Andes keep out moist air from the Amazon Basin. Along the coast, especially north of Chile in Peru, cold ocean currents make the climate cool and foggy but almost rainless. In some areas, no rain has ever fallen. In most places, 20 years will pass by before a drop of rain is felt. However, when it does rain, the desert comes alive with a wide variety of colorful flowers and bushes. An occasional **oasis** (oh-AY-sihs) can be found in places where short, swift rivers flow from the Andes into the Pacific ocean. An oasis is a place in a desert where there is enough water for people and crops. These islands of green are planted with cotton, sugar, and tropical fruits.

Farther south along the Pacific coast is Chile's Central Valley, a rich farming area where most of the Chilean people live. Chile's capital, Santiago, is located here.

OTHER REGIONS

The topography, landforms, climate, and resources of other parts of Latin America are as varied as those of the vast continent of South America.

Central America.   Central America is a long ribbon of land that connects North and South America. It extends from the Isthmus of Tehuantepec (tuh-WAHN-tuh-pek), in Mexico, to the Isthmus of Panama.

The land is mountainous, and many of the mountains are volcanic. The highest volcano, Tajumulco (ta-hoo-MOOL-koh), in Guatemala, is 13,816 feet high, and is extinct. However, many of Central America's 250 other volcanoes are still active. (You will read more about them on page 23).

The climate of Central America varies greatly, depending on altitude. The highlands have moderate temperatures and sufficient rainfall, carried in by **trade winds** from the Caribbean Sea. Trade winds are winds that blow steadily toward the equator. In Costa Rica the highlands support an important cattle industry, and coffee is grown on the hills of Nicaragua, Honduras, El Salvador, and Costa Rica.

On either side of the highlands, bordering the Pacific Ocean in the west and the Caribbean Sea in the east, are narrow coastal plains. Much more rain falls on the Caribbean side than on the Pacific coast. This is because the Pacific side is in a rain shadow created by the central mountains.

The Caribbean coastal plain is the site of lush tropical rain forests, where Central America's important banana crop is grown. Banana plants are very tall, reaching 10 to 20 feet. After a year of growth, they produce flowers on a stem. It is from these flowers that bananas grow. As the bananas grow larger, the stem becomes very heavy and bends toward the ground. Workers cut the whole stem from the plant while the bananas are still green. The unripe bananas are transported by railroad to the coast and then shipped by boat to the United States. Banana boats are refrigerated to keep the fruit from ripening too quickly.

Mexico.   Mexico is mainly a mountainous country with narrow coastal plains on the east and west. The climate is diverse, varying with altitude as well as location. As in the other mountainous regions of Latin America, there are three vertical climate zones: **tierra caliente, tierra templada,** and **tierra fría.**

The **tierra caliente** (TYEHR-uh kah-LYEN-tuh), or "hot land," is found at the lowest altitudes, from sea level to 3,000 feet. In the east, the tierra caliente extends from the Isthmus of Tehuantepec to the Tropic of Cancer and includes the coastal plain along the Gulf of Mexico and the Yucatán (yoo-kuh-TAN) Peninsula. The climate on the Gulf coastal plain is a tropical savanna type—warm and dry in winter and warm and wet in summer. The major port on the Gulf coast, Vera Cruz, has an average daily temperature that seldom goes below 68°F or above 85°F. The city gets about 60 inches of rain yearly, mostly in the wet season, which occurs in summer. From the Tropic of Cancer northward to the border of the United States, the Gulf coast is cooler and drier, with rainfall more frequent in the cool winter months.

The Yucatán Peninsula is located to the east of the Gulf coast. It is a low-lying plain that juts out into the Gulf of Mexico. In the north, horizontal beds of limestone lie immediately below the peninsula's surface, making it difficult to find water there. As a result, the land can support only small shrub trees, brush, and cactus. The southern part of the Yucatán Peninsula has a tropical wet climate, and rain forests cover most of the area. The Yucatán Peninsula was once a center of civilization of the Maya Indians, but today it is sparsely populated.

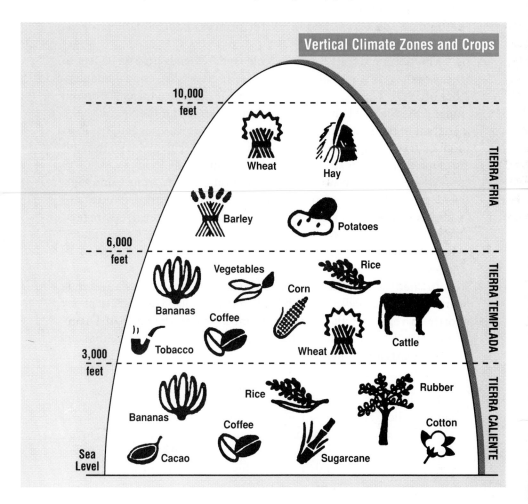

Vertical Climate Zones and Crops

The **tierra templada** (tem-PLAH-duh), or temperate zone, includes most of Mexico's Central Plateau region, which lies between the two ranges of the Sierra Madre mountains. This zone rises to 6,000 feet, and the climate is mild. Central Mexico is actually a valley located in a high volcanic area. As in most of Mexico, rainfall is light, since the winds lose most of their moisture by the time they pass over the mountains to reach the plateau. The rainy season is from June through September, when it usually rains once a day. Mexico's principal industries, as well as much of its agricultural land, are located in the Central Plateau.

The principal city of the Central Plateau is Mexico City, the nation's capital and major population center. Located at 7,200 feet above sea level, Mexico City has a cool climate that varies only slightly during the year. On the road out of Mexico City, one can see the two snowcapped volcanoes, the warrior Popocatépetl (poh-puh-kah-TAY-petl), 17,887 feet high, and his Aztec princess Ixtaccihuatl (ees-tahk-SEE-wahtl), 17,342 feet high.

The **tierra fría** (FREE-uh), or "cold land," extends from 6,000 feet to the snow line. It is cold all year round, with an average annual temperature of 59°F. This area lies primarily in Mexico's two major mountain ranges: the Sierra Madre Occidental in the west, and the Sierra Madre Oriental in the east. These mountains are steep and rugged, rising as high as 10,000 feet. Indeed, the Sierra Madre Occidental is so difficult to climb that it is crossed by only three communications lines.

Mexico's Pacific northwestern region extends from Cape Corrientes (kawr-ee-EN-tays) in the south to the border of the United States in the north. The Sierra Madre Occidental runs through this region, merging with the Rocky Mountains when it reaches the United States. Most of the land in this region is arid desert, receiving less than 10 inches of rain a year.

Isolated along the eastern side of the Gulf of California is a long narrow peninsula called Baja (BAH-hah) California. The climate in the northern region of Baja California is similar to that of San Diego, California. However, the southern half receives little rainfall. Several tourist resorts are located in this region.

Caribbean America: West Indies. The West Indies includes all the islands in the Caribbean Sea. These islands stretch between North and South America in the shape of a crescent for approximately 1,500 miles. The largest island is Cuba, with an area of over 42,000 square miles. Many of the smaller islands are only a few square miles in area.

Most of the islands of the West Indies are mountainous, and some are volcanic. The highest peak, Pico Duarte (PEE-koh DWAHRT-ay) is in the Dominican Republic, a country on the island of Hispaniola. Cuba is the only country in the West Indies with large level areas.

Some of the islands of the West Indies, such as the Cayman Islands and the Bahamas, are formed of tiny sea animals called **coral**. The skeletons of these animals are made of limestone. Over the centuries, billions of these coral skeletons piled up, forming islands. The coral formations give the islands a rugged appearance. They have also resulted in the creation of many underground caverns and streams.

All the islands of the West Indies have a rainy season and a dry season. The rainy season lasts from May through October. Although the rain falls in torrents, it lasts only for a short time each day. Seasonal hurricanes begin to arrive in August, and they bring high winds and heavy, concentrated rainfall. There is little variation in temperature, which averages 80°F.

Most of the West Indies lack natural resources. Agriculture no longer is the principal source of employment on most of these islands. Because of the mountainous terrain, farmers have a difficult time earning an adequate living. For generations, sugar cane, grown on large plantations, has been the primary export crop. Most people now live in the towns and cities.

Although some of the West Indian islands have tried to industrialize, tourism is the mainstay of most island economies. With their sun-drenched beaches, tropical seas, green mountains, and warm breezes, the islands seem a tropic paradise. They are popular winter vacation spots for North Americans seeking refuge from the cold.

NATURAL RESOURCES

Minerals are an important resource in many parts of Latin America. You will learn more about how these resources are used and which Latin American industries depend on them when you study later chapters in the book. For a brief summary of which countries produce what, look at the chart on page 22. You will see that Latin American countries are among the world leaders in the production of oil and natural gas. The same holds true for other materials needed by modern industrial societies. These include iron, needed to make steel for building and machinery, and bauxite, used to make aluminum for airplanes, buildings, and other products.

Mineral Resources of Latin America	
COUNTRY	MINERAL RESOURCES
Antigua & Barbuda	none
Argentina	lead, zinc, tin, copper, iron, manganese, oil, silver, copper, gold, uranium, sulfur
Bahamas	salt
Barbados	lime
Belize	limestone
Bolivia	tin, natural gas, oil, zinc, tungsten, antimony, columbium, silver, iron
Brazil	iron, manganese, bauxite, tungsten, nickel, uranium, gemstones, chromium, diamonds, coal, oil, tin, titanium, gold
Chile	copper, iron, nitrates, molybdenum, iodine, coal, cobalt, zinc, oil, gas, gold
Colombia	oil, natural gas, coal, iron, nickel, gold, copper, salt, emeralds, lead
Costa Rica	gold, salt, sulfur, iron
Cuba	nickel, cobalt, iron, copper, manganese, salt
Dominica	pumice
Dominican Republic	nickel, bauxite, gold, silver
Ecuador	oil, natural gas, copper, iron, lead, coal, sulfur
El Salvador	none
Grenada	none
Guatemala	oil, nickel
Guyana	bauxite, gold, diamonds
Haiti	bauxite, copper, gold, silver
Honduras	gold, silver, copper, lead, zinc, iron, antimony, coal
Jamaica	bauxite, gypsum, limestone
Mexico	oil, silver, copper, gold, lead, zinc, natural gas, iron, manganese, tungsten
Nicaragua	gold, silver, copper, tungsten
Panama	copper
Peru	oil, copper, lead, molybdenum, silver, zinc, iron, tungsten
Saint Christopher & Nevis	none
Saint Lucia	pumice
Saint Vincent & the Grenadines	stone and gravel
Suriname	bauxite, iron
Trinidad and Tobago	oil, natural gas, asphalt
Uruguay	none
Venezuela	oil, natural gas, iron, gold, bauxite

Note: An underlined resource means that the country next to it is one of the world's major producers of the mineral and/or has major supplies of it.

NATURAL DISASTERS

Latin America is second only to East Asia in the number and type of natural disasters by which it is afflicted. Floods, droughts, and mountain avalanches are commonplace. Even more terrible are the hurricanes, earthquakes, and volcanic eruptions to which the area is prone. Natural disasters have resulted in thousands of deaths and the destruction of entire villages and major urban neighborhoods. In the aftermath of massive destruction and loss of life, the governments of Mexico, Colombia, and Nicaragua have been forced to undertake major reconstruction programs.

Hurricanes strike primarily in the Caribbean basin and occasionally along the Pacific coast of Mexico. They occur mostly from August through November.

Earthquakes are common along all of Latin America's major mountain ranges, from Central America south through Chile. In recent years, serious quakes have occurred in Peru (1970), Nicaragua (1972), Guatemala (1975), Chile (1971 and 1985), and Mexico (1985). After a major quake, it is common to see people camping out on the streets to avoid becoming trapped in falling buildings during further tremors.

There are also many active volcanoes. In 1981, an eruption of El Chichon, in an isolated region of southern Mexico, spewed out 10 million tons of volcanic ash. One of the deadliest volcanic eruptions in Latin America occurred in Colombia when the Nevada del Ruiz peak exploded in 1985. Two sudden blasts sent steam and ash into the air, but almost no lava flowed. Instead the superheated molten rock inside the volcano melted the snow and ice that capped the peak. This caused a mud avalanche that raced down the mountain at speeds of 30 miles per hour. Within hours, it had completely covered the tiny town of Armero. Other villages in the region were also heavily damaged. More than 20,000 people were dead or missing. Almost all the buildings in the path of the mud flow were destroyed, and an estimated 150,000 people were left homeless.

AGRICULTURE

Agriculture is still an important way of life for many of the people of Latin America. Even in 1965 half of the population depended on the soil for a living. By the mid-1980s, however, only Haiti, Honduras, Guatemala, and Ecuador had over 50 percent of their labor forces working in agriculture. Most Latin American countries now have between

CASE STUDY:

An Earthquake in Chile

Earthquakes are a part of life in Latin America. Pablo Neruda, a Chilean poet and Nobel Prize winner, remembers the terror he felt as a young boy during an earthquake in the port city of Valparaiso.

> Every native of the city carries in him the memory of an earthquake. There is the shudder of the earth as it quakes and the rumble that surfaces from deep down as if a city under the sea, under the land, were tolling the bells in its buried towers to tell man that it's all over.
>
> Sometimes when the walls and the roofs have come crashing down in dust and flames, down into the screams and the silence . . . when everything seems to have been silenced by death once and for all, there rises out of the sea . . . the mountainous wave, the immense green arm that surges, tall and menacing, . . . to sweep away whatever life remains within its reach.
>
> Sometimes it all begins with a vague stirring, and those who are sleeping wake up. . . .
>
> And then, during the great tremor, there is nowhere to run, because the gods have gone away. . . .
>
> This is not the terror felt by someone running from a furious bull, a threatening knife, or water that swallows everything. This is a cosmic terror, an instant danger, the universe caving in and crumbling away. And, meanwhile, the earth lets out a muffled sound of thunder, in a voice no one knew it had.
>
> The dust raised by the houses as they came crashing down settles little by little. And we are left alone with our dead, with all the dead, not knowing how we happen to be still alive.

Pablo Neruda. *Memoirs* (New York: Farrar, Straus and Giroux, 1976).

1. What happened to the earth and sea during the earthquake? What happened to the houses?
2. According to this excerpt, what could the residents of Valparaiso do to save themselves from the earthquake?

These bananas have been harvested and are awaiting shipment to market. They are shaded to prevent premature ripening. Bananas, coffee, and other crops are grown on large plantations.

one or two out of every four workers working in agriculture. (That compares with about one farmer in fifty workers in the United States.) The majority of Latin American farmers are subsistence farmers with small plots of land. They grow just enough food for their families. Many must farm on small patches on steep hillsides. **Terraces**, flat sections of soil held in place by stone walls, increase the area that can be cultivated on the mountain slopes.

Latin American countries are among the world leaders in the production of wheat, soybeans, coffee, cattle, dairy products, wool, cotton, hogs, sugar, fish, rice, and corn and other grains. Latin America's most fertile land is used for commercial agriculture. However, the products of the region's large commercial plantations—coffee, bananas, and sugar—are used mainly for export. These cash crops dominate the economies of many countries. Despite the fact that agriculture is a very important economic activity, many Latin American countries have to import food to feed their populations.

25

Land Reform.   The problems of Latin American agriculture have numerous causes. Among them are the lack of modern technology and the continued use of inefficient farming techniques. However, the most important cause can probably be traced to the history of the region and the traditional pattern of landholding.

Beginning in colonial times, land ownership in Latin America was concentrated in the hands of a wealthy few. Favorites of the Portuguese or Spanish king were granted huge tracts of land. Organizing this land into vast agricultural estates, the landowner employed peasants under almost slavelike conditions to work the land with primitive agricultural implements. These vast estates, which continued to exist into the twentieth·century, are called **latifundia.**

During the past 50 years, this pattern of land ownership has been one of the most controversial issues in Latin America. Some people feel the solution to the problem is **land reform**, the break-up of the large plantations and the redistribution of the land to the peasants. The first Latin American nation to try land reform was Mexico, in 1917. The results were mixed.

Today, most Latin American nations have some kind of land reform program. However, the controversy surrounding land reform still rages. Supporters of land reform mount several arguments in its favor. They believe redistribution of the land will result in improved crop yields. They also believe that it will help prevent revolution, by giving a larger number of people a stake in society. Those who oppose land reform say that large estates are more efficient in terms of production than a lot of small farms. Perhaps the greatest problem of land reform, however, is the difficulty of ensuring fair enforcement.

REVIEWING THE CHAPTER

I. Building Your Vocabulary

In your notebook, write the numbers from 1 to 5. After each number, write the term that matches the definition.

estuary	latex	oasis
yerba maté	altiplano	coral

1. a bitter tea

2. a partially enclosed body of water, connected with the open sea and affected by the tides

3. a place in a desert where there is water for people and crops

4. animals whose skeletons pile up, forming islands

5. the sap from which rubber is made.

II. Understanding the Facts

In your notebook, write the numbers from 1 to 5. Select the sentence of each pair that is a true statement, and write its letter after the number.

1. **a.** Latin America is located north and west of the United States.
   b. Latin America is located south and east of the United States.

2. **a.** The Rio de la Plata is the longest river in Latin America.
   b. The Amazon is the longest river in Latin America.

3. **a.** In July, it is winter in Chile.
   b. In July, it is summer in Chile.

4. **a.** Corn is the mainstay of the Indian population of the altiplano.
   b. Potatoes are the mainstay of the Indian population living in the altiplano.

5. **a** The islands of the West Indies are mainly level land.
   b. The islands of the West Indies are mainly mountainous.

III. Thinking It Through

In your notebook, write the numbers from 1 to 5. After each number, write the number of the correct answer to the question.

1. Which of the following is a description of the Orinoco River?
   a. It rises in the Andes and flows across Venezuela before emptying into the sea.
   b. Rapids and high falls made it hard for explorers to use to penetrate Brazil's interior.
   c. The river carries 20 percent of the world's fresh water.
   d. It is an important commercial waterway for Paraguay and Argentine.

2. All of the countries of South America except Chile have
   a. earthquakes.   c. mountains.
   b. jungles.   d. deserts.

3. Which of the following pairs of regions are most alike?
   a. the Gran Chaco and the Andean Highlands
   b. the Southern Pacific Coast and the Guianas
   c. the Pampas and the Llanos
   d. the Patagonian Plateau and the Amazon Basin

4. How might a region be affected by being in a rain shadow?
   a. Floods might destroy villages and crops.
   b. High humidity might make it an uncomfortable place to live.
   c. There might not be enough water to grow crops.
   d. Continuous cloud cover might reduce sunlight.

5. Why are most of Mexico's industries and agricultural land located in the tierra templada?
   a. The region has a mild climate.
   b. The limestone beds underlying the region hold plentiful water supplies.
   c. The region is on the coast and is well served by many rivers.
   d. The region's rugged terrain protects it from outside attack.

DEVELOPING CRITICAL THINKING SKILLS

1. Show how landforms and climate determine population patterns and economic development in Latin America.

2. Describe the geography and climate of each of Argentina's regions.

3. Explain why the Brazilian highlands have a large population and are home to Brazil's richest farmlands.

4. Discuss the effects of natural disasters on Latin America.

INTERPRETING A GRAPH

Leading Mineral and Food Producers

BAUXITE (ALUMINUM ORE)	Australia 40%	Russia* 7.5%	Guinea 10%	Jamaica 9%	Other
CATTLE	Russia* 9.5%	US 8%	China 10%	Brazil 7%	Other
COCOA BEANS	Ivory Coast 30%	Brazil 16%	Ghana 13%	Malaysia 10%	Other
COFFEE	Brazil 27%	Colombia 14%	Indonesia 7%	Mexico 5%	Other
COPPER	Chile 10%	US 19%	Russia* 10%	Japan 9.6%	Other
CORN	US 30%	China 8%	Brazil 6%	Romania 5%	Other
HOGS	China 41%	Russia* 9%	US 5%	Brazil 4%	Other
IRON ORE	Russia* 27%	China 18%	Brazil 17%	Australia 12%	Other
MANGANESE	Russia* 40%	Gabon 10%	Brazil 9%	China 7%	Other
SUGARCANE	Russia* 13%	India 9%	Brazil 7%	Cuba 6.7%	Other
FISH	Japan 12%	Russia* 11%	China 10%	Peru 7%	Other

*Includes other nations of the former Soviet Union.   Source: U.S. CIA.

1. Of which product does Latin America produce a greater share than any other world region?
   a. cocoa beans
   c. copper
   b. coffee
   d. iron ore

2. A valid conclusion based on the chart is that
   a. most of the world's sugarcane is produced by two countries.
   b. China is a declining world power.
   c. Brazil has greater resources than other Latin American nations.
   d. The world's major industrial nations also dominate its agricultural production.

INTERPRETING A MAP

Study the map on page 12. Then answer the following questions.

1. The climate of São Paulo is
   a. tropical savanna.   **c.** humid subtropical.
   b. marine.   **d.** Mediterranean.

2. The area around which city would probably be best for growing bananas?
   a. Mexico City   **c.** Lima
   b. Buenos Aires   **d.** Manaus

ENRICHMENT AND EXPLORATION

1. Make a chart of the major physical regions of Latin America. For each region, indicate its location, climate, principal cities, and products.

2. Collect pictures of a West Indies coral reef, including some of the colorful and unusual fish that are found there. Label the pictures and arrange them in a bulletin-board display to share with the class.

2 The First Americans

Many historians believe that human beings first set foot in North America during the Ice Age, about 30,000 years ago. During that period, huge sheets of ice, or **glaciers**, covered about one-third of the earth's surface. Since large quantities of ocean water were used to form the ice, which was as much as two miles thick, the levels of the oceans became lower. In some places, land was uncovered.

One newly uncovered strip of land lay between Asia and North America, where the Bering Strait flows today. Herds of moose, caribou, and mammoths began to cross this **land bridge** from Asia to North America in search of food and warmer temperatures. The hunters who depended on these animals for food, shelter, and clothing soon followed. These were probably the first Americans.

THE GREAT MIGRATION

The migration from Asia to America did not take place all at once, but occurred in a series of waves. The migration took thousands of years, ending when the glaciers finally melted and the sea once more covered the land between the two continents, as it does today.

The first Americans continued to live as nomads, wandering from place to place in search of food. Some moved into eastern and central North America. Others drifted southward, through Mexico and Central America, on into South America. These journeys took a long time, but it is generally accepted that humans lived in Peru 14,000 years ago. Pottery found in a cave in Brazil has been dated as 9,000 years old.

During the thousands of years that the nomads wandered through the Americas, the world changed. The glaciers melted, tundra became

THE FIRST AMERICANS AND THE WORLD

2500 B.C.–A.D. 1546

c. 2500 B.C.	Slash and burn agriculture in Guatemala
c. 1500 B.C.	Mayan civilization begins.
1500–1400 B.C.	Olmec civilization thrives in Mexico.
700–200 B.C.	Chavin civilization flourishes in Peru.
480 B.C.	*Golden Age begins in Greece.*
c. 300 B.C.	Maya begin to build cities.
c. A.D. 30	*Jesus put to death.*
A.D. 300–900	Mayan Classic Period Teotihuacán civilization in Mexico
c. A.D. 500	Tihuanaco built by Aymara people.
c. A.D. 800	Tikal in decline; Maya migrate to Yucatán.
c. A.D. 1000	Aymara culture spreads to Bolivia, Chile, and Peru. Toltecs gain in Mexico's Central Valley.
A.D. 1066	*William the Conqueror leads Norman invasion of England.*
c. 1100	Mayan culture weakened by civil war and attacks by neighbors.
c. 1200	Chimu culture appears in Peru. Chibcha arise in Colombian mountains. Aztecs arrive in Mexico. Inca spread their rule.
1325	Aztecs build capital city at Lake Texcoco.
mid-1400s	Nomadic attacks cause fall of Toltec empire.
late 1400s	Inca conquer most of South America.
1492	*Columbus lands at San Salvador.*
1500s	Civil war divides Inca.
1519–1521	Spanish conquest of the Aztecs
1533–1535	Spanish conquest of the Inca
1546	Maya conquered by Spanish.

forest, and grassland became desert. Entire species of animals, such as the giant bison, the three-toed horse, the mastodon, and the mammoth became extinct.

Development of Farming.   The change in climate and the disappearance of the large animals which were their main source of food forced the nomads to learn new ways of life. People living around lakes and rivers began to fish and to trap ducks and other birds. Those living along the coasts gathered shellfish for food. In some regions, people began to eat more and more plant foods. They ground seeds to make flour, gathered berries and bulbs, and ate nuts.

Then, in the area that is now Mexico, people began to plant crops. At first they cultivated certain grains. These grains, early forms of **maize**, or corn, along with beans and squash became the main source of food. From Mexico, farming spread both north and south. In the Andean Highlands, the potato was cultivated. In other parts of South America and on the Caribbean islands, people raised manioc and other root crops similar to the sweet potato.

A major development was **irrigation.** This was a system of human-made ditches and canals that carried water from rivers and streams to the fields. Irrigation was important because it made it possible for farmers to water their crops even during the dry season.

Civilizations Emerge.   When people learned to grow food, they took a major step toward what we call civilization. Since they no longer needed to follow after herds of game, they could begin to settle permanently in one place and to build homes. Fewer people died of hunger, and populations increased. Food production took less time and labor. That meant that some people were able to specialize in work other than farming, such as the creation of beautiful pottery or the crafting of new tools.

People began to live together in larger communities, and governments were organized to regulate their activities and relationships. Religion became important as people looked to priests to help control the environment. Calendars, marking the changes of seasons, and systems of writing, to preserve ideas and pass on information, were developed.

Over the years, powerful city-states and empires appeared. These states were based on irrigation agriculture, and they supported large populations. A variety of goods was produced by highly skilled craftspeople. Public building projects were completed with the work of many laborers. These included many temple mounds, irrigation networks, roads, bridges, and reservoirs. To control this large work force, a rigid class structure developed. Priests and nobles, defended by warriors, ruled and regulated large numbers of farmers, craftspeople, and laborers.

THE EARLIEST CIVILIZATIONS

Archaeologists have found traces of civilizations that existed several thousand years ago in the Americas. By carefully analyzing the evidence, historians are able to recreate what life may have been like among these earliest peoples.

The Olmecs (about 1500 B.C.-400 B.C.). The first major civilization in the Americas was the Olmec (OHL-mek), in Mexico, which flourished from 1500 B.C. to 400 B.C. Not very much is known about the Olmecs. Living along the Gulf of Mexico, near the present-day city of Veracruz, the Olmecs reached a very high level of culture. They built stone temples and possibly developed some form of **hieroglyphic** writing and a calendar. They may have introduced corn to their Gulf Coast neighbors. There are signs that the Olmecs may have worshiped the jaguar. The figure of a creature, half-human, half-jaguar, thought to be a god, occurs in their art. The Olmecs left many small objects of jade, as well as perfectly ground mirrors made of hematite, a form of iron. Perhaps best known are their colossal stone sculptures of heads, weighing over 20 tons each, which can still be seen in Mexico today.

The Chavin (about 700 B.C.-200 B.C.). The earliest civilization to appear in South America was the Chavin (shuh-VEEN), which flourished in the northeastern highlands of Peru from about 700 B.C. to 200 B.C. Highly developed and sophisticated, the Chavin built large temples with painted sculptures and produced beautiful ceramics, gold objects, and textiles.

Tiahuanaco (about A.D. 500-1200). Tiahuanaco (tee-ah-wah-NAH-koh), an ancient ruin in western Bolivia, near Lake Titicaca, is believed to have been the center of a culture originated by a people called the Aymara (eye-mah-RAH). Building was begun some time before A.D. 500. Around A.D. 1000, the culture spread to eastern Bolivia, northern Chile, and Peru, where it flourished for some 200 years. The great temples at Tiahuanaco are noted for their massive stones, weighing up

The Olmecs carved stone heads out of huge boulders. This carving is in the village of Villahermosa, near Palenque, in Mexico.

to 100 tons each and fitted together with extraordinary precision without the use of cement. The creators of Tiahuanaco also excelled at ceramics, and their painted pottery is considered among the finest examples of Indian art before the arrival of Europeans.

Teotihuacán (about A.D. 300-900). Between A.D. 300 and 900, a civilization flourished in the central valley of Mexico. Its commercial center was Teotihuacán (tay-oh-tee-wah-KAN), about 30 miles northeast of where Mexico City stands today. At its peak, Teotihuacán had a population of almost 100,000, and the civilization exerted influence in such far-off places as the Guatemalan Highlands and the valley of Oaxaca (wah-HAH-kah). The people grew corn, were skillful sculptors and stone cutters, and appear to have been peace-loving.

The ruins of Teotihuacán are among the most impressive in the Americas. Among these is the Pyramid of the Sun, Mexico's tallest pyramid, which stands 216 feet high and covers approximately ten acres at its base.

The Toltecs (about A.D. 1000-1400). After the fall of Teotihuacán in around A.D. 900, the Toltecs (TAHL-teks) gained influence in Mexico's Central Valley, making their capital at Tula (TOO-lah). By the year 1100, they had spread their influence as far south as the Yucatán Peninsula. The Toltecs were very different from the people of Teotihuacán. Their rulers were warriors, and their god, Quetzalcoátl (ket-sahl-koh-AT'l), demanded human sacrifice.

The Toltecs excelled at architecture and the arts, were advanced workers of metal and stone, and developed a sophisticated calendar. Attacks by nomadic peoples brought about the fall of the Toltec empire in the 1400s and paved the way for the rise of the Aztecs (see page 40).

The Chimu (A.D. 1200-1400). The Chimu (chee-MOO) first appeared around 1200 on the northern coast of Peru. The area is desert, and the Chimu developed a system of irrigation to improve the soil. The Chimu were city-dwellers. They had a highly structured society. They built many well-planned cities, including Chan Chan, their capital. The Chimu were conquered and absorbed by the Inca in the mid-1400s.

The Chibcha (about A.D. 1200-1541). The Chibcha (CHIB-chah) appeared in the mountains of Colombia at about the same time the Chimu appeared in Peru. The most highly developed of the Colombian Indians, the Chibcha were skilled farmers and weavers. They are best known, however, for their beautiful gold and copper ornaments. They had a well-organized government and a highly developed religious system that included human sacrifice. The Chibcha were conquered by the Spanish between 1536 and 1541.

THE MAYA (ABOUT 1500 B.C.-A.D. 1546)

As you have read, there were many great Indian civilizations that rose and fell in the Americas before the arrival of Columbus. All of these civilizations are called **pre-Columbian civilizations**, or "civilizations before Columbus." Perhaps the best known of the pre-Columbian civilizations, and the most highly developed, are the Maya, in Guatemala; the Aztec, in Mexico; and the Inca, in South America.

Mayan Beginnings. Mayan civilization developed in the rain forests of Guatemala. As early as 2500 B.C., people were cultivating corn in

36

this area, using the **slash-and-burn method** of agriculture. Trees were cut down and burned, and the ashes from the burned trees fertilized the soil. Using sharp sticks, farmers loosened the soil and planted seeds or roots.

The agricultural methods of the Maya quickly exhausted the soil, and Mayan villages had to be moved very frequently. This discouraged the building of cities. However, by 300 B.C., the Maya began to erect cities with centers for religious ceremonies and to house their priests and rulers. These ceremonial centers were made up of many small, steep pyramids. The graceful stone temples that stood atop these pyramids were all the more remarkable because they were made without stone tools. Each Mayan center also had a ball court where war prisoners competed with each other for their lives. The Maya built about 40 cities with more than 20,000 people in each.

The greatest Mayan city and ceremonial center was Tikal (tee-KAHL), already flourishing in the first century A.D., in what is now northeastern Guatemala. The hub was the Great Plaza. Surrounding the plaza were several large temple-pyramids, a cluster of smaller temples, and a large palace complex. Other temples and palaces, along with ball courts, reservoirs, and causeways, occupied the surrounding area. By A.D. 800, Tikal had begun to decline. Today, the ruins of the abandoned center are an impressive sight.

Social Structure.   The society of the Maya was organized like a pyramid. At the apex, or narrow top, were a king or queen and a small number of priests and nobles, who made all major decisions in each city-state. Below the priests and nobles were a larger number of merchants and artisans who handled the day-to-day affairs of the community. At the broad base of the pyramid were farmers, workers, and slaves.

Because they lived in a tropical climate, the Maya wore clothing for personal adornment rather than for warmth. The men wore sleeveless jackets, loin cloths, and sandals. Women wore skirts and shawls or simple long dresses, but went barefoot except when they went on long journeys.

Economy.   The agricultural economy of the Maya was based on corn, or maize, and tending the **milpas,** or cornfields, was the most important daily activity. The Maya also raised sweet potatoes, beans, onions, and squash. However, the average Mayan family probably had to work only 120 days per year in order to produce more than twice the amount of food it needed. This left time for other activities, usually religious.

CASE STUDY:

A Mayan Legend

Popul Vuh is a collection of Mayan stories and legends that were passed down orally from generation to generation. In the mid-1500s, a Mayan Indian used the Spanish alphabet to record these legends. Much of the original manuscript has been lost. However, the stories that remain help us gain a better idea of the Mayan's view of the world.

(A macaw is a kind of parrot common in South and Central America. It is one of the largest parrots, and its plumage is especially colorful.)

> This was when there was just a trace of early dawn on the face of the earth. There was no sun. But there was one who magnified himself. Seven Macaw is his name. The sky-earth was already there, but the face of the sun-moon was clouded over. Even so, it is said that his light provided a sign for the people . . .
>
> "I am great. My place is now higher than that of the human work, the human design. I am their sun and I am their light, and I am also their months.
>
> "So be it: my light is great . . . because my eyes are of metal. My teeth just glitter with jewels, and turquoise as well: they stand out blue with stones like the face of the sky.
>
> "And this nose of mine shines white into the distance like the moon. Since my nest is metal, it lights up the face of the earth. When I come forth before my nest, I am like the sun and the moon for those who are born in the light. It must be so, because my face reaches into the distance," says Seven Macaw.
>
> It is not true that he is the sun, this Seven Macaw, yet he makes himself bigger, his wings, his metal. But his face extends no farther than his perch; his face does not reach everywhere beneath the sky. The faces of the sun, moon, and stars are not yet visible, it has not yet dawned.
>
> And so Seven Macaw puffs himself up as the days and the months, though the light of the sun and moon has not yet dawned. He only wished for . . . greatness . . . This was when the flood was worked upon the people, the wooden dolls . . .

Popul Vuh. Translation by Dennis Tedlock (New York: Simon and Schuster, 1985), p. 86.

Like Tikal, Chichén Itzá is a famous Mayan center. The temple pyramid of El Castillo (Spanish for fortress) stands in the center of the photograph. Statues of gods surround the area.

1. At what time in history does the story occur?

2. Describe the physical appearance of Seven Macaw. How does this show how the Maya combined real things with magical things in their legends?

3. What does Seven Macaw claim to be? What facts are given in the legend to disprove Seven Macaw's claim?

Religion.   Religion was a very important part of Mayan life. The Maya believed that the earth had been created and destroyed four or five times, and that it would be destroyed again. To persuade the gods to delay this destruction, the Mayan rulers prayed, fasted, burned incense, and shed their own blood in self-mutilation. Cities fought each other in order to capture, torture, and sacrifice the rulers of opposing cities. The principal gods were the gods of rain, the heavens, corn, and death.

Cultural Achievements.   The Maya had the most highly developed Indian culture in the Americas. They developed a system of arithmetic that included the concept of zero. To mathematicians, the use of the zero indicates highly advanced thinking. They also had an accurate calendar of 365 days. Each of the 18 months in the calendar year consisted of 20 days, with an extra month made up of the remaining 5 days. This system enabled the Maya to predict eclipses and to track comets. In addition, they were the only pre-Columbian people to create a true system of writing. It combined phonetic symbols standing for sounds and **ideographic** (picture) symbols standing for words. (Experts are now translating this writing.)

Mayan civilization lasted from about 1500 B.C. to A.D. 1546. It was at its height between A.D. 300 and 900, an era known as the Classic Period. Around the year 800, the Maya suddenly abandoned their great cities in Guatemala and moved northward into the Yucatán Peninsula of Mexico. The reason for this migration is unknown. Among the possibilities suggested by historians are a volcanic eruption, a sudden change in climate, a civil war, or a foreign invasion.

Decline.   The years in the Yucatán are known as the Late Period of Mayan history. During this period, the Maya began to rebuild their culture, and their new empire reached great heights. Beginning around 1100, however, the Maya were weakened by civil wars and attacks by other Indian groups. Mayan civilization continued in decline for the next several hundred years and finally came to an end when the Maya were conquered by the Spanish in 1546 (see Chapter 3).

Today, the great cities of the Maya are nothing more than beautiful ruins, some of which are in the Yucatán. However, several million descendants of the Maya live in Guatemala and Mexico.

THE AZTECS (A.D. 1200-1521).

The Aztecs were relative newcomers to Mexico, arriving there from the north in around A.D. 1200. A fierce people, they had lived as wandering

This Mayan stone carving shows a priest holding a ceremonial staff over a sacrificial victim. What role did religion play in the daily life of the Maya?

warriors, traveling from place to place and fighting for anyone who would pay them.

The chief Aztec god was Huitzilpochtli (wee-tsee-lah-POHKT-lee), the god of sun and war. According to legend, Huitzilpochtli had instructed the Aztecs to wander until they came to a place where an eagle perched on a cactus was eating a snake. After years of wandering, the Aztecs reached the Central Valley of Mexico. On a marshy island in Lake Texcoco (TES-koh-koh), they saw their sign. There, in about 1325, they began to build their capital city.

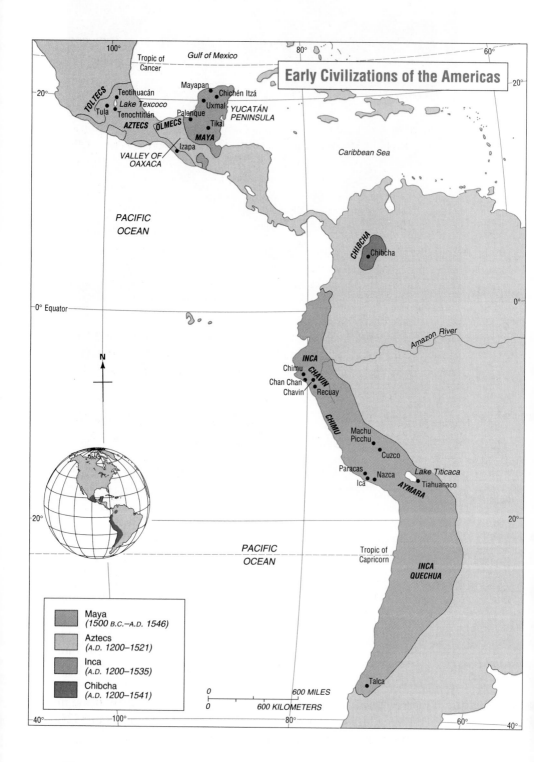

Early Civilizations of the Americas

Tropic of Cancer

Gulf of Mexico

100°   80°   60°

20°   20°

TOLTECS
Teotihuacán
Mayapan
Lake Texcoco
Chichén Itzá
Tula
Tenochtitlán
Uxmal
YUCATÁN
Palenque
PENINSULA
AZTECS   OLMECS
Tikal
MAYA

Caribbean Sea

Izapa

VALLEY OF
OAXACA

PACIFIC
OCEAN

CHIBCHA
Chibcha

0° Equator   0°

Amazon River

N

INCA
Chimu   CHAVIN
Chan Chan
Chavin   Recuay

CHIMU

Machu
Picchu

Cuzco

Paracas
Nazca   Lake Titicaca
Ica   Tiahuanaco
AYMARA

20°   20°

PACIFIC
OCEAN

Tropic of
Capricorn

INCA
QUECHUA

Maya
(1500 B.C.–A.D. 1546)

Aztecs
(A.D. 1200–1521)

Inca
(A.D. 1200–1535)

Chibcha
(A.D. 1200–1541)

Talca

0   600 MILES
0   600 KILOMETERS

40°   100°   80°   60°   40°

Gradually, the Aztecs began to spread their power as they conquered and enslaved the neighboring tribes one by one. By the late 1400s, they had become the dominant force in Mexico, controlling all the land between the Gulf of Mexico and the Pacific Ocean.

Tenochtitlán. The center of the Aztec empire was Tenochtitlán (tay-noch-tee-TLAHN), built on the site of present-day Mexico City. At the period of greatest Aztec power, Tenochtitlán had more than 100,000 inhabitants. It was a magnificent city. Built on islands in the middle of Lake Texcoco, it was connected to the mainland by movable bridges. These bridges could be raised in case of enemy attack. Within the city were streets, canals, large stucco houses, rooftop flower gardens, and pyramidlike temples to the gods. Arriving in the 1500s, some of the first Spanish explorers wondered if the city "was not a thing in a dream."

At Tenochtitlán, the Aztecs perfected an unusual method of farming. They built huge rafts, covered them with earth, and floated them on the lake. On these **chinampas**, or "floating islands," they grew enough maize and vegetables to feed their expanding population comfortably. Eventually, roots from the tree rafts attached themselves to the bottom of the shallow lake to become permanent foundations for buildings.

Social Structure. Like most early civilizations in America, Aztec society was rigidly organized, with each person assigned a specific role. At the top was the emperor, who was considered divine and treated as a living god. Warfare was the most highly respected activity, and the great warriors were the nobles of the empire. Below them were the merchants and traders, who provided the community with great wealth. Then came the free peasants and artisans. At the bottom of the social scale were the slaves, who were usually prisoners of war.

The Aztecs had an elaborate law code, and a sophisticated system of courts. Punishments for crime were severe: a thief was enslaved for a first offense and hanged for the second. Murder and rebellion were punished by death.

Daily Life. The Aztecs lived very comfortable lives. They dwelled in thatch-roofed huts and wore roughly woven cotton clothing. Food was plentiful. Maize, beans, and peppers were grown for trade as well as for home consumption. Most people also ate avocados, pineapples, squash, fish, turkeys, geese, and ducks. From the agave, or century, plant, they made strong thread and brewed an alcoholic beverage called *pulque*.

This drawing of the great Temple of Tenochtitlán was constructed from descriptions by Spanish conquerors and through study of existing Aztec monuments.

The nobles drank hot chocolate, which was considered a divine drink and forbidden to the lower classes

Aztec children attended school. Boys started their formal education when they were 10 or 12 years old. Sons of commoners, merchants, and artisans were taught religion, grammar, and the art of war. The sons of the nobility went on to higher schools, remaining in them until they were in their early twenties. They learned public speaking, religion and philosophy, mathematics, astrology, history, and moral conduct. They were instilled with an awareness that life is short and filled with hardships. After graduation, they could choose careers as soldiers, priests, or government officials.

Girls attended separate schools. They were taught religious duties, such as sweeping the temples, and the rites for offering incense and food to the idols. They also learned weaving and other domestic chores. Girls remained in school until they were about 16 or 17, when their families would arrange marriages for them. The Aztecs adopted many of the inventions of the tribes they conquered or traded with. They took over the calendar and mathematics of the Maya. From other groups, they learned the use of metals, weaving, and pottery making. Their artists and artisans produced beautiful gold and silver jewelry, carved jade and crystal, and lovely lacquer work. The Aztec garments made of cotton and feathers are quite amazing.

Religion and Decline. The fall of the Aztec empire in the early 1500s came about almost as rapidly as its rise a brief 200 years before. The Aztecs' religious beliefs played an important role in their downfall. The Aztecs believed that death and destruction were inevitable, and that the gods enjoyed warfare among people. To remain in favor with the gods, the Aztecs offered human sacrifices. The victims were prisoners captured in wars with neighboring tribes. Because they could never be certain that the gods were satisfied, the Aztecs offered more and more sacrifices. It has been estimated that as many as 20,000 persons were sacrificed by the Aztecs each year. It is not any wonder that many of the Aztecs' neighbors welcomed the arrival of the Spanish in 1519 and eagerly assisted them in defeating their oppressors.

The Aztecs' religious beliefs led to their downfall in another way. One of the Aztec gods was Quetzalcoátl, who according to legend was the original Aztec ruler. He had white skin and a light beard. One day, Quetzalcoátl sailed away on a magic raft. He promised to "return out of the water of the east, as a bearded man riding on an animal." When reports were heard in 1519 of the arrival of the Spanish, led by white-skinned, bearded Hernán Cortés riding on a horse, there was no doubt that Quetzalcoátl had returned to claim his throne. The Aztecs welcomed the "god," and by 1521, the Spanish conquest of their empire was complete. (You will read more about the conquest of the Aztecs in the next chapter.)

Today, many of the people of Mexico are descendants of the Aztecs. More than a million people throughout the country speak only Nahuatl (NAH-waht'l), the Aztec language.

THE INCA (ABOUT A.D. 1200-1535)

At about the same time that the Aztecs were building their empire in Mexico, another group was creating a great civilization in South America. This was the Inca empire. The religion of these people was based on sun worship. The name Inca was first given to the emperor, who was believed to be descended from the sun god. Eventually, all the people of the empire were called Incas, or "children of the sun."

The Incas lived in the Andean mountains of Peru. In about A.D. 1200, they began to spread their rule over other groups in the area, sometimes peacefully, sometimes with the use of force. By the late 1400s, they had conquered many of the peoples of South America. Their empire covered much of present-day Peru, Ecuador, Bolivia, and Chile. At its height, the Inca empire had a population of 5 to 16 million people.

Economy and Cultural Achievements.   The Incas were farmers who grew potatoes, cotton, maize, peanuts, squash, tomatoes, and beans. They built irrigation systems to bring water to the coastal deserts. They cut terraces on the mountain slopes to increase the amount of cultivable land and to prevent the soil from washing away. They domesticated the alpaca and the llama, animals that they used for meat and as sources of very fine wool.

The Inca empire was rich in gold and silver, and the Incas mined and worked the gold. Inca gold jewelry shows a very high level of skill. The Incas also developed various industries, including the spinning and weaving of cotton and wool and pottery making. The Incas had no formal system of writing, but kept records and sent messages by means of intricate bundles of knotted and colored string, called a **quipu** (KEE-poo). The Incas were quite advanced in the practice of medicine, having knowledge of the use of anesthetics and even performing brain surgery.

Social Structure.   Inca society was rigidly organized, much like that of the Maya and Aztecs. Authority was centered in the emperor, or Lord Inca, who had absolute power over the lives of his people from birth to death. The Inca distributed the land and supervised the cultivation of crops. Individual land ownership was prohibited, but each family was allotted a plot of land, which was enlarged as the family grew.

The emperor was assisted in his duties by the nobles, priests, and government officials. Merchants and traders had a favored social position, below the nobles. At the bottom of the scale was a large group made up of free farmers, artisans, and slaves.

The daily activities of the Inca people were constantly supervised and regulated. Officials chose the districts in which people lived and the occupations they followed. The Incas did not use money, and taxes were paid in the form of labor or goods. Farmers had to turn over a portion of their crops to the emperor. Inca men had to work on any project the government decided to undertake, such as the building of temples, roads, bridges, and fortresses.

Organization of the Empire.   The Inca capital was Cuzco (KOOS-koh), the "city of the sun." The Inca rulers tried to unify the people of their vast empire. Conquered peoples had to learn Quechua (KECH-wah), the Inca

The Incas fashioned many objects from silver and gold. This statue of an Inca corn god is made of silver and stands about 2 inches tall.

language. People were sent to live among newly conquered tribes to teach them Inca customs and laws. They established public schools that taught the Inca religion and history. The subject peoples tended to be loyal and obedient.

The Incas were great builders. They constructed a vast system of roads connecting all parts of their far-flung empire. Besides roads and bridges, they built great temples and palaces. Stone was cut and transported by human labor, and the stone blocks fitted together without cement. The Incas may have learned this skill from the people of Tiahuanaco.

In 1911, an American explorer, Hiram Bingham, discovered the ruins of Machu Picchu (MACH-oo PEEK-Choo), about 50 miles northwest of Cuzco. Built 6,750 feet above sea level, this fortress city was never discovered by the Spanish. Today, many of its beautiful stone structures still stand, visible monuments to the skill of their Inca builders.

47

Machu Picchu, an ancient fortress city of the Incas in the Andes Mountains.

Decline of the Inca Empire.   In the early 1500s the Inca empire was divided by civil war. The ruler, Huayna Capac (WYE-nah-KAH-pak), had died in 1525, and his two sons, Huáscar (WAHS-kahr) and Atahualpa (at-uh-WAHL-puh), fought for control of the empire. Atahualpa was eventually victorious, but the fighting had taken its toll. When the Spanish arrived in 1533, they found the empire greatly weakened. Within two years, the Spanish were able to conquer the great Inca empire.

The sophisticated civilizations of the Incas, the Maya, and the Aztecs had developed in isolation from the rest of the world. In the early 1500s, however, a new age was beginning in Europe. It would bring great change to the Western Hemisphere. The age of exploration was under way. Contact with the Europeans would alter forever the way of life of the peoples in Central and South America.

REVIEWING THE CHAPTER

I. Building Your Vocabulary

In your notebook, write the numbers from 1 to 5. After each number, write the term that best completes the sentence.

chinampas	milpas	glaciers
quipu	maize	irrigation

1. The Inca sent messages and kept records with the help of a (an) _____ .

2. During the Ice Age, huge sheets of ice called _____ covered much of the earth's surface.

3. Many Native American peoples developed _____ systems that carried water from rivers or streams to fields.

4. The Maya based their economy on growing _____ , or corn.

5. Tending the _____ , or cornfields, was the most important daily activity of the Maya.

II. Understanding the Facts

In your notebook, write the numbers from 1 to 5. After each number, write the letter of the word or phrase that best completes the sentence.

1. People began to settle permanently in one place when they began to
   a. live in the Americas. b. grow food. c. hunt animals.

2. The civilization that left colossal stone sculptures of heads is the
   a. Olmec. b. Aztec. c. Chimu.

3. The most highly developed Indian civilization in the Americas was the
   a. Incan. b. Aztec. c. Mayan.

4. The capital of the Aztec empire was
   a. Chan Chan. b. Teotihuacán. c. Tenochtitlán.

5. The Incas lived in
   a. Guatemala. b. the Andean mountains of Peru. c. the Yucatán.

III. Thinking It Through

1. Why did the first people come to the Americas?
   a. They wanted to escape persecution by powerful tribes in Asia and Europe.
   b. They were looking for a new place to build their capital city.
   c. They followed herds of animals which they depended on for food and clothing.
   d. Disease drove them out of their old continent.

2. Which of the following civilizations survived long enough to be conquered by the Spanish?
   a. the Olmec   c. the Chimu
   b. the Chibcha   d. the Toltecs

3. One result of the slash-and-burn method of agriculture of the Maya was the
   a. increased use of burned trees for fertilizer.
   b. expansion of forests in Mexico and Central America.
   c. decision to organize society under the rule of women priests.
   d. building of cities.

4. What role did chocolate play in Aztec civilization?
   a. It was a drink of the nobility, forbidden to the lower classes.
   b. It was a ceremonial drink offered to the gods.
   c. It was made into coins and used as money.
   d. The Aztecs formed it into bricks and used it to erect buildings.

5. The Inca were like the Aztecs in that they
   a. sacrificed thousands of people to their gods.
   b. were ruled by an emperor.
   c. spread their empire into northern South America.
   d. domesticated alpacas and llamas for use as sources of food and wool.

DEVELOPING CRITICAL THINKING SKILLS

1. We use the term *civilization* to describe a culture or society that has reached an advanced state. Usually, a civilization possesses four characteristics. These are (a) complex technical skills; (b) community living; (c) advanced learning; and (d) advanced intellectual and cultural achievements. Select one of the societies discussed in this chapter. Using the characteristics above, explain why it is considered an advanced civilization.

2. Describe how the Aztecs and the Incas treated the peoples they conquered.

3. Show how the use of a calendar would be important to the civilizations of the Americas.

4. Discuss the reasons why the Aztecs' religious beliefs contributed to their downfall.

READING A TIMELINE

Use the Time Box on page 32 to find answers to the following questions. Write the answers in your notebook.

1. What event occurred closest to the time of the fall of the Teotihuacán civilization?
   a. the death of Jesus
   b. the building of the Tihuanaco
   c. the decline of Tikal
   d. the establishment of the Aztec capital city at Lake Texcoco

2. What event or events contributed most to the 16th century occurrences shown in the Time Box?
   a. the collapse of the Toltec empire
   b. the civil war between Huayna Capac and Atahualpa
   c. the movement of the center of Mayan civilization from Guatemala to the Yucatán Peninsula.
   d. the voyages of Christopher Columbus to the Americas

ENRICHMENT AND EXPLORATION

1. In 1911, an American archaeologist named Hiram Bingham discovered Machu Picchu, the "lost city" of the Inca, high in the Andes Mountains of Peru. Read more about this fabulous city of the Inca empire and write a report on your findings. One possible source is Bingham's own story of his discovery, *Lost City of the Incas*. Also useful might be *Making the Past: The New World*, by Warwick M. Bray.

2. Select one of the major Indian groups—Maya, Aztecs, Inca—discussed in this chapter. Use reference sources and current magazines to find out about the descendants of the group living in Latin America today. Report to the class on your findings. Be sure to include information on the ways in which the people today continue the traditions of their ancestors.

LATIN AMERICA AND THE WORLD
1096–1824

1096	Europeans begin Crusades.
1416	Portuguese Prince Henry establishes school for sailors.
1488	Dias rounds Cape of Good Hope.
1492	Columbus lands at San Salvador.
1494	Spain and Portugal sign Treaty of Tordesillas.
1497–1498	Vasco da Gama sails to India.
1497–1503	Amerigo Vespucci visits the Caribbean.
early 1500s	Europeans bring enslaved Africans to Latin America.
1502–1504	Vasco Nuñez de Balboa lands in Panama.
1516–1556	King Carlos I rules Spain.
1519–1521	Cortés conquers Aztecs.
1519–1522	Magellan's ship circumnavigates the earth.
1535	Pizarro defeats Inca.
1542	New Laws of Indies proclaimed.
after 1550	Portuguese use enslaved Africans.
1776	*U.S. Declaration of Independence*
1791	Toussaint L'Ouverture leads revolt of enslaved Africans in Haiti.
1804	Haiti gains independence from France.
1818	Chile achieves independence.
1821	Mexico and New Grenada independent.
1822	Brazil becomes independent empire.
1823	United Provinces of Central America formed.
	U.S. proclaims Monroe Doctrine.
1824	Mexico becomes a republic. All Spanish colonies in South America free.

3 Colonization and Independence

As you read in Chapter 2, three major Indian civilizations were flourishing in the Americas in 1500—the Maya in Central America, the Aztec in Mexico, and the Inca in Peru. At the same time, on the other side of the Atlantic Ocean, major changes were taking place in Europe. These changes would have far-reaching consequences for the peoples of the Americas.

THE AGE OF EXPLORATION

During the Middle Ages, as the period from about 500 to 1450 is called, Europeans had limited contact with the rest of the world. Most people were concerned mainly with what happened in their own lives and in their own villages. In an entire lifetime, few people ever left their village. Indeed, most people might not know what was happening a mere fifteen or twenty miles away.

European Interest Awakens. Gradually, all this changed. Beginning about 1100, thousands of Europeans joined the Crusades, marching to Palestine to reclaim the Holy Land from the Muslims. At the same time, merchants and adventurers traveled to China and India and other Asian lands. Besides tales of wonderful sights and strange customs, these travelers brought back exotic treasures. There were spices to preserve and improve the taste of food and drugs to relieve pain. Thick rugs arrived to warm cold stone floors, and luxurious silks and velvets were imported to be used for clothing. Rare fruits such as lemons, apricots, and melons were introduced to Europe. Quickly, a demand arose for these goods, and an active and profitable trade with Asia began.

The overland trade route between Asia and Europe was long and dangerous. Further, almost all goods brought from Asia into Europe passed through Italy, which had a **monopoly**, or total control of, trade with the East. Soon, people in other European nations began to seek a new, all-water, trade route to Asia.

Portugal Takes the Lead in Exploration.   For many years, Portuguese seamen had sailed along the Atlantic coast. However, their knowledge of the sea was very limited, and they never ventured far from land, for fear of getting lost.

In 1416, Prince Henry, a son of the Portuguese king, established a school for sailors. Henry, later known as Henry the Navigator, had a number of aims. He wished to gain a share in the profitable African slave trade that was then controlled by the Muslims. He was also interested in obtaining gold from kingdoms in West Africa. Finally, he wanted to acquire new lands and peoples in Africa for Portugal and, thus, for Christianity.

At Prince Henry's school, Portuguese seamen learned to read maps and to use the latest navigational instruments, such as the **compass** and the **astrolabe**. With these new instruments they could determine the relative distance of the stars and the planets. They used the measurements to calculate their ship's position on the seas. Portuguese shipbuilders also developed the **caravel**, a ship that, unlike other European vessels of the time, was not only swift but could sail against the wind.

Soon, Portugal's sea captains began venturing farther and farther south along the African coast. This required a lot of courage, for many sailors believed that if they went too far, their ship would fall off the edge of the earth. In the years after Henry's death, Portuguese rulers wished to find a way to sail directly to India and the East Indies. This would enable Portugal to trade directly with Asia, bypassing the Muslim traders and Italian merchants who controlled the overland routes. The Portuguese persevered, and in 1488 Bartholomeu Dias (DEE-ahsh) rounded the southern tip of Africa, now called the Cape of Good Hope. Ten years later, in 1497-1498, another Portuguese sea captain, Vasco da Gama (dah-GAH-mah), sailed southward along the west coast of Africa, around the Cape of Good Hope, and eastward across the Indian Ocean to India. Nearly forty years after his death, Prince Henry's dream of an all-water route to the East was fulfilled.

Spain Finances the Voyages of Columbus.   Spain, Portugal's neighbor, was also interested in finding an all-water trade route to the East. The Spanish rulers, King Ferdinand and Queen Isabella, decided to finance a voyage of exploration by an Italian navigator and geographer named Christopher Columbus.

54

An artist's version of the landing of Columbus in America. The explorer kneels under the flag as a priest raises the Holy Eucharist in thanksgiving.

The Portuguese planned to reach Asia by sailing southward around Africa and then eastward to India. Columbus had a different plan. He believed he could reach Asia quickly and easily by sailing directly westward. There were two important facts that Columbus did not know. The earth is much larger than Columbus believed it was. And a large mass of land—North and South America—lay between Spain and Asia.

On August 3, 1492, Columbus set sail from Spain with three small ships, the *Niña*, the *Pinta*, and the *Santa Maria*. After two months at sea, on October 12, 1492, Columbus landed on a tiny island, which he named San Salvador (today, one of the Bahama Islands). Of the people he encountered there, he wrote in his journal, "They came swimming to the ships' boats . . . and brought us parrots and cotton thread in balls, spears, and many other things . . . and we exchanged for them . . . small glass beads and small bells. They took all and gave what they had with good will. . . ." Continuing southward, Columbus explored the coasts of two other islands, Cuba and Hispaniola. On the voyage he wrote a letter to the queen describing Hispaniola:

> This island, like all the others, is extraordinarily large. In the interior there are many mines and an [immense] population. [Hispaniola] is a wonder. Its mountains and plains, meadows, and fields are beautiful and rich for planting and sowing, and for raising cattle of all kinds, and for building towns and villages. The harbors on the coast, and the number and size and purity of the rivers, most of them bearing gold, surpass anything that would be believed by one who had not seen them.

Columbus was convinced he had reached "the Indies," islands off the coast of Asia. He called the people he found there "Indians." Taking with him several Indians he had captured, a few parrots, and some of the Indians' gold ornaments obtained on Hispaniola, he returned triumphantly to Spain.

King Ferdinand and Queen Isabella welcomed Columbus warmly. Impressed with the gold that Columbus had brought, the Spanish rulers agreed to finance new, bigger expeditions to bring back gold and slaves. Columbus made three more voyages, reaching the Lesser Antilles and Puerto Rico in 1493 and Jamaica in 1494, the north coast of South America and the island of Trinidad in 1498, and Jamaica and the coast of Central America in 1502-1504. His men forced the Indians to search for gold and killed those who would not cooperate. Thousands of people were murdered or cruelly worked to death within a few years.

The Line of Demarcation.   With both Spain and Portugal exploring the seas it was clear that conflicts were bound to arise about ownership of newly "discovered" lands. To avoid such quarrels, King Ferdinand and Queen Isabella turned to the pope for help. In 1493, the pope drew an imaginary line down the middle of the Atlantic Ocean, from the North Pole to the South Pole. This was known as the **Line of Demarcation.** All newly discovered lands to the west of the line were to belong to Spain; all lands to the east could be claimed by Portugal. However, the Portuguese became dissatisfied with the line because they thought it gave Spain too much territory. In 1494, Spain and Portugal signed the Treaty of Tordesillas, which moved the line farther west.

A "New World."   Other explorers soon followed Columbus's westward route across the Pacific Ocean. One of the first people to realize that the land on the other side of the Atlantic Ocean was not Asia was Amerigo

Vespucci (ves-POO-chee) an Italian sea captain in the service of Portugal. Vespucci, who visited the Caribbean and explored the northern coast of South America between 1497 and 1503, described the lands he saw as a "New World," to distinguish them from India. A German mapmaker read Vespucci's reports and named the lands "America," after him.

Other discoveries soon proved that Vespucci was correct. In 1513, a Spanish adventurer named Vasco Nuñez de Balboa (bal-BOH-uh) landed in Panama. Setting out from the Atlantic coast, Balboa crossed the narrow Isthmus of Panama. Reaching the other side, he looked out on a great body of water. This was the Pacific Ocean. Balboa's sighting of the huge ocean made it clear that the "New World," bordered by water on both sides, was indeed a separate land mass, unconnected to Asia.

Any remaining doubts were ended by the voyage of Ferdinand Magellan (ma-JEL-an), a Portuguese navigator sailing for Spain. In 1519, Magellan and his crew set out on a voyage around the world. Sailing westward from Spain, they crossed the Atlantic and sailed southward along the coast of South America. Passing through what is today called the Strait of Magellan, they sailed into the Pacific Ocean and continued westward, finally returning to Spain in 1522. Magellan himself, who was killed in the Philippines in 1521, and four of his five ships never completed the voyage. However, those who survived became the first people in history to **circumnavigate**—sail completely around—the earth. They proved, once and for all, that the land Columbus had reached was not Asia.

THE CONQUISTADORS

The Spanish explorers who reached the Americas soon began to hear tales of **El Dorado**, a fabulous city of gold. These tales told of a South American Indian chieftain who each year covered himself with gold dust, then washed it off in a lake into which his subjects threw gold and jewels.

Fired by dreams of great riches, many Spanish adventurers set off in search of El Dorado. As they journeyed through Central and South America, they encountered many Indian groups, often fighting and conquering them. As a result, they came to be called **conquistadors** (kong-KEES-ta-dours), or conquerors. The conquistadors were usually accompanied by priests, for the Spanish desire for gold was matched by the desire to replace the Indians' religions with Christianity. The Spanish believed it was their duty to "deliver" the Indians to God.

Cortés in Mexico. One of the conquistadors was a Spanish captain named Hernán Cortés (kor-TEZ). While on the island of Cuba, Cortés heard of the rich Aztec empire, and in 1519, with 700 men, 17 horses, and 13 guns, he set out for Mexico.

For a while, Cortés and his men traveled along the Mexican coast. They traded and sometimes fought with the local Indians, and from them learned all they could about the Aztecs. During this time, Cortés gained the services of two people who enabled him to communicate with the Indians. One was a shipwrecked Spanish sailor, who had learned the Mayan language. The other was an Aztec woman, La Malinche (lah mah-LEEN-chuh), called Doña Marina by the Spanish, who spoke both Maya and Nahuatl, the Aztec language. Through Doña Marina, Cortés learned of the Aztec belief that he was Quetzalcoátl, coming to save them. (As you recall, Quetzalcoátl was the Aztec god-king who had promised to return to reclaim his throne and redeem his people.)

Reports of the Spanish soldiers were soon carried back to Tenochtitlán by an Aztec tax collector named Pinotl. Moctezuma (mahk-tuh-ZOO-muh), the Aztec emperor, sent scouts for further information. Their eyewitness accounts filled him with alarm:

> Their trappings and arms are all made of iron. They dress in iron. . . . Their swords are iron, their bows are iron, their spears are iron. Their deers carry them on their backs wherever they wish to go. These deers, my lord are as tall as the roof of a house. . . . Their dogs are enormous, with flat ears and long, dangling tongues. The color of their eyes is a burning yellow; their eyes flash fire and shoot off sparks.

The other peoples ruled over by the Aztecs, however, secretly rejoiced in the whispered news that Quetzalcoátl was coming to save them from their hated rulers.

Cortés entered Aztec territory on April 20, 1519. Moctezuma sent ambassadors with golden gifts to meet the Spanish. He hoped these gifts would satisfy the strangers and persuade them to leave. However, the sight of the gold merely deepened Cortés's resolve to gain control of the Aztec empire.

Burning his ships to prevent his men from deserting, Cortés began the long and difficult march inland to Tenochtitlán. Bernal Diaz del Castillo, who accompanied Cortés, left this account:

> We came to a very strong fortress built of stones and mortar and some other cement so hard that it was difficult to demolish with

iron pickaxes. Indeed it was so well constructed for offense and defense that it would have been very difficult to capture. We halted to examine it, and Cortés asked the [Indians] . . . for what purpose it had been built in this way. They answered that since there was continuous war between their Lord Moctezuma and the Tlascalans [an enemy group], the latter had built this fortress to defend their towns, this being their territory. We rested awhile, and this information gave us plenty to think about.

Making certain to approach from the east, as Quetzalcóatl was supposed to do, Cortés and his men arrived in the Aztec capital in November. They captured and imprisoned Moctezuma, and for a while Cortés tried to rule through the emperor. However, in 1520 the Aztecs attacked the Spanish, killing half of them. Cortés escaped at night with the remainder of his men.

In 1521, Cortés returned with a force of about 1,000 men and many Indian allies. After a three-month siege, the Aztecs surrendered. Tenochtitlán was destroyed, and Cortés began to ship the Aztec treasure back to Spain.

This drawing shows the Spanish attack on Tenochtitlán. After conquering the Aztecs, Cortés went on to subdue the Mayas in the Yucatán Peninsula.

Cortés set about building Mexico City upon the ruins of the Aztec capital. He brought the Aztecs' former subjects under Spanish control and went on to conquer the Maya in Yucatán. Soon, all of Mexico was firmly in the control of Spain.

Pizarro in Peru.   Francisco Pizarro (pih-ZAHR-oh) was one of the Spanish settlers in Panama. There he heard rumors of a fabulous land, high in the mountains far to the south. This land, called Peru, was said to be so rich that the floors of its palaces were paved with gold.

Pizarro was a poor man. As a youth in Spain, he had earned his living by tending pigs. He decided to find Peru. Setting out in 1524, Pizarro encountered incredible hardships—storms, shipwreck, near-starvation. Finally, in 1532, on his third expedition, he landed on the northern coast of present-day Peru. With his small band of 160 men, he began the climb up the Andes Mountains, where Atahualpa, the new Inca emperor, awaited him.

As you read in Chapter 2, Atahualpa had just defeated his brother in a civil war to gain control of the Inca empire. When Pizarro arrived, Atahualpa was in camp, surrounded by his army. Pizarro occupied the little town of Cajamarca (ka-huh-MAHR-kuh) and, pretending friendship, invited Atahualpa to visit him. The Inca emperor arrived with his bodyguard of thousands of picked troops. Without warning, the Spanish charged from ambush, firing guns and cannons. The bodyguard was routed with heavy casualties, and Atahualpa was captured.

With Atahualpa in his power, Pizarro controlled Peru. The Incas offered to fill a large room with gold and another with silver if Pizarro would release their ruler. Pizarro agreed. Runners were sent to all parts of the vast empire to collect the treasure. But when the ransom was delivered, Pizarro did not release Atahualpa. Instead, he had the emperor killed.

The Incas tried to retaliate against the Spanish. However, already weakened by civil war, and now leaderless, they had little success. Pizarro left Cajamarca and marched on the capital of Cuzco. By 1535, he had defeated the Incas and set up a new Spanish capital at Lima (LEE-muh) on the Pacific coast. From here, treasure ships carried Inca silver and gold back to Spain.

THE PORTUGUESE SETTLE BRAZIL

In 1500, a Portuguese sea captain, Pedro Alvares Cabral (kuh-BRAHL), was sailing for India. Strong winds blew him off course and forced him westward to the land that is now Brazil. Cabral claimed this land for Portugal.

The Portuguese were slow to establish settlements in Brazil. In 1555, however, the French tried to establish a colony in the area of present-day Rio de Janeiro. The Portuguese responded quickly, crushing the French colony and settling the area themselves.

Unlike the areas of the Americas settled by the Spanish, Brazil had no great Indian empires and no rich treasures of silver and gold. It was, however, a rich source of brazilwood, a tree from which red dyes popular in Europe could be made. The Portuguese settlers cut the brazilwood and shipped it back to Portugal. They also began to grow sugar cane.

Favored by the soil and climate, northeastern Brazil soon became the site of enormous sugar plantations, or **fazendas**. The labor force on these plantations consisted almost entirely of slaves. At first, the planters relied on raids on Indian villages for their slave labor. However, the Indians did not adjust to this system and often ran away into the heavy forest. Some even committed suicide. After 1550, Portuguese planters turned increasingly to the use of enslaved people from Africa. They had already been using Africans to work their sugar plantations on an island off the coast of West Africa. Since they were in a strange land, the Africans could not disappear so easily into the forest. They had to work or be killed.

LIFE IN THE COLONIES

When the conquest was over, the Spanish and Portuguese settled down to agriculture and mining. The shores of the area from Brazil to the West Indies were carved up into sugar plantations. On the highlands and grasslands the newcomers created vast cattle ranches. Toward the middle of the eighteenth century, coffee cultivation was introduced in the tropical highlands. Gold, silver, and diamonds were discovered and mined in Colombia and Brazil.

As in the rest of the world at the time, most of the population of Latin America was rural. However, cities did arise. The largest city in South America in 1650 was the silver mining center of Potosí, in Bolivia, which had a population of 160,000. Mexico City had a population of 200,000 at the close of the seventeenth century. By 1788, in Spanish America there were over thirty institutions of higher learning authorized to award college degrees. There were also several universities that awarded doctorates in medicine, law, and philosophy.

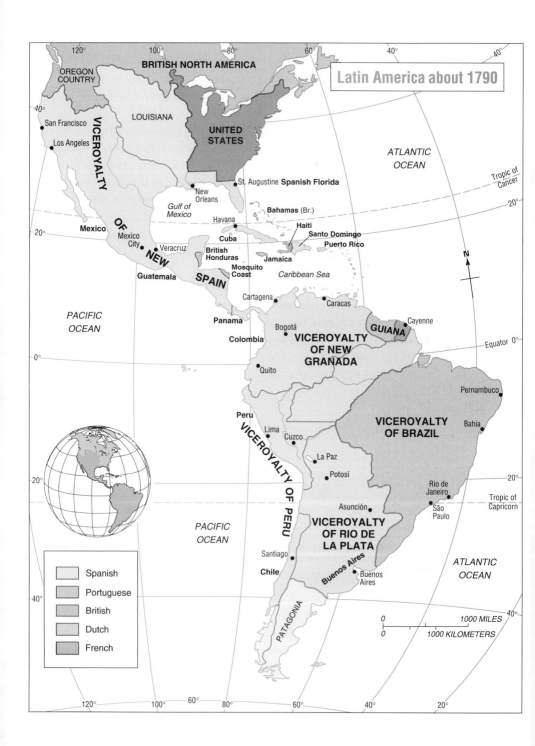

Latin America about 1790

OREGON COUNTRY

BRITISH NORTH AMERICA

LOUISIANA

UNITED STATES

San Francisco

Los Angeles

VICEROYALTY OF NEW SPAIN

Mexico

Mexico City

Veracruz

Guatemala

Gulf of Mexico

New Orleans

Havana

Cuba

British Honduras

Mosquito Coast

Panama

St. Augustine Spanish Florida

ATLANTIC OCEAN

Bahamas (Br.)

Haiti

Santo Domingo

Puerto Rico

Jamaica

Caribbean Sea

Cartagena

Colombia

Bogotá

VICEROYALTY OF NEW GRANADA

Quito

Caracas

Cayenne

GUIANA

Equator 0°

PACIFIC OCEAN

Peru

Lima Cuzco

La Paz

Potosí

VICEROYALTY OF PERU

Pernambuco

VICEROYALTY OF BRAZIL

Bahia

Rio de Janeiro

São Paulo

Asunción

VICEROYALTY OF RIO DE LA PLATA

Santiago

Chile

Buenos Aires

Buenos Aires

PACIFIC OCEAN

ATLANTIC OCEAN

PATAGONIA

Tropic of Cancer

Tropic of Capricorn

Spanish

Portuguese

British

Dutch

French

0   1000 MILES

0   1000 KILOMETERS

62

Government.   The Spanish king was an **absolute monarch**. This means that the king was all-powerful. He made all decisions and approved all laws. His subjects owed him total and unquestioning loyalty.

The Spanish kings organized their empire for their own benefit. They wished to keep tight control over their colonies. However, the colonies were too far away for the king to govern directly. Therefore, he appointed a **viceroy,** or person who acted in the place of the king, to govern the colonies for him. Each viceroy governed a large area called a **viceroyalty.**

The king, assisted by a group of Spanish nobles called the Council of the Indies, made all the laws for the colonies. It was the viceroy's job to enforce these laws. An **audiencia,** or court, was appointed by the king to make sure that the viceroy carried out his orders. The only elected body was the town council, chosen by a small group of wealthy colonists.

The system of government in the Spanish colonies was very rigid. It took a long time to bring about change or to respond to new conditions. In many cases, this hindered colonial development

Colonial governments were often corrupt. Wealthy landowners bribed officials to look the other way when they cheated or abused the Indians. The king himself could be bribed. King Carlos I, who reigned from 1516 to 1556, made laws to protect the Indians from slavery. However, the wealth of the empire, and thus of the king, depended on the forced labor of the Indians. Therefore, the laws protecting the Indians were frequently overlooked.

Settlement in Brazil.   The government established by the Portuguese in Brazil was much less centralized. Most of the settlements in Brazil hugged the coast. Winds and ocean currents made transportation and communication among the various settlements very difficult. As a result, a much greater degree of local rule was allowed than in the Spanish colonies.

As you read, settlement of Brazil proceeded slowly at first. To encourage settlement, the king of Portugal divided Brazil into districts called **captaincies.** These captaincies were awarded by the king as favors to his friends, who became known as **captains.** The captains were given the right to build settlements, collect taxes, and govern their own districts.

Colonial Economic Policy.   The economic policy of Spain and Portugal regarding their colonies was known as **mercantilism.** Under this policy, which was followed by most European nations at the time, the colonies were to provide the home nation with raw materials. They were also to serve as markets, buying the manufactured goods that the home country produced. All goods entering the colony had to be carried by the home country's ships. As a result of this mercantilist policy, Spain and Portugal's American colonies were forbidden to buy foreign manufactured goods or to sell raw materials to anyone but the home country. They were also forbidden to manufacture any products that would compete with those produced by the home country. Thus, Spain and Portugal became wealthy, while their American colonies remained undeveloped and dependent on imports. Except for minor industries such as pottery, weaving, and tanning, little opportunity was provided for industrial development.

The basis of Spanish wealth in the Americas was rich mineral deposits, mainly silver but also gold in what is now Bolivia and Mexico. Spanish treasure ships carrying cargoes of silver and gold back to Spain were frequently attacked by pirates who prowled the seas, as well as by ships of other European nations. Late in the 1500s, the Spanish developed a **convoy** system to protect their ships. Under this system, Spanish warships escorted the treasure ships on the homeward voyage across the Atlantic.

Agriculture, while not as profitable as mineral resources, also played a role in the colonial economy. Wheat and maize were grown on a large scale in Mexico and Peru. Sugar cultivation, first introduced in the West Indies, spread rapidly to other colonial areas. Wine and olives were produced in the irrigated valleys of Peru. The colonists also produced important quantities of tobacco, cacao, and indigo. A particularly im-

The Spanish used the conquered Indians in Mexico and elsewhere in Latin America as slave laborers. This picture shows the treatment the Indians received at the hands of their Spanish masters.

portant Spanish contribution to American economic life was the introduction of various domestic animals, including chickens, mules, horses, cattle, pigs, and sheep.

Social Structure. Society in the American colonies of Spain and Portugal was divided into distinct and separate classes. A person was born into a social class and remained in that class for life. There was little or no chance to move from one class to another. At the top were those who had been born in Spain or Portugal. Because these countries are located on a piece of land called the Iberian Peninsula, the people who came from there were known as **peninsulares** (puh-NIN-suh-lar-us). The peninsulares were few in number, but they dominated society, controlling most of the power and wealth. Of the 170 viceroys that governed the colonies during Spanish rule, only four were not peninsulares.

Below the peninsulares were the **criollos** (kree-OH-yos), those people who were born in America but whose parents or grandparents were Spanish. The criollos managed the farms and directed the mining of silver and gold. However, although many criollos were wealthy, they could not hold any important positions in the government.

Below the criollos were the **mestizos,** people of mixed Spanish and Indian parentage, and the **mulattoes,** people of mixed Spanish and African parentage. At the bottom were the Africans brought as slaves, and the Indians, who were treated little better than slaves.

Indians and Africans. In order to develop their colonial mining and plantation economies, the Spanish and Portuguese needed cheap and abundant labor. They turned to the native populations, forcing them to work in the mines and fields. At first, they developed a system known as the **encomienda** (en-KOH-mee-en-doh). Under this system, a colonist was granted a deed, or *encomendar,* assigning him a group of Indians who were to serve him as laborers. In return, the colonist, or *encomendero,* pledged to protect his Indians, pay their wages, and encourage their conversion to Christianity. However, the settlers often mistreated their charges, and the system turned out to be little more than a thinly disguised form of slavery. Indeed, the system was so harsh that its practice in the West Indies resulted in the almost total destruction of the Indian population there.

Protests against the encomienda were led by a Catholic missionary named Bartolomé de Las Casas (lahs KAH-sahs). In 1542, the Spanish king proclaimed the New Laws of the Indies, which resulted in the eventual disappearance of the encomienda.

CASE STUDY:

A Lost Indian Heritage

Guamán Poma de Ayala was an Indian who lived in Spanish South America during the seventeenth century. Guamán, who had learned to speak and write Spanish, wrote an account of Indian life under Spanish rule. In the following selection, Eduardo Galeano, a twentieth-century Uruguayan novelist, imagines Guamán's thoughts as he wrote the book. The sentences in italics are direct quotes from Guamán's work.

Today, Guamán Poma de Ayala finishes his letter to the king of Spain. At the start it was addressed to Philip II, who died while Guamán was writing it. Now he wants it delivered into Philip III's own hand. He has trekked [walked] from village to village, *the author walking over mountains with much snow,* eating if he could and always carrying on his back his growing manuscript of sketches and words.

To write this letter is to weep . . .

The Indians are the natural owners of this kingdom and the Spaniards, natives of Spain, are strangers here in this kingdom. *Also, it is God's punishment that many Indians die in mercury and silver mines. In all Peru, where there were a hundred not ten remain.*

Today, Guamán finishes his letter. He has lived for it. It has taken him half a century to write and draw. It runs to nearly twelve hundred pages. Today, Guamán finishes his letter and dies.

Neither Philip III nor any other king will ever see it. For three centuries it will roam the earth, lost.

Eduardo Galeano. *Memory of Fire* (New York: Pantheon, 1985).

1. How does Guamán's letter describe the Spanish treatment of the Indians?

2. What percentage of Indians does Guamán say died under Spanish rule?

3. Why did no king see Guamán's letter?

Although the encomienda disappeared, the mistreatment of the Indians did not. A new system, the **repartimiento** (ray-par-TEE-mee-en-toh), required all male Indians to work for a certain amount of time each year in Spanish mines, factories, farms, and ranches. The repartimiento did not provide a dependable and continuing supply of labor, however. Soon the colonists turned for a steady supply of cheap labor to a new system, known as debt **peonage.**

Because the arrival of the Europeans had robbed them of their usual means of livelihood, many of the Indians often found themselves in debt to the colonists. In order to repay the debt, they were forced to become **peons,** working for a colonial employer until the debt was paid—an event so rare it might be considered a miracle! The practice of debt peonage continued into the twentieth century.

European colonization had a disastrous effect on the Indians of the Americas. One cause, as you have read, was the harsh conditions of near-slavery. Another less obvious cause was disease. The Spanish and Portuguese brought with them germs that were new to the Americas. The Indians had no resistance to these germs, especially smallpox, and millions of them died. Between enslavement and disease, whole tribes were wiped out. When the Spanish arrived in 1519, the Indian population of the area of New Spain was about 25 million. Less than 100 years later, in 1605, there were a little more than 1 million left. This was one of the greatest population disasters the world has ever seen.

Europeans brought the first enslaved people from Africa in the early 1500s. As the Indian population declined, the slave trade increased. In many areas, the African population eventually outnumbered the white and mestizo populations. Most of the African slaves worked on the sugar plantations. Many Spanish and Portuguese believed that the Africans were better able than the Indians to withstand the hardships of plantation labor. Therefore, there was little attempt, even among the missionaries, to defend the Africans against abuses.

The Church in Latin America. Roman Catholicism was the official religion both of the Spanish colonies and of Brazil. The king was the head of the church and appointed all priests and bishops. Special taxes were collected to support the church.

The Spanish and Portuguese kings were interested in converting the Indians to Roman Catholicism; that is, they wanted to bring God to the Indians and to have them become Catholics. Hundreds of **missionaries** were sent to the colonies to teach the Indians about Christianity. The

A Brazilian plantation. The main house often had many wings. Farm buildings and slave quarters were located nearby.

missionaries also tried to teach the Indians the Spanish and Portuguese language and customs.

The missionaries often tried to protect the Indians from oppression. In many cases, their attempts antagonized the peninsulare or criollo landowners and got the missionaries into trouble with the government. Many of the priests and missionaries were brave men who even dared to accuse the king of committing a grave sin by allowing the mistreatment of the Indians.

The missionaries built churches and schools for the Spanish and Portuguese as well as for the Indians. However, there were never enough priests to serve all the people. The empires were simply too big, and transportation across the rough terrain too difficult. Thus, many people throughout the colonies seldom saw a priest. They spent most of their lives without contact with the major cultural institution of the colonizing countries.

Role of Women. Males dominated Latin American colonial life. Women were not permitted to control their dowries or inheritances. Fathers arranged marriages for their daughters, and men could easily obtain an end to marriage, while women could not.

However, some colonial women operated their own businesses, and several rose to positions of political and intellectual leadership. Perhaps the best known is the Mexican nun, Sor Juana Iñes de la Cruz (1651-1695), who was a noted mathematician and author of some exceptionally beautiful poetry.

THE STRUGGLES FOR INDEPENDENCE

By the early 1800s, Spain and Portugal controlled all the lands of Latin America except for a few scattered settlements. They had controlled these colonies for nearly 300 years. Beginning in the late 1700s, discontent with European rule began to grow. By 1824, most of the colonies had fought wars that freed them from Spanish and Portuguese rule.

Reasons for Discontent.   There were a number of causes for Latin American discontent with Spanish and Portuguese rule. One of the most important was the colonial social structure. The more numerous criollos and wealthier mulattoes and mestizos resented being ruled by the few privileged peninsulares. These groups felt they were entitled to an active role in the government. The lower classes—the Indians and Africans— wanted their freedom and rights. All began to see independence as the way to improve their lives.

Another important cause of discontent was the mercantile trade policy of the parent countries. The colonists felt that the Spanish and Portuguese trade laws limited their economic development and prevented them from becoming prosperous.

Finally, as time passed, the colonists began to think of America as their home country, and themselves as Americans, rather than Europeans. These feelings of patriotism were further sparked by events in other parts of the world. In particular, the colonists were fired in their desire for freedom by the American War for Independence, in which the thirteen English colonies revolted against Great Britain, and by the French Revolution, in which the French overthrew the king and declared their political rights.

Haiti.   The first Latin American war for independence was not fought against Spain or Portugal, but against France, which had only a few colonies in the region. In 1791, African slaves who worked on the sugar cane plantations in Haiti on the island of Hispaniola revolted against colonial rule, which had begun there nearly 100 years earlier. They were led by a self-educated former slave named Toussaint L'Ouverture (loo-ver-TOOR). L'Ouverture was captured in 1802 and died in a French prison. However, under the leadership of Jean-Jacques Dessalines (day-sah-LEEN), another former slave, the colonists succeeded in defeating the French. In 1804, Haiti thus became the first Latin American nation (and the second, after the United States, in the Western Hemisphere) to gain independence.

Mexico.   The first uprising against Spanish power in the Americas took place in Mexico. In 1810, a criollo priest, Miguel Hidalgo (ee-THAHL-goh), led an enormous army of Indian peasants in an attack against the criollos and peninsulares. Hidalgo was a strong believer in liberty and equality. He wanted not just independence, but a complete restructuring of government and society.

After some victories, in 1811 Hidalgo was captured and executed. Another priest, José Morelos (moh-RAY-lohs), took his place. Despite some early successes, Morelos, too, was captured and executed by Spanish forces in 1815. With Morelos's death, hope for social improvements for the lower classes came to an end, and Mexico returned to its status as a Spanish colony.

Finally, in 1821, the peninsulares and criollos carried out a revolution of their own. A rebellion in Spain that had overthrown the king had made these people fear that their privileged position in the colonies might be threatened. Banding together behind a Spanish officer named Agustín de Iturbide (ee-toor-BEE-thay), they declared independence from Spain. Iturbide proclaimed himself emperor of Mexico, but was soon overthrown, and in 1824 Mexico became an independent republic.

Central America briefly was part of Iturbide's Mexican empire. But by 1823, representatives from Guatemala, El Salvador, Honduras, Nicaragua, and Costa Rica had met to form the United Provinces of Central America, a federation with a constitution, a president, and an assembly.

Brazil.   In Brazil, independence was won without bloodshed. In 1807, when Napoleon invaded Portugal, the Portuguese king, John IV, fled to Brazil with his family and royal court. Once there, he declared Brazil a kingdom equal in status to Portugal, and opened its ports to foreign trade.

John returned to Portugal in 1821, but left his son Pedro to rule in his place. The Brazilians became angry when John, no longer in Brazil, tried to turn the nation back into a colony. They persuaded King Pedro to declare Brazil independent. Pedro agreed, and in 1822 Brazil became an independent empire, with Pedro as emperor. (Brazil became a republic in 1889.)

Spanish South America.   Many leaders played a role in the movement for South American independence. None were more important, however, than Simón Bolívar (boh-LEE-vahr) and José de San Martín (san mahr-TEEN). Bolívar, the son of a wealthy Venezuelan criollo family, had been educated in Europe, where he became a strong supporter of the ideals of the French and American revolutions. San Martín, also a criollo, had been born in Argentina, but served with the Spanish army in Europe. The personalities of the two leaders were sharply different. Bolívar was passionate and emotional, while San Martín was humble and modest. However, both were committed to driving the Spanish out of South America.

Bolívar led the struggle for independence in northern South America. Returning to Venezuela in 1810, Bolívar organized a revolt in his native city of Caracas. The revolt was unsuccessful, as were further revolts in 1813 and 1815. Finally, in a daring move, in 1819, with a large army of patriots, he succeeded in climbing and crossing the rugged and bitterly cold Colombian Andes. The Spanish forces lay below. On

Simón Bolívar is called "the Liberator" of South America. Who were some of the other leaders in the movement for Latin American independence?

the field of Boyacá, the patriot band defeated the surprised Spanish in a short, sharp battle. Bolívar then entered Bogotá (capital of present-day Colombia). Three years later, in 1821, he defeated the last major Spanish force in northern South America at Carabobo. The entire Viceroyalty of New Granada was free. Hailing Bolívar as "the Liberator," the people elected him the first president of a new republic called Gran Colombia, which included present-day Colombia, Venezuela, Ecuador, and Panama.

While Bolívar was fighting to free northern South America, San Martín was leading the struggle in the south. Returning home from Europe in 1812, San Martín trained a rebel army in Argentina. Deciding to join forces with another South American patriot, Bernardo O'Higgins, he led his forces over the snow-covered Andes into Chile. The patriots fought long and hard, and in 1818, Chile became independent, with O'Higgins as its governor.

From Chile, San Martín's forces sailed north to drive the Spanish from Peru. They captured the capital, Lima, but the Spanish remained entrenched in the nearby mountains. Simón Bolívar now journeyed southward with his army to meet San Martín, and to help continue the battle for freedom. On December 9, 1824, the patriots defeated the Spanish at the battle of Ayacucho. This was the last major engagement of the war. All the Spanish colonies in South America were now independent.

Effects of Colonialism. For much of Latin America, the colonial era was over, but the legacy of 300 years of colonial rule remained.

The colonial record in Latin America is mixed. The Spanish and Portuguese were harsh in their treatment of the great Indian civilizations of the Americas. And they exploited both human and natural resources to attain their ends. Armed with the slogan "for God, gold, and glory," anything that they might do became permissible for the Spanish and the Portuguese.

However, the European influence was not all negative. To the people of Latin America, Spain and Portugal bequeathed their languages, literature, religion, and customs. Over 100 million Latin Americans today speak Spanish. They still admire *Don Quixote* and other Spanish literary classics, and build churches and cathedrals in the Spanish style. European powers also passed on to their American possessions their creative ideas about learning, beauty, artistic expression, and individualism. In an infinite number of ways the European—especially the Spanish—imprint is indelibly fixed on the land and people of Latin America.

REVIEWING THE CHAPTER

I. Building Your Vocabulary

In your notebook, write the numbers from 1 to 5. After each number, write the term that best matches the definition.

monopoly	mestizos	viceroy
criollos	conquistadors	caravel

1. governor of a Spanish colony appointed by the king to act in his place
2. total control of something, such as trade
3. people born in America but of Spanish origin
4. people of mixed Spanish and Indian parentage
5. Spanish adventurers who led the conquest of the Indian civilizations of the Americas

II. Understanding the Facts

In your notebook, write the numbers from 1 to 5. After each number, write true or false for each of the sentences below. If the statement is false, replace the underlined name or term with the correct name or term.

1. The arrival of the Spanish filled the Aztec emperor Atahualpa with fear.
2. The Spanish, led by Francisco Pizarro, conquered the Inca.
3. Hundreds of mulattoes were sent to the colonies to convert the Indians to Christianity.
4. The leaders of the Mexican struggle of independence were Toussaint L'Ouverture and José Morelos.
5. Simón Bolívar and José de San Martín were the principal leaders in the movement for South American independence.

III. Thinking It Through

In your notebook, write the numbers from 1 to 5. After each number, write the letter of the best answer to the question or the best ending to the sentence.

1. One important result of the Crusades, beginning around 1100, was that
   a. Christians gained control over Palestine for 500 years.
   b. Europeans grew increasingly interested in contact with other parts of the world.
   c. France held a monopoly on trade with eastern countries.
   d. Fruits such as lemons, apricots, and melons were introduced to Asia.

2. What did Magellan's voyage prove?
   a. that the Americas were two continents, not one
   b. that the world was round
   c. that Columbus had circumnavigated the earth
   d. that Muslim sailors had reached the Americas before Columbus

3. In the report about the Spanish sent by Aztec scouts to Moctezuma, what are the scouts referring to by the statement, "their eyes flash fire and shoot off sparks?"
   a. the weapons of the Spanish
   b. the drunkenness of the Spanish troops
   c. the weariness of the Spanish after their journey to the Aztec empire
   d. the anger of Spanish leaders at the Aztec religion

4. Which group would be most in favor of the peonage system?
   a. peons   b. criollos   c. mulattos   d. missionaries

5. As a result of the battle of Ayacucho,
   a. the Incas surrendered their empire to the Spanish.
   b. the Line of Demarcation was moved westward.
   c. José de San Martín was put in charge of all forces fighting the Spanish in Gran Colombia.
   d. all South America became independent of Spain.

DEVELOPING CRITICAL THINKING SKILLS

1. Describe the government and social structure in the Spanish colonies.

2. Show how Spain and Portugal benefited from the economic policy known as mercantilism.

3. Explain why the Spanish and Portuguese treated Native Americans and Africans in their colonies so harshly.

4. (a) Discuss the reasons why the colonies of Spain and Portugal in the Americas revolted against the mother countries. (b) What might these countries have done to prevent the revolutions that cost them their colonies?

INTERPRETING MAPS

Study the map on page 76. Then answer the following questions.

1. What two modern countries were once parts of Gran Colombia?
   a. Ecuador and Costa Rica
   b. Cuba and Brazil
   c. Venezuela and Panama
   d. Colombia and Peru

2. Which statement is best supported by information on the map?
   a. Spain still had a small colonial empire in the Americas.
   b. Borders between Latin American nations were well defined by 1850.
   c. Brazil was the most powerful nation in Latin America.
   d. Guatemala and Nicaragua were provinces of Mexico in 1850.

Latin America in 1850

UNITED STATES

Gulf of Mexico

Tropic of Cancer

MEXICO

Cuba (Sp.)

Bahamas (Br.)

SANTO DOMINGO

Puerto Rico (Sp.)

Jamaica (Br.)

British Honduras (Br.)
HONDURAS
GUATEMALA
EL SALVADOR
NICARAGUA
COSTA RICA
Panama

HAITI

Guadeloupe (Fr.)
Martinique (Fr.)

Caribbean Sea

Mosquito Coast (Br.)

ATLANTIC OCEAN

PACIFIC OCEAN

N

VENEZUELA

(Br.) (Neth.)
(Fr.)
Guiana

NEW GRANADA (COLOMBIA)

ECUADOR

Equator 0°

PERU

EMPIRE OF BRAZIL

BOLIVIA

PARAGUAY

Tropic of Capricorn

PACIFIC OCEAN

CHILE

ARGENTINE CONFEDERATION

URUGUAY

ATLANTIC OCEAN

0   1000 MILES
0   1000 KILOMETERS

United Provinces of Central America (1823–1838)

Gran Colombia (1819–1830)

Borders in dispute

ENRICHMENT AND EXPLORATION

1. Write a short play dramatizing the fall of the Aztec or Incan empires to the Spanish. Choose students to play the various roles, rehearse the play, and then present it to the class. You might wish to ask students with artistic talent to design scenery and costumes for the play.

2. Use encyclopedias and other library sources to find out more about the daily life of the Indians in the Spanish and Portuguese colonies of Latin America. In particular, look for information about conditions under the *encomienda*, or debt peonage. Then imagine you are an Indian in one of the colonies, and write a diary covering a week in your life.

4 *People and Culture*

Latin America is a rich mix of peoples and cultures. Reflecting the area's history, this mix has three main elements—Indian, European, and black African. Each of these groups has added its own colors and patterns to the fabric of contemporary Latin American culture.

ORIGINS AND LANGUAGE

Ethnic Groups.   People of many different ethnic and racial backgrounds live in Latin America. The major groups are people of European descent, Indians, people of African descent, people of mixed European and Indian descent, and people of mixed European and African descent.

Most of Latin America's Indians live in Mexico, Peru, Guatemala, Bolivia, and Ecuador. Many of the Indian groups inhabit remote villages, apart from the rest of the population. They speak only their native languages and take little part in the affairs of the country in which they live. Some of them live almost exactly as their ancestors did hundreds of years ago.

Africans first came to Latin America as slaves during the colonial era. Forced to leave their homelands in Africa, they were imported by the Spanish and Portuguese colonists to work on the plantations and in the mines. It is estimated that more than 5 million black Africans were brought to Latin America as slaves between the early 1500s and late 1800s. About two-thirds of them went to Brazil. Today, people of African descent live in almost all areas of Latin America. The largest numbers are in Brazil, Haiti, Cuba, Jamaica, Venezuela, Colombia, and Ecuador, as well as on some of the islands of the Caribbean region.

The Spanish and Portuguese who colonized Latin America inter-

Students in Mexico City. About 55 percent of the Mexican people are mestizos and about 29 percent are American Indians.

married fairly freely with the Indian peoples they met there. As a result, about one-third of the population today are mestizos, (as you remember, people of mixed Indian and European ancestry). The majority live in Mexico, Colombia, Venezuela, Chile, Peru, Ecuador, El Salvador, Honduras, Paraguay, Guatemala, and Nicaragua. Large numbers of mulattoes, descendants of Africans and Europeans who intermarried, live in Brazil, Cuba, the Dominican Republic, and other areas.

In southern South America, Argentina and Uruguay are predominantly European. Most of the inhabitants of these countries are descendants of the large numbers of Spanish, Italian, German, and Portuguese immigrants who poured in during the late nineteenth and early twentieth centuries. It is estimated that between 11 and 12 million immigrants arrived in South America during this period.

Like the United States at this time, South America was seen as a haven from persecution and a land of opportunity. This sentiment was expressed by Rubén Darío, a Nicaraguan-born poet who had made Argentina his "second motherland." In "Hymn to Argentina," a poem written in 1910 to celebrate the one-hundredth anniversary of Argentina's independence, Darío appealed to "all the disinherited of the earth" to come to Argentina where everyone was promised a full life.

Welcome all nations to the new promised land!
Here is the region of El Dorado,
Here is the terrestrial paradise.
Here the longed-for good fortune,
Here the golden fleece.

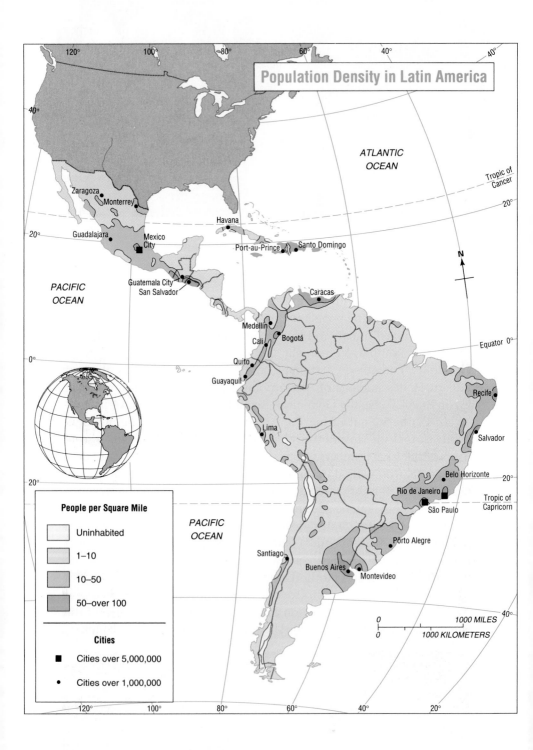

Population Density in Latin America

ATLANTIC OCEAN

PACIFIC OCEAN

Tropic of Cancer

Tropic of Capricorn

Equator 0°

PACIFIC OCEAN

Zaragoza
Monterrey
Havana
Guadalajara
Mexico City
Port-au-Prince
Santo Domingo
Guatemala City
San Salvador
Caracas
Medellín
Cali
Bogotá
Quito
Guayaquil
Recife
Lima
Salvador
Belo Horizonte
Río de Janeiro
São Paulo
Pôrto Alegre
Santiago
Buenos Aires
Montevideo

N

People per Square Mile

	Uninhabited
	1–10
	10–50
	50–over 100

Cities

■ Cities over 5,000,000

• Cities over 1,000,000

0   1000 MILES
0   1000 KILOMETERS

The arrival of new immigrant groups in recent years has further enriched Latin America's population. Many Japanese live in southern Brazil. Chinese live in Mexico, Peru, and Cuba. On some Caribbean islands, Indians from Asia make up half or more of the population, while in several countries, there are sizable numbers of people from Lebanon and Eastern Europe.

Racial Groups.   Race plays a smaller role in Latin American life than in most multiracial areas of the world. Generally, life-style, education, and occupation are more important than skin color in determining status. However, prejudice based on color does exist. In all countries with large Indian populations, Indians remain near the bottom of the social scale. Even in Brazil, which has a large, racially mixed population, there are serious economic and social differences among racial groups. In Venezuela, however, a multiracial society enjoys a great degree of openness with a minimum of discrimination.

A Kuna Indian woman of the San Blas islands off Panama with her grandchild. Her clothing is typical of the Indians of the Panamanian region.

Language.   Spanish is the language spoken by most of the people of Latin America. However, it is not the Spanish of Spain, but an American version that has developed over the years. In Argentina and Uruguay, for instance, the Spanish has been heavily influenced by Italian, the language of many nineteenth- and twentieth-century immigrants to those countries. Indian dialects have affected the local Spanish of Mexico, Guatemala, and Peru. Many everyday words are derived from Indian languages: *hamaca* (hammock), *huracán* (hurricane), *tabaco* (tobacco), and *chicle* (chewing gum) are just a few.

Within Latin America, the Spanish spoken is not uniform either. Intonation and accent—even some words—vary from country to country, sometimes from region to region. For example, in Cuba, "bus" is *guagua*; in Chile, it is *micro*; in Mexico, *camión*; in Argentina, *colectivo*. Ask for a *torta* in Mexico, and you will be served a sandwich. Ask for the same thing in Chile, however, and you will receive a slice of layer cake!

In Brazil, which was colonized by Portugal, Portuguese is the official language. English is the official language of Belize, Guyana, and a number of the Caribbean nations, including Jamaica, Grenada, Trinidad and Tobago, and the Bahamas. It is also spoken by people of African descent who settled on the coast of Central America. French is the official language of Haiti and of the islands of the French Antilles, while Dutch is the tongue of Suriname and the Netherlands Antilles. Chinese, Hindi, Arabic, and Slavic languages are also spoken in some areas of Central and South America.

In addition, numerous native American languages are spoken by nearly 24 million Indians in Latin America. The most important are Nahuatl, Quechua, Aymará, and Guaraní. In Peru, both Spanish and Quechua are official languages. In Paraguay, although Spanish is the official language, Guaraní is formally recognized as the everyday language spoken by most of the people.

DAILY LIFE

As you have read, Latin America is a vast region of great cultural and ethnic diversity. However, certain patterns of living are common to a majority of the people.

The Family.   In Latin America, the family is the single most important social institution. Each family member has a clearly defined role. In the traditional home, the father is the head of the household and is expected to support the family. The mother is responsible for raising the children and maintaining the family's links with the church. Children are expected to care for their parents in old age. In many urban households, live-in servants help with the cooking and washing.

The Latin American family unit is usually an **extended family.** This means that households consist of grandparents, parents, children, and cousins. In addition, other relatives usually live nearby, and families spend holidays and vacations together. The interests of the family come first, and assistance is provided for any family member facing economic difficulty or illness. Most of a child's early years are spent with the members of the extended family.

A unique feature of the Latin American family is the concept of godparenthood. The godparent, or *padrino*, assumes the role at the child's baptism. The *padrino* is loved, respected, and honored, and recognized as a family member. In the event of the death of the child's parents, or *padres*, the *padrino* assumes the responsibility of raising the godchild, or *ahijado*.

The Home.   The home is the center of most social activity in Latin America. Birthdays, weddings, and saints' days are all occasions for family get-togethers and celebrations. It is common for parties, with sumptuous sit-down feasts served by the hosts, to last all night. Guests are welcomed with the greeting, "*Mi casa es su casa,*" "My house is your house." Hospitality reaches its greatest heights in rural areas, where peasants treat visitors almost as royal guests.

Houses in the rural areas of Latin America have undergone little change over the years. Most rural houses are made of logs or sun-dried bricks of earth or clay. Roofs are of any available material—leaves, grass, or branches. The interiors have earthen floors and lack water or sanitary facilities. Not all modern conveniences are lacking, however, and it is not unusual to find a radio or television set next to a primitive stove.

In the cities, the older houses are modeled on the typical houses of Spain. Most of the houses are one-story buildings. Adobe walls, painted white, keep out the heat. Most of the rooms open onto a central patio that serves as a cool place for family activity. The patio is often decorated with lush gardens. Newer city houses are built with modern materials and conveniences. Many urban Latin Americans live in high-rise apartment buildings.

Food.   Most Latin Americans eat their main meal at midday. This meal consists of several courses, including soup, rice or beans with meat or fish, and dessert. Dinner, usually a simple dish or snack, is not served until 8 or 9 P.M.

Given the size of the region, it is not surprising that food varies from place to place in Latin America. However, tomatoes, beans, rice, potatoes, maize (corn), chicken, and cocoa are common to all countries. A wide variety of fresh fruits is available, among them apples, pineapples, papayas, and mangoes. A special treat is the cherimoya, or custard apple, a heart-shaped green fruit that tastes something like vanilla ice cream mixed with a bit of strawberry, pineapple, and banana.

Dishes that are regarded as typically Latin American usually blend Spanish with **indigenous,** or native, ingredients. One of the most popular is guacamole, mashed ripe avocados seasoned with hot peppers and tomatoes. Another is seviche (say-VEE-chay), fish or shrimp that is cooked not over heat but by soaking it in lime juice. This "cooking" technique was developed before the invention of refrigeration to prevent fish from spoiling.

Each country has its own food specialty. In Argentina and Uruguay, which produce fine beef cattle, this is the *asado* (ah-SAH-doh), a marvelous outdoor barbecue of spit-roasted meats. Chile is famous for its seafood as well as for *pastel de choclo,* (Pah-STEL day CHOK-loh), a hearty casserole of stewed chicken stuffed with meat and topped with corn pudding. The national dish of Brazil is *feijoada* (fay-ZWAH-dah), black beans cooked with sausage, beef, and bacon. *Llapingachos* (lyah-pin-GAH-chos), enjoyed in Ecuador, consists of potatoes stuffed with cream cheese and eggs and served with a sauce of onions and tomatoes. All over Latin America, small meat pies called *empanadas* (em-pahn-AH-thahs) are popular snacks, while *flan,* or baked custard, is a favorite dessert.

Dress.   Most Latin Americans dress conservatively. In the tropics, the men usually wear white trousers and shirts. The women wear loose white blouses and full dark skirts. In the cities, people dress more formally. The men wear suits and ties, the women, the latest fashions from all over the world. Children usually wear smocks or uniforms for school.

Garments of traditional design are still worn by many Indians in Latin America. In the Andes, the hats of the Indian women indicate the particular region in which they live. The *quexquemel,* worn in Mexico, is a long piece of cloth with an opening for the head; it is worn over the shoulders as a cape. A similar garment, called a *poncho,* is

84

commonly worn as protection from the cold by Indian men of the mountain regions. The Indian men of the Chiapas region of Mexico carry leather pocketbooks over their shoulders.

Marriage.   In the past, boys and girls could date only with parental permission. They were accompanied by a chaperon, or older person who ensured proper behavior. Today, however, the traditional patterns are changing, and young people are beginning to meet on their own. Most children live at home until they get married. The wedding ceremony is elaborate and usually takes place in church. A Latin American girl does not give up her family name when she marries. If Maria Leyva marries José Paso, she becomes Maria Leyva de Paso. All children bear a given name, the father's family name, and the mother's family name, in that order. Thus, if Maria Leyva and José Paso have a son whom they name Ernesto, the child's full name would be Ernesto Paso Leyva.

EDUCATION

Most Latin American countries have a 12-year school program. This is divided into six years of primary and six years of secondary instruction. Kindergartens are usually private and found only in urban areas. The school year is from March to November. Vacation falls in December, January, and February, when it is summer in Latin America. School is usually held six days a week, from 7 A.M. to 12 noon.

Education is controlled by a government agency, generally called the ministry of public education. This ministry makes the major decisions about primary and secondary education in both public and private schools. All students must pass official examinations prepared by the ministry .

By law, school attendance is required for all Latin American children. In actuality, however, only about half of the children ever attend school. A principal reason for this is poverty. In poor rural areas, children often have to help support their families by working in the fields and cannot go to school.

Literacy.   As would be expected in so large a region, educational facilities and achievement vary widely in Latin America. The **literacy rate**—the proportion of people who can read and write—ranges from about 90 percent in Chile, Argentina, Uruguay, Cuba, and Costa Rica, to less than 60 percent in Guatemala and Honduras, and 21 percent in

Haiti. Several countries have made tremendous strides in recent years in increasing the literacy rate. Most dramatic is the case of Mexico. In 1970, almost 35 percent of Mexicans were **illiterate**, or unable to read and write. Today, only 12 percent are illiterate. This change came about as a result of government efforts to improve adult education.

The Indians. For many Indians, especially those living in remote areas, the tribal village is the center of their lives. They take little or no part in the political or economic activity of the larger nation in which they live, and they rarely participate in formal schooling. Several countries, particularly Peru, Mexico, and Brazil, are trying to encourage their Indian populations to become active citizens. To achieve this goal, the governments of these nations have undertaken large-scale programs of Indian education.

Mexico's Indian-education program is typical. Specially trained teachers are sent to the Indian villages. At first, they teach in the local Indian language, then gradually switch to Spanish. Each Indian man or woman who is taught to read or write promises to teach someone else in their family or in their village. The government of Mexico hopes that knowledge of the national language—Spanish—will provide a stepping stone for the entrance of the Indians into the nation's mainstream.

The Universities. The university system of Latin America has long been the training ground of the professional classes. Entrance to the university is based on an examination taken upon completion of an academic secondary school program. In the past, entrance was limited to the upper classes of Latin American society. However, in recent years, young people from the urban middle class have begun to attend the universities. Many countries have actively worked toward this expansion of educational opportunity. In Argentina and Chile, for instance, the government passed university reform laws. In other nations, the number of state universities was increased.

In many Latin American countries, the universities play an important political role. Students are active in politics and often form a center of opposition to oppressive dictatorships or military governments. In several instances, students have banded together and have taken part in the successful overthrow of a nation's government. Sometimes, a nation's leader who feels threatened by student political groups will shut down the university.

URBAN AND RURAL LIFE

Latin America has many large cities, which are home to the majority of its population. Many of these urban metropolises are very modern, with futuristic skyscrapers, bustling superhighways, and busy international airports. They are in sharp contrast with the remote rural villages that are almost unchanged from colonial and precolonial times.

Cities. Latin America has more than 20 cities with populations that exceed one million people. About two-thirds of the population lives in cities, and almost one out of every three Latin Americans lives in a city of over one million people. The urban population continues to grow as more and more people flock to the cities from farms and villages. In the 1980s, Latin American cities were growing at a rate of 12 million persons a year.

In many Latin American countries, the urban population is concentrated in a single city. These cities also are the site of the country's government offices, major transportation lines, and industrial services. **Demographers,** people who study population growth and patterns, call these cities **primate cities.** Some of Latin America's primate cities are Caracas, Venezuela, with a metropolitan area population of almost 4 million, and Rio de Janeiro, Brazil, São Paulo, Brazil, Buenos Aires, Argentina, and Mexico City, Mexico, with populations ranging from 12 to 18 million. The concentration of population and services in a single place has led to many problems in recent years, and efforts are under way to develop other urban centers. In Brazil, for example, the government built an entirely new capital city, Brasília, and encouraged government officials and diplomats to move there.

Many present-day Latin American cities were originally established by the Spanish in the sixteenth and seventeenth centuries. The government of the time set forth elaborate rules for the establishment of such cities. Each town had to have a central square, arcades, a church, a jail, and a government house. The instructions were so detailed that the Spanish settlers were even told how to locate buildings to take advantage of prevailing wind patterns. Consequently, the downtown sections of almost all older Latin American cities have exactly the same layout.

Today, however, the order of the Spanish colonial towns has vanished. Latin American cities are infamous for gigantic traffic jams and high levels of air pollution. Industrial zones are often located dangerously close to residential housing, while highways pass through the centers of many of the major cities. Urban squatters live in shacks sandwiched between modern skyscrapers and enormous public housing complexes.

The Barrio. The cities are divided into neighborhoods, or **barrios**. The barrios are usually segregated by income levels. Because of the tremendous traffic congestion, it is not uncommon for workers to spend two or three hours riding the bus from the barrio to their place of work. Some cities have tried to ease the congestion by building subway systems, but without great success. During rush hours, the streets are still jammed, and people are squeezed inside the buses and hang out the doors and windows.

Slums. Approximately 20 to 30 percent of Latin America's urban population lives in squatter developments. Many of these squatters are workers with low-level jobs or recently arrived immigrants from rural areas. Moving in during the night, they illegally occupy sites on public land. They hurriedly construct makeshift shacks before dawn from whatever material is either available or affordable—sheet aluminum, scraps of lumber, or, if they are lucky, cement blocks. There are no water and no sanitary facilities. Cooking is done with kerosene or bottled gas. These shantytowns have different names in different countries—*villas miserias* in Argentina, *favelas* in Brazil, *callampas* in Chile, and *ranchos* in Venezuela—but few Latin American nations have escaped their blight.

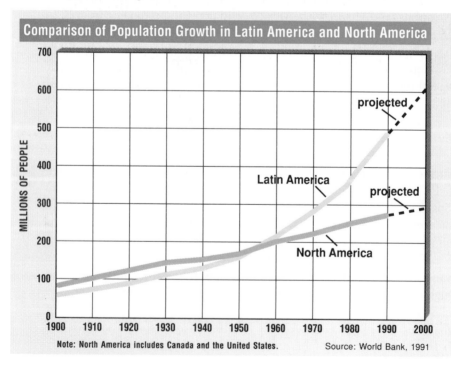

Comparison of Population Growth in Latin America and North America

Note: North America includes Canada and the United States.   Source: World Bank, 1991

The contrast between rich and poor is very sharp in many cities of Latin America. In Rio de Janiero, shown here, the slums of the poor stand next door to the high-rise apartments of upper-income people. About what percentage of the people in Latin America live in cities and towns?

Rural Villages.   For the Latin American peasant, or *campesino*, life continues much as it has for centuries. Most villages have fewer than 400 people, and the pace is slow. Pigs, dogs, and chickens roam the streets. At midday, when the sun is hottest, no one is to be seen. There may be no school or, if there is, children must often walk miles to attend. Very few people can read or write. They learn about the outside world by listening to the radio or attending movies, mostly imported from the United States.

A mountain village in Colombia. The houses are made of sun-dried bricks with roofs of thatch or tiles.

Land Reform.   Agriculture is the way of life for many of the people of Latin America. However, despite the fact that agriculture is a major economic activity, most Latin American countries have to import food.

The problems of Latin American agriculture have numerous causes. Among them are the lack of modern technology and the continued use of inefficient farming techniques. However, the most important cause is rooted in the region's history. It is the traditional pattern of landholding.

In colonial times, favorites of the Portuguese or Spanish king were often granted huge tracts of land in Latin America. Land ownership soon became concentrated in the hands of a small group of wealthy people. The landowners, or *terratenientes*, organized their land into vast agricultural estates called latifundia (see page 26). They employed peasants under slavelike conditions to work the land with primitive agricultural implements.

The latifundia system, established more than 300 years ago, continues into the twentieth century. Today, as in the 1600s, a privileged few own most of Latin America's fertile land. The remainder of the rural population works subsistence farms on small plots of land, growing barely enough food to feed their families.

During the past 50 years, the pattern of land ownership has been one of the most controversial issues in Latin America. Some people feel the solution to the problem is land reform. Under land reform, the government breaks up the large plantations and distributes the land among the peasants.

The first Latin American nation to undertake a formal program of land reform was Mexico, in 1917. Today, most Latin American nations have established some kind of land reform. The most significant programs, besides that in Mexico, are in Nicaragua, El Salvador, Cuba, Chile, Peru, and Bolivia.

The controversy surrounding land reform still rages. Supporters of land reform believe redistribution of the land will result in improved crop yields. They also believe that by giving a larger number of people a stake in society, land reform will help prevent revolution. Those who oppose land reform say that large estates are more efficient in terms of production than a lot of small farms. Perhaps the greatest problem of land reform, however, is enforcement.

RELIGION

The overwhelming majority of Latin Americans are Roman Catholics, and the Roman Catholic Church plays a major role in the region. Church attendance, however, is generally low, and the practice of the religion centers around the traditional ceremonies relating to birth, marriage, and death. Other religious groups are also present, although their members are relatively few.

The Roman Catholic Church.   Roman Catholicism, the religion of Spain and Portugal, was carried to America by the friars who accompanied the conquistadors across the Atlantic Ocean. These Catholic

Religious processions are part of the culture of many Latin American countries. These villagers in El Salvador are carrying statues of saints as part of their observance of Easter week, the holiest time in the Christian calendar.

missionaries spread out over the continent. They worked intensively among the Indians, and by the end of the sixteenth century, numerous converts had been made. Today, more than 90 percent of all Latin Americans are Roman Catholics.

Over the years, the church in Latin America became very wealthy. As its wealth grew, it became more conservative. In the past, the missionaries and priests had fought for the rights of the Indians and other exploited people. Now, however, church leaders began to lend support to the privileged and moneyed classes. They taught that the poor should accept their condition without complaint as God's will. In many ways, they were successful in imparting this idea. But eventually, some people began to question the church's position. These individuals tried to find ways to reduce the power of the church and the clergy.

Beginning in the 1960s, the Roman Catholic Church began to rethink its role. A group of Latin American priests proposed a new doctrine that came to be known as **liberation theology**. According to this doctrine, the condition of poverty is not something to be accepted by the poor humbly and uncomplainingly. Rather it is a condition caused by those with power in society, who stand to profit from its continuation. It is the responsibility of the church, said the liberation theologists, to take an active role in helping to change the conditions that lead to poverty. They tried to move the church into the forefront of the struggle for social justice in Latin America.

Liberation theology created some problems within the Roman Catholic Church. In 1979, Pope John Paul II addressed a meeting of Latin American bishops in Mexico. He agreed that the workers and peasants had the right to organize to better their economic condition. At the same time, however, he urged that priests avoid becoming too involved in social and political issues. In 1983, the Pope strongly condemned the activist position of certain Latin American priests with regard to social issues.

Today, the Roman Catholic Church is acknowledged as the chief protector of human rights in Latin America. It is one of the few institutions in the region with sufficient prestige to check the power of the state. In Chile, in the 1970s and early 1980s, it was the church that led the opposition to the oppressive military regime of General Augusto Pinochet (see Chapter 9).

Protestants and Jews.   Protestantism first came to Latin America with the large numbers of immigrants who arrived from Europe in the nineteenth century. Liberal leaders who were unhappy about the growing power of the Catholic Church encouraged the establishment of Protestant missions. Protestant churches have been successful in many regions. Most notable, perhaps, is Nicaragua, where today 10 percent of the population is Protestant.

In the 1930s, many Jews fleeing persecution in Europe found a haven in Latin America. Today they freely practice their religion there.

African-influenced Religions.   In the Caribbean and in Brazil, the African influence has led to the development of a variety of religious rituals that combine African and Catholic traditions. These rituals have various names: in Haiti, voodoo; in Cuba, santería; in Trinidad, sango; and in Brazil, candomblé and macumba.

We can learn much about Latin America from its writers, artists, and philosophers. In their works, they share their vision of the land in which they live. The Latin American artist often portrays a world where nothing is secure, where force rules and civil war is an everyday occurrence. Frequently occurring natural disasters and the enormous contrast between rich and poor are central themes. Sometimes the poor are seen as having no salvation except death. In one of the classic novels, *Pedro Paramo*, by the Mexican writer Juan Rulfo, all the characters are dead.

Literature. The first Latin American colonial authors were the Spanish explorers and conquistadors. Writing of their experiences, they produced a literature about heroes, wars, Indian civilizations, and the New World. The most notable was *La Auracana*, by a Spanish captain named Alonso de Ercilla y Zúñega. In this epic poem, Ercilla y Zúñega praises the heroic resistance of the Araucanian Indians of Chile against the Spanish.

Perhaps the most important work to appear in the years following independence was *Martín Fierro*, by José Hernández, which celebrated the life of the Argentine gaucho (see Chapter 8). In the later part of the nineteenth century, a new artistic movement developed in Latin America. This movement was called **modernism.** Led by such writers as Rubén Darío of Nicaragua, the modernists denounced the concern with material things and championed the doctrine of art for art's sake.

Twentieth-Century Novelists. By the first quarter of the twentieth century, the United States had emerged as a world power. The fear, resentment, and jealousy felt by many Latin Americans for their powerful Yankee neighbor was expressed by the Uruguayan novelist José Rodó in a work called *Ariel*. In this book, Rodó contrasts North and South Americans. He portrays North Americans as lacking in culture and interested only in money and the things money can buy. Latin Americans, on the other hand, although economically poorer, are seen as spiritually richer than their North American rivals. This book influenced the thinking of Latin Americans for generations.

Latin Americans also began looking inward at their own culture. Writers such as José Carlos Mariátegui of Peru wrote of the problems of integrating the Indians into society. Regionalist writers from northeastern Brazil, including Jorge Amado and Rachel de Queirós, wrote about subjects such as plantation life, the role of Brazilian women, and social problems. In Mexico, Rosario Castellanos wrote about the clash of cultures between the Indians and Europeans, while in Cuba, Nicolás Guillén described the life and sufferings of Africans.

Writers also began focusing on the problems of Latin American cities. Juan Carlos Onetti and Mario Benedetti of Uruguay, Julio Cortazar of Argentina, Octavio Paz and Carlos Fuentes of Mexico, and Guillermo Cabrera Infante of Cuba describe the complexities of urban life. Loneliness and despair are familiar themes in their writing.

The Literary Boom. Two giants of Latin American letters emerged in the early years of the twentieth century. They were Jorge Luis Borges of Argentina, and Miguel Angel Asturias of Guatemala. Borges, born in 1899, was blind. His highly imaginative poems and short stories range from fantasies to sophisticated detective yarns. Asturias, also born in 1899, was an avid student of Mayan religion and society. Two of his novels, *Guatemalan Legends* and *Men of Maize*, explore the Indian culture and its tremendous influence on Latin America. Asturias received the Nobel Prize for Literature in 1967.

In the last 25 years, the novelists and poets of Latin America have experienced a great surge in international popularity and recognition. Perhaps the most popular author is Gabriel García Márquez. Born on the steamy Caribbean coast of Colombia in 1928, García Márquez was one of the 16 children of a poor telegraph operator. Raised by his grandparents, he grew up listening to his grandmother's tales of civil war, ghosts, and vanished wealth. His epic novel, *One Hundred Years of Solitude*, incorporates some of these elements. Full of imagination and magic, it traces the lives of the eccentric Buendia family in the mythical town of Macondo over a period of 100 years.

The work of García Márquez—and many other modern Latin American writers—is characterized by a technique known as **magic realism.** This technique mixes dreams with reality. Myth, fantasy, and humor are used to chronicle everyday life. Dead husbands return as ghosts to frighten and embarrass their wives. People fly off into the darkness, and women live on a diet of dirt. Strange animals fill the landscape, and it rains for four years. In addition to García Márquez, two of the best known magic realists are the novelists Demetrio Aguilera Malta of Ecuador and Isabel Allende of Chile.

Another major group of modern novelists explores the events of Latin American history. Alejo Carpentier of Cuba writes of the conflict of modern and primitive cultures in Latin America. Eduardo Galeano of Uruguay has produced a creative narrative of Latin America from its origins to the present day.

CASE STUDY:

An Argentine Vacation

Latin Americans, like everyone else, enjoy taking a break from the routine of everyday life. The following newspaper article describes vacationing in Argentina.

As the weather turns warm in South America, . . . one idea takes hold of most Argentines—it's time for the annual vacation. . . .

In Argentina, it is not only the rich who travel. The powerful [labor] unions made the summer vacation a holiday for all in the 1940s by building huge seaside hotels for their members. Since then the Argentine summer season has become a sacred tradition. . . .

Argentines prefer traditional rather than unusual vacations. The idea . . . is to travel to a nearby place where friends and neighbors will also vacation. . . . Despite the expanse and variety available in the more than 2,000-mile-long country, Argentines rarely go more than 500 miles for a vacation.

The isolated regions of Patagonia in the south are visited by only 150,000 people a year, compared with more than 4 million who go to the beaches. . . . Camping and hiking are virtually nonexistent. For the most part, Argentines prefer the beaches, especially those packed with other Argentines.

"The Argentine is a very traditional and conservative person and doesn't like to do what is out of the normal," says one businessman. "We like to follow what is in style." Says another Argentine: "Argentines have a tendency to seek out summer places that are like the places they have always lived."

The majority of the working-class vacationers go to the seaside resort of Mar del Plata, called "the pearl of the Atlantic," 200 miles south of the capital. The rich escape Argentina and take a 40-minute flight across the Rio de la Plato to [the beaches of] Uruguay.

The population of Mar del Plata swells to more than 2 million in the summer, from 350,000 in the off-season. Even during the economic crisis that plagued Argentina in the 1980s, this resort continued to attract large numbers of workers. This is because the [labor] unions

*Mar del Plata is Argentina's major resort. It is crowded
during the warm months from November to April.*

control tens of thousands of hotel rooms that are rented exclusively
to their members. The government helps to keep costs [low] by
excluding the union hotels from the taxes paid by regular hotels. . . .

With much of Buenos Aires transferred to Mar del Plata in the
summer, business and politics need not stop. The Peronists [political
party] were in the middle of a political battle when summer arrived
in 1984. Instead of putting off their vacations, they just moved the
meetings to a Mar del Plata hotel.

"The Lure (and the Lore) of Argentina's Summer," by Lydia Chavez. *The New York
Times,* Dec. 2, 1985.

1. Where do most Argentines go for vacation?

2. Based on this article, how would you describe the vacation prefer-
ences of most Argentines?

3. Why are working-class Argentines able to afford vacations even during times of economic crisis?

Poetry. Latin America has also produced its share of world-renowned poets. The most famous, Pablo Neruda, was born in Chile in 1904. The son of a poor railroad worker, his success as a writer allowed him to escape poverty. Another Chilean poet is Gabriela Mistral. Whereas Neruda's poetry is of an epic nature, Mistral, a teacher, describes the children with whom she worked. Mistral received the Nobel Prize for Literature in 1945 (the first Latin American to be so honored), Neruda, in 1971. Other poets of stature include César Vallejo of Peru and Ernesto Cardenal of Nicaragua.

Art and Architecture. Graphic arts and drawing have traditionally flourished in Latin America. The best-known Mexican illustrator, José Guadalupe Posada, drew cartoons poking fun at everyday life. His caricatures of contemporary revolutionary and government leaders earned him immense popularity with the masses of Mexican people.

Perhaps the best-known works of modern Latin American art are the murals produced by Mexican artists after the Mexican revolution of 1910. The Mexican muralists combined traditional Indian designs with modern forms. They created a vigorous national style that influenced artists throughout the world. The "Big Three" who led the muralist movement were Diego Rivera, José Clemente Orozco, and David Alfaro Siqueiros. For these men, the purpose of art was to educate. Although each emphasized different aspects, their paintings all told the story of the Indians, their enslavement by the Spanish, and the struggle of the modern working class. Murals by these artists adorn the walls of many public buildings in both Mexico and the United States.

Some Latin American artists moved away from nationalist themes and realist techniques. Roberto Matta of Chile and Wilfredo Lam of Cuba were identified with **surrealism.** This artistic style, related to the literary technique of magic realism, seeks to portray life as if it were a dream. Two fine artists from Uruguay are Pedro Figari and Joaquín Torres García. Modern Argentine artists include Rómulo Maccío, Antonio Seguí, Julio Le Parc, and Luis Felipe Noé. Well-known women artists are Raquel Forner of Argentina and Frida Kahlo of Mexico.

Latin American art owes much to the area's rich folklore and the African influence. Haiti is recognized for its primitive painters whose work is influenced by the rituals of voodoo

Latin America, particularly Mexico and Brazil, has pioneered in the integration of art and architecture. One hundred architects worked together to produce the magnificent buildings of the National University in Mexico City. Perhaps most impressive is the central library, designed

Brazil's National Congress building in Brasília, the nation's capital since 1960. The main public buildings in Brasília were designed by Oscar Niemeyer.

by Juan O'Gorman. The architects of Brazil have made that country's public buildings the envy of the world. Best known are the futuristic constructions of the capital city, Brasília, designed by Oscar Niemeyer.

Music and Dancing. The music of Latin America mingles European, African, and Indian influences. Since the early 1960s, there has been a revival of interest in the area's folkloric traditions. Each country has its national dance. A characteristic step is the *zapateado*, or heel-beating, which is incorporated into the *cueca* of Chile, the *sanjuanito* of Ecuador, the *maninera* of Peru, and the *seis zapateo* of Puerto Rico. Perhaps the most famous Latin American dance internationally is the Argentine *tango*, which became a world craze in the 1920s. Other Latin American dances that have enjoyed popularity in the United States are the *cumbia* from Colombia, the *samba* from Brazil, and the *merengue* and *salsa* of the Caribbean.

99

In addition to folk and dance music, musical life also flourishes in concerts, operas, and symphony orchestras. Large cities, such as Buenos Aires, have some of the finest opera houses in the world. Many Latin American composers have won international fame. Among the best-known is Heitor Villa Lobos of Brazil. Inspired by Indian and African folk music, Villas Lobos composed a series called *Chôros* that is based on the popular urban music and dance of the time. Other important musicians include the pianist Claudio Arrau of Chile and the composers Silvestre Revueltas and Carlos Chávez of Mexico and Amadeo Roldan of Cuba.

Sports. There is no question that *futbol*, as soccer is called in Spanish, is the most popular sport in Latin America. Indeed, for many Latin Americans, soccer is more than a game; it is almost a way of life. Each year, contests pit one country's best players against another's. The rivalries are so intense that victory is accompanied by a national celebration. Defeat brings practically a day of national mourning. In the 1930s, Argentina and Uruguay dominated Latin American soccer, but Brazil has recently also had winning teams. Perhaps the greatest soccer player who ever lived was born in Brazil. He is Edson Arantes do Nascimento, known to the world as Pelé.

A soccer match in Buenos Aires. Soccer is a national passion in many Latin American nations. The players have the status of celebrities.

The main house of a large hacienda *(ranch) in Argentina.*
Compare and contrast this house with the dwellings
shown in the photographs on pages 89 and 90.

Several of the more northern Latin American countries have adopted baseball (*beisbol* in Spanish) as their national sport. Among these countries are Cuba, Venezuela, Panama, and the Dominican Republic. Many professional baseball players in the major leagues in the United States come from Latin America.

Several sports, introduced by the Spanish, date from the colonial era. Bullfighting is popular in Mexico and Panama. Cockfighting is a popular spectator sport throughout the Caribbean. Betting on the winner is an important part of this sport, in which specially trained gamecocks fight to the death. Jai-alai (hy-LIE), a game resembling handball and played by two or four players with a ball and a long curved basket strapped to the wrist, is another favorite sport.

Life in Latin America is a rich blend of social and cultural traditions. Although they may vary somewhat from country to country, these traditions form a tie that binds together the people of the region.

REVIEWING THE CHAPTER

I. Building Your Vocabulary

In your notebook, write the numbers from 1 to 5. After each number, write the word that matches the definition.

indigenous   mestizo   latifundia
illiterate   barrios   surrealism

1. unable to read or write
2. artistic style that seeks to portray life as if it were a dream
3. large estates owned by the wealthy few
4. native
5. neighborhoods in Latin American cities

II. Understanding the Facts

In your notebook, write the numbers from 1 to 5. After each number, write the letter of the correct answer to the question.

1. Which of the following statements best describes the ethnic background of Latin America's people?
   a. of Indian and African descent   b. of European, Indian, African, and mixed descent   c. of European descent

2. What is the center of the social structure in Latin America?
   a. church   b. school   c. family

3. Before land reform began in the twentieth century, who owned most of the land in Latin America?
   a. Indians   b. large landowners   c. groups of farmers

4. What is the religious faith of the overwhelming majority of Latin Americans?
   a. Roman Catholicism   b. Protestantism   c. Judaism

5. Which of the following statements best describes the way Latin American writers portray the world?
   a. Good people tend to be rewarded.   b. Life is insecure.
   c. Life is basically happy.

III. Thinking It Through

In your notebook, write the numbers from 1 to 5. After each number, write the number of the correct answer to the question.

1. In Latin American society, social status depends on
   a. ethnic background more than education or skill.
   b. education and occupation more than race.
   c. whether or not one can trace ancestry to the conquistadors.
   d. how many languages one can speak.

2. The statement "Mi casa es su casa" means habit of
   a. owning land and other property in common.
   b. living in individual homes rather than apartment buildings.
   c. welcoming strangers with generous hospitality.
   d. lavishing expensive gifts on important visitors.

3. A key reason for the rapid growth of Latin American cities is that
   a. rural poverty has forced millions of people off the land.
   b. immigrants have been pouring in from other continents.
   c. housing is readily available in cities.
   d. air pollution in rural areas is intolerable.

4. The idea behind liberation theology is that
   a. poor people should accept their lot because they will one day go to heaven.
   b. wealthy people should give away their riches to help the poor.
   c. poor people should revolt against their rulers.
   d. the church should work to change social conditions that lead to poverty.

5. The paintings of Mexican muralists stress such themes as
   a. the heroism of the Spanish conquistadors.
   b. the injustices suffered by Indians and other poor people.
   c. the technological advances of Mexican industry.
   d. the doctrines of the Roman Catholic Church.

DEVELOPING CRITICAL THINKING SKILLS

1. Show the importance of the extended family in Latin American society.
2. Explain how the breaking up of large estates might affect the lives of all Latin Americans.
3. Describe how the role of Latin America's Roman Catholic Church has changed over time.

103

READING A CHART

The chart contains information about the population of the nations of South America. Use the chart to answer the questions that follow it. Then, use the material in the chapter, as well as encyclopedias and other library reference sources, to make a similar chart for the nations of Central America.

Countries of South America

COUNTRY	POPULATION	CITIES OVER 1 MILLION	OFFICIAL LANGUAGES	LARGEST ETHNIC GROUP
Argentina	32.7 million	Buenos Aires	Spanish	Europeans (Spanish, Italian)
Bolivia	6.4 million	None	Spanish (official), but Quechua, and Aymara widely used	Indians
Brazil	155.6 million	São Paolo, Recife, Rio de Janeiro, Belo Horizonte, Brasilia, Salvador, Fortaleza, Porto Alegre, Novo Iguaco, Curitiba	Portuguese	Europeans (Portuguese, Italian, German, Spanish), Africans
Chile	13.0 million	Santiago	Spanish	Mestizos
Colombia	33.0 million	Bogotá, Cali Medellin	Spanish	Mestizos
Ecuador	10.5 million	Quito, Guayaquil	Spanish	Indians, Mestizos
Guyana	1.0 million	None	English	East Indians, Africans
Paraguay	4.2 million	None	Spanish (official) but speak Guarani	Mestizos
Peru	22.3 million	Lima	Spanish and Quechua (both official). Aymara also widely used.	Indians, Mestizos
Suriname	.4 million	None	Dutch	East Indians
Uruguay	3.1 million	Montevideo	Spanish	Europeans (Spanish, Italian)
Venezuela	19.7 million	Caracas	Spanish	Mestizos

Source: CIA, 1991.

1. Rank the South American nations in order of population, from largest to smallest.

2. Which South American nations do not use Spanish as an official language?

3. Which South American country has the largest proportion of Africans?

ENRICHMENT AND EXPLORATION

1. Use library resources to learn how the expansion of settlement and economic activity in Latin American countries has affected the lives of people in remote Indian villages. Choose one Indian group for close-up study. Present a written or oral report on how the group's life has changed.

2. Collect information about the ethnic composition of one of the following countries: Argentina, Brazil, Costa Rica, Cuba, Guyana, Peru. Using library resources, write a report describing the relations among ethnic groups within the country you have chosen. Answer such questions as: Which ethnic group contains the most people? Does one ethnic group have more power or status than others? How well do the different groups get along?

3. As a class project, collect information about how Latin American culture influences music, dance, literature, and other aspects of life in the United States. Use books, encyclopedias, newspapers, magazines, and similar sources. Make a bulletin board display.

4. Use your school or public library to obtain a short work by one of the writers mentioned in this chapter. Read the work. Prepare a written or oral report.

5. Make a bulletin board display on Latin American art and architecture, using photographs or drawings. To each item, attach a brief critique saying what you like or dislike about its style.

6. Collect five or more recipes describing the preparation of Latin American dishes. Choose one of the recipes and prepare it at home, with the help of an adult. (You may have to find substitutes for some of the ingredients.) Present an oral report to the class on your experience.

MEXICO AND THE WORLD

1810–Today

1810	Miguel Hidalgo launches War for Mexican Independence.
1821	Mexico gains independence.
1823	*U.S. proclaims Monroe Doctrine.*
1824	Mexican republic established.
1833–1855	Presidency of Antonio López de Santa Anna
1836	Texas wins independence from Mexico.
1845	*U.S. annexes Texas.*
1846–1848	War with the United States; loss of huge territory under Treaty of Guadalupe Hidalgo.
1853	Mexico sells Gadsden Purchase to U.S.
1855–1872	Presidency of Benito Juarez
1861–1865	*U.S. Civil War*
1863	France installs Maximilian as emperor.
1867	Maximilian is captured and executed.
1876–1910	Dictatorship of Porfirio Díaz
1910–1911	Revolution overthrows Díaz.
1914–1918	*World War I*
1917	New liberal constitution
1926–1929	Conflict between Mexican government and Roman Catholic church.
1929	Institutional Revolutionary Party (PRI) is organized.
1938	Mexico nationalizes oilfields.
1939–1945	*World War II*
1940s	Many *ejidos* (collective farms) are established.
1970s	Large deposits of oil are discovered.
1982–1991	Mexico in economic crisis
1991	Amendment proposed to end land distribution program.

5 Mexico

Mexico, the northernmost country of Latin America, is the only Latin American nation that shares a border with the United States. With an area of some 761,000 square miles, it is the third largest nation in Latin America (after Brazil and Argentina), and the thirteenth largest nation in the world.

Mexico's border with the United States is about 2,000 miles long. The Rio Grande, which separates Mexico from Texas, forms over half of that boundary. On the east, Mexico is bordered by the Gulf of Mexico, on the south by Guatemala and Belize, and on the west by the Pacific Ocean.

THE LAND

Mexico is a country with a generally rugged terrain. Two massive mountain ranges, the Sierra Madre Occidental, on the west, and the Sierra Madre Oriental, on the east, extend through the country from north to south. Between the mountains is the Central Plateau, actually a high fertile valley. Most of the nation's population lives in the Central Plateau. The capital, Mexico City, the oldest city on the North American continent, is located here.

On Mexico's extreme west is a long, narrow peninsula called Baja (BAH-hah) California, or Lower California. This long, narrow strip of land extends from the southern border of the U.S. state of California 760 miles into the Pacific Ocean. It is separated from the mainland of Mexico by the Gulf of California. In the east, another peninsula, the Yucatán Peninsula, juts into the Gulf of Mexico. The Yucatán, a flat, jungle-like area that is barely above sea level, was an important center of the great Maya civilization.

The climate of Mexico varies sharply from region to region. These differences are most pronounced in the south. There the climate is affected by the wide variety in altitude. In the most heavily populated parts of the Central Plateau, the climate is generally pleasantly cool. The rainy season is from June through September, when it usually rains once a day. (For details on the land and the climate of Mexico, see Chapter 1.)

PEOPLE AND CULTURE

Mexico's culture is a rich mixture of Spanish and Indian influences. The heritage of the Maya and Aztecs who once ruled the region is reflected in all areas of Mexican life. Indeed, Mexico is named for the Aztec god Mexitli.

Population.   Mexico has a population of more than 84 million. Among the nations of the Western Hemisphere, only the United States and Brazil have more people. Mexico's population is growing at a rate of 3.9 percent a year, one of the highest growth rates in the world. If this growth rate continues, by the year 2000 Mexico's population will exceed 120 million.

The great majority—80 percent—of Mexico's population are mestizos. (As you recall, mestizos are people of mixed European and Indian background.) Indians make up approximately 12 percent of the population. (The Mexican government defines Indians as people who live in isolated areas, follow traditional customs, and speak an Indian language rather than Spanish.) The remaining 8 percent of Mexicans are of unmixed European—mainly Spanish—backgrounds. It is estimated that 96 percent of Mexicans are Roman Catholics.

The Indians.   Although their numbers are relatively small, there are many different Indian groups in Mexico today. Among them are descendants of the ancient Maya, who live mainly in the Yucatán; the Chol Indians, in the state of Tabasco; and several groups in Oaxaca.

Most of the Indians work subsistence farms, and some of them depend on handicrafts to make a living. The Indians keep largely to themselves, and many groups have strict rules against marrying anyone from outside the village. Indians generally follow traditional customs and religious rituals. For example, some of the Maya sacrifice turkeys to their gods in order to promote rainfall. When an Indian dies, the land and other property are distributed among the survivors.

Open-air Indian markets attract tourists and Mexicans alike. Among the most popular are the markets in Oaxaca and Patscuaro, where booths are piled high with an amazing assortment of goods. Chickens, fish, pots and pans, and clothing, as well as a variety of colorful handicrafts are displayed for sale.

Standard of Living. One of Mexico's most urgent problems is the low standard of living of a large portion of its population. Although **per capita income**—the average income of each person in a place—is higher than that of many Latin American countries, wealth is very unevenly distributed. Some 40 percent of the population shares only 9 percent of all income. The average Mexican, especially in rural areas, is very poor.

A major factor contributing to poverty in Mexico is a severe shortage of jobs. As a result, tens of thousands of Mexicans illegally enter the United States each year in search of employment. Another major problem is the lack of fertile land. Only 15 percent of Mexico's land can be cultivated. Moreover, despite a 50-year program of land reform, many peasants are still landless.

Mexican market in Oaxaca. All kinds of farm produce as well as handcrafted items are sold in the open-air markets.

Major Cities. More than 70 percent of Mexico's population live in urban areas, and the nation has some of the world's fastest-growing cities.

Mexico City, the capital, has more people than any other city in the world. In 1985, at least 10 million people lived within its boundaries. Mexico City is the economic, political, and cultural center of Mexico. Popular with tourists, it has long, broad avenues and many buildings of unusual interest. Chapultepec (chuh-POOL-tuh-pek) Park, a favorite recreation spot, was once the summer retreat of the Aztec emperor, Moctezuma. Mexico City was built on the site of Tenochtitlán, the Aztec capital, and Aztec ruins are still being uncovered. In 1978, for example, workers constructing a subway in the heart of downtown Mexico City accidentally found the ruins of the Aztec Great Temple.

Mexico City faces many problems, however. Most serious is severe overcrowding. It is estimated that a thousand migrants from rural areas arrive in Mexico City each day, establishing themselves in shantytowns on the city's outskirts. One of the largest of these shantytowns, Ciudad Nezahualcóyotol (see-oo-DAD nez-ah-wahl-KOH-yoh-tohl), has 3.5 million inhabitants. This is about the same number of people that live in the entire city of Los Angeles.

The avenues and roads are not adequate to handle the number of vehicles that enter and leave the city every day. Efforts to improve transportation by building a subway system had little effect. The subway, like the roads, is unable to absorb the constantly growing population, and both are packed during rush hours.

The heavy concentration of industry in the area and the constant automobile traffic have made Mexico City one of the most polluted cities in the world. Many of the city's residents suffer from respiratory illnesses and heart disease caused by the polluted air.

Guadalajara (gwahd-uh-luh-HAHR-uh), Mexico's second largest city, is a rich mining and agricultural center, as well as a major tourist attraction. It is famous for its pottery. *Veracruz*, on the southeast coast, is the site of the landing of Hernan Cortés in 1519. *Cuernevaca* (kwehr-nuh-VAH-kuh), the "city of eternal spring," and *Acapulco* (ah-kuh-POOL-koh), with its beautiful beaches on the Pacific coast, are two of Mexico's most popular vacation resorts.

Holidays. Mexicans celebrate their many religious and national holidays with **fiestas,** or festivals, filled with music, dancing, and feasting. Every Mexican town, city, and village holds a fiesta to honor its patron saint. The fiesta begins before daylight with fireworks and the ringing of church bells. People pray and light candles in colorfully decorated

Traffic in downtown Mexico City. Population experts predict that the city will be the most highly populated city in the world by the year 1995.

churches. They dance in the streets and buy refreshments from stands in the market square. Professional cockfights and bullfights provide additional entertainment. Fireworks at night mark the end of the fiesta.

On the nine nights before Christmas, in a ceremony called the *posada*, friends and neighbors act out the journey of Joseph and Mary to Bethlehem. Each night after the *posada*, the children play the **piñata** game. The piñata is a gaily decorated papier-maché or clay container that is filled with toys, candies, and coins, and hung from the ceiling. After being blindfolded, the children take turns trying to break the piñata with a stick. After the piñata breaks, everyone scrambles for the presents.

One of Mexico's most unusual religious festivals is the Day of the Dead. It begins on the night of Halloween and continues through the next day, All Saints Day. On this holiday, people attend candle-lit vigils in the local cemeteries. Shops sell *pan de muerto*, or "bread of the dead," bread baked in the shape of a skull and crossbones. Brightly decorated skull cookies and candies are also popular.

Mexico's most important national holiday is Independence Day. Celebrated on September 16, it commemorates the day in 1810 when a criollo priest named Miguel Hidalgo launched the Mexican War for Independence (see page 70). In the town of Dolores, Hidalgo rang the bell to gather the local Indians and mestizos to church. He then raised the **Grito de Dolores** (Cry of Dolores), in which he demanded that Spain grant Mexico its freedom—"Down with bad government, death to the Spanish!" Today, to mark the beginning of the holiday, the Mexican president each year rings the Liberty Bell and repeats the Grito de Dolores.

CASE STUDY:

Mexican Fiestas

The Labyrinth of Solitude, by one of Mexico's leading authors, Octavio Paz, describes the Mexican people—their character, traditions, and culture. The following excerpt explores the Mexican love of public festivals—in Spanish, *fiestas*.

> The Mexican loves fiestas and public gatherings. Any occasion for getting together will serve, any excuse to stop the flow of time and commemorate men and events with festivals and ceremonies. . . . There are few places in the world where it is possible to take part in a spectacle like our great religious fiestas with their violent primary colors, their bizarre costumes and dances, their fireworks and ceremonies, and their inexhaustible . . . surprises: the fruit, candy, toys, and other objects sold on these days in the plazas and open-air markets.

> But the fiestas which the Church and State provide for the country as a whole are not enough. The life of every city and village is ruled by a patron saint whose blessing is celebrated with devout regularity. Neighborhoods and trades also have their annual fiestas, their ceremonies and fairs. And each one of us . . . has his own saint's day, which he observes every year. It is impossible to calculate how many fiestas we have and how much time and money we spend on them. I remember asking the mayor of the village near Mitla, several years ago, "What is the income of the village government?" "About 3,000 pesos a year. We are very poor." . . . "And how are the 3,000 pesos spent?" "Mostly on fiestas, señor. We are a small village, but we have two patron saints."

> This reply is not surprising. Our poverty can be measured by the frequency and luxuriousness of our holidays. Wealthy countries have very few; there is neither the time nor the desire for them, and they are not necessary. The people have other things to do, and when they amuse themselves they do so in small groups.

Octavio Paz. *The Labyrinth of Solitude* (New York: Grove Press, 1961).

1. List the events mentioned by Paz that are celebrated with a fiesta.

2. What are some of the features of a fiesta?

3. How does Paz relate poverty in Mexico to the nation's love of fiestas?

The Arts.   The arts have been important in Mexico since the days of the ancient Indian civilizations. Great pyramids and temples near Mexico City and in the Yucatán are impressive evidence of Maya and Aztec architectural skill. The Aztecs also composed music and poetry, and a few fragments of sacred Mayan writings still survive.

Architecture continued to thrive during the colonial period, as the Spanish built thousands of churches throughout the colony. In the small town of Cholula, alone, the Spanish built 365 churches! The Spanish also produced important literature. One of the most outstanding colonial writers was Sor (Sister) Juana Inés de la Cruz (HWAH-nah ee-NES day lah KROOS). A Mexican by birth, Sor Juana entered a convent at the age of 18. Her concern with women's rights was unusual for the era, as illustrated by the following poem:

> Oh stupid men, unreasonable
> In blaming woman's nature
> Oblivious [unaware] that your acts incite [encourage]
> The very faults you censure [condemn].

In the 1900s, Mexico has given the world many important architects, artists, composers, and writers. Particularly noteworthy are the muralists who portrayed Mexico's history on the walls of some of its public buildings. For many years, the Mexican Revolution dominated the nation's literature. But today, writers such as Octavio Paz and Carlos Fuentes (FWEN-tays) have turned their attention toward urban Mexico and its role as a modern nation. (For details about the arts in Mexico, see Chapter 4.)

Crafts.   Mexico is sometimes called the "land of handicrafts." Some of the objects produced combine Indian artistry with Spanish techniques and materials. One finds silver jewelry in Taxco, black pottery in Oaxaca, glazed blue and white pottery in Puebla, and hand-tooled leather goods in Jalisco. Mexican craftsworkers still continue the centuries-old traditions of dying and weaving reeds, painting on bark, and carving musical instruments out of wood.

Education.   Formal education in Mexico dates to colonial times, when Franciscan missionaries established schools to educate the Indians in the Christian way of life. Education remained in the hands of the Roman Catholic Church for many years. Following independence, the government took control of the schools. However, the illiteracy rate remained

Diego Rivera was one of the most famous Mexican muralists. His works celebrate the life, history, and social problems of Mexico and can be seen in many government and official buildings. This one is in the Palace of the Governors in Mexico City.

extremely high. One of the principal goals of the Mexican revolution of 1910 was to bring education to the masses.

Today, the Mexican government spends more than 12 percent of its budget on education. All children between the ages of 6 and 15 are required to attend school. Great strides have been made in expanding educational opportunity. The nation's literacy rate has climbed from 65 percent in 1970 to over 88 percent in the early 1990s. While only 9.4

percent of the school age population completed high school in 1970, over 23 percent did so in 1983.

Through education, the government is making a great effort to bring Mexico's Indians into the mainstream of national life. Many Indians are distrustful of the government's motives, however. To overcome this, the government encourages Indian communities to build their own schools. It also teaches the Indians how to improve their immediate environment, and offers free meals to schoolchildren. When the Indians' suspicions are laid to rest, government schoolteachers provide instruction in reading both the native language and Spanish.

Public Health. As a result of modern medical practices, epidemic diseases are rapidly disappearing. **Life expectancy,** the average number of years a person in a place usually lives, is now 66 years. However, the **infant mortality rate**—the percentage of children who die before reaching the age of one—is still high.

Malnutrition is a serious problem. Most low-income families live on a diet of corn, beans, and **chilis,** a kind of hot pepper. To combat malnutrition, a government-sponsored chain of supermarkets distributes food at discount prices. The government also encourages Mexican families to eat foods such as fish and vegetables that would provide a more balanced diet.

Labor. Mexico's constitution guarantees all workers an eight-hour day and a weekly day of rest. There are minimum wage and workmen's compensation laws. Labor is guaranteed the right to organize unions, and management has the right to form associations to protect its interests. Mexico's social security law guarantees medical and financial assistance to all workers.

THE ECONOMY

In the past, Mexico's economy centered on agriculture and mining. However, the economy has developed more rapidly and consistently than that of most other Latin American nations. This growth is due in large part to government policies that successfully promoted the development of large-scale industry. Great prosperity accompanied the discovery of oil in the 1970s. But world economic developments in the 1980s made it hard to know whether this newly found resource was a blessing or a burden.

Oil drilling platforms in the Gulf of Mexico. The discovery of oil meant high-paying jobs for Mexicans willing to endure the long hours and dangerous environment.

Oil and Natural Gas.   In October 1974, large oil deposits were discovered in the southern Mexican states of Chiapas and Tabasco. By the 1980s, Mexico was the third largest oil exporter to the non-Communist countries, and oil accounted for 70 percent of the nation's export income.

The discovery of oil marked a major shift in the Mexican economy. During the energy shortage of the 1970s, oil exports of some 1.5 million barrels a day brought Mexico huge profits and prosperity. In the mid-1980s, however, market supplies of world petroleum increased and prices began to fall. For example, it was projected that petroleum in 1986 would cost $26 per barrel; before January was over, the price for a barrel of oil had slipped to the low $20s and was expected to drop even further. Every $1 drop in price for a barrel of oil cost Mexico more than half a billion dollars a year. The country's future growth is dependent on the price of oil in the world market.

Agriculture.   About 35 percent of Mexico's people are engaged in agriculture. About one-half of the farmers work on **ejidos** or collective farms. On a collective farm, the land is owned and worked by the community, which shares the products of the farm. Most of the ejidos were created after 1940, when the government distributed nearly 45 million acres of land to the nation's peasants. However, the ejidos are generally poor. They do not have modern equipment and ejido farmers rarely use chemical fertilizers. While ejido farmers generally raise enough food to feed their families, they seldom have anything left over for market.

116

The most productive farms are the **haciendas.** These are commercial farms, usually owned by wealthy landowners or large corporations. They use the latest machinery and equipment to produce a wide variety of crops for export.

The most important export crops are coffee, fruits and vegetables, and cotton. Because of its tropical location, Mexico is able to grow fruits and vegetables all year, and the export of tomatoes, lettuce, peas, and citrus fruits to the United States during the winter is an important source of income. Mexico supplies more than half of the world's **sisal,** a fiber from a plant grown on the Yucatán Peninsula that is used to make heavy twine. Cattle ranching is another important part of Mexican agriculture.

Despite Mexico's thriving agriculture, the nation is unable to feed its population and must import a number of basic foods. Corn, used to make **tortillas,** pancakes eaten with almost every Mexican meal, was long the basis of the Mexican diet. To keep corn affordable, for years the Mexican government kept corn prices low.

Today, many middle-class Mexicans are eating more meat. As a result, farmers have shifted from corn to sorghum, a grain which is easier to grow, brings higher prices, and is sold as feed to livestock raisers. The government has had to increase corn imports to provide food for the rural poor, who are unable to afford meat and continue to exist on a diet of corn and beans. As part of an effort to encourage corn production, the government has raised corn prices for the first time in decades.

Independence Day Parade crowd, Mexico City.

Mining. Mexico has vast mineral deposits, and mining is carried on in almost every state. Mexico is the world's fifth largest producer of silver. Other important metals mined for export are gold, lead, zinc, and copper. Iron and coal are mined for domestic use, and are more than sufficient to support the nation's steel industry. For many years, foreign corporations owned 97 percent of Mexico's mines. However, legislation passed in 1960 brought the mines under Mexican control.

Manufacturing. Manufacturing has grown rapidly in Mexico in recent years. Mexico City is the leading manufacturing center, followed by Monterrey and Guadalajara. Steel, textiles, and sugar processing are the major industries, with chemicals, industrial machinery, agricultural products, road building, and oil refining close behind. A recent shift from automobile assembly to automobile manufacture has stimulated growth in the production of plastics and chemicals. For many years, Mexico encouraged foreign, particularly American, investment to develop new industry. However, in 1973, a new law required that all new industry have at least 50 percent Mexican ownership.

Tourism. Mexico earns more from tourism than any other Latin American nation. Its balmy climate, sunny beaches, ancient ruins, and many quaint towns make this country a favorite for foreign visitors, especially Americans.

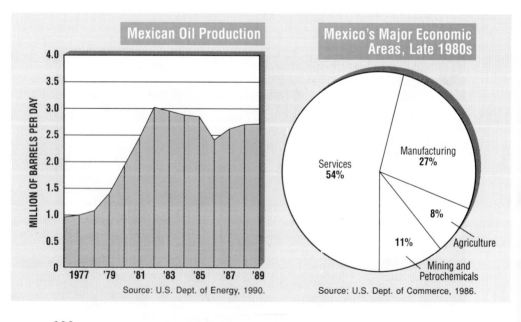

Source: U.S. Dept. of Energy, 1990.

Source: U.S. Dept. of Commerce, 1986.

118

As you read in Chapter 2, pre-Columbian Mexico was the center of three highly developed civilizations. The Toltecs, the first in the region, excelled at architecture. The Maya, in the Yucatán, are considered the greatest of the early American civilizations. They developed a system of mathematics and an advanced system of writing. The Aztecs, a more warlike people, extended their rule throughout central Mexico. Their capital city, Tenochtitlán, was a marvel of engineering and artistry.

The Spanish first arrived in Mexico in the early 1500s. By 1521, the conquistador Hernan Cortés, at the head of a small group of soldiers, had conquered the Aztecs, killed their emperor, destroyed their capital city, and begun to ship their gold and silver treasure back to Spain.

Thus began a period of Spanish rule that lasted 300 years. The Spanish rebuilt the capital, which they named Mexico City. They used the stones of the Aztec temples for churches, schools, and government buildings. They forced the Aztecs to labor for them, and a great many Indian deaths resulted from overwork and disease.

The Spanish introduced a system of high taxes and economic and political restriction. Dissatisfaction with Spanish rule reached a climax in the 1800s. In 1810, Mexico became the first colony in Latin America to rebel against Spanish rule. After years of struggle, Mexico finally gained independence in 1821. For a brief period, Mexico was an empire, under Agustín de Iturbide. It became an independent republic in 1824.

(For details on pre-Columbian Mexican civilizations, Spanish colonization, and independence, see Chapters 2 and 3.)

The Young Republic. In the years following independence, Mexico was torn by power struggles. From 1833 to 1855, the country was controlled largely by General Antonio López de Santa Anna, who ruled sometimes as an elected president, sometimes as a dictator who had seized power. Santa Anna's rule was marked by waste and corruption. The problems of the large numbers of poor were ignored. However, Santa Anna was a colorful leader and there are many stories about him. One tale tells how the general walked out of an important meeting with the Catholic bishop with the excuse that his favorite fighting cock was sick and needed attention.

War with Texas. In the 1820s, many Americans began to settle in Mexico's sparsely populated northern region, called Texas. The settlers soon grew discontented with Mexican rule. In 1835, fighting broke out.

119

In February, Santa Anna's army surrounded a force of almost 200 settlers in the Alamo, an empty mission in San Antonio. The outnumbered Texans refused to surrender. After nearly two weeks, the Mexicans stormed the fort, and all the Texans were killed.

A month later, crying "Remember the Alamo," the Texans defeated the Mexicans at San Jacinto and captured General Santa Anna. Santa Anna was released after signing a secret treaty recognizing Texas as an independent republic. The Mexican government, however, refused to accept the treaty.

War with the United States.   Tension with the Texans continued. Many Texans wanted their region to become part of the United States, and in 1845 the U.S. Congress voted to **annex** Texas. This means that the United States incorporated Texas in its own territory. Mexico had already declared that the annexation of Texas would mean war, and Mexican patrols and U.S. troops were soon clashing along the border. In 1846, the United States declared war on Mexico.

American armies drove deep into Mexico and occupied much of the country. U.S. General Zachary Taylor defeated Santa Anna at Buena Vista in February 1847, and a month later U.S. General Winfield Scott captured the Atlantic port city of Veracruz. Despite these and other defeats, the Mexicans continued to fight.

In one of the bloodiest battles of the war, the Americans stormed the fortress of Chapultepec in Mexico City. Preferring death to surrender, the young military cadets defending the fortress refused to leave. They were all killed. Today, the Niños, or Children's, Monument at the entrance to Chapultepec park celebrates the bravery of Mexico's "boy heroes."

On September 14, 1847, the Americans captured Mexico City, and Mexico surrendered. The Treaty of Guadalupe Hidalgo (gwah-dah-LOO-pay ee-DAHL-goh) was signed in 1848. Under the terms of this treaty, Mexico recognized Texas as a state of the United States. It also gave up its land north of the Rio Grande. This territory, known as the **Mexican Cession,** included the present-day states of California, Nevada, and Utah, most of Arizona, and parts of New Mexico, Colorado, and Wyoming. In return, the United States paid Mexico $15 million. Five years later, in the Gadsden Purchase of 1853, Mexico sold the United States an additional strip of land in Arizona and New Mexico for $10 million.

Reform and Civil War.   After the Mexican War, Santa Anna returned to power as "perpetual dictator." However, in 1855, he was overthrownby a liberal group led by a Zapotec Indian named Benito

The fortress of Chapultepec under attack by American forces in 1847. The castle atop the rocky hill was built in the 1700s as a summer home for the Spanish viceroys. Today, the castle is a museum of colonial history and ethnography.

Pablo Juárez (HWAH-rehs). The liberals enacted a new constitution that provided for a more democratic government. They also announced plans for reform. In particular, they wanted to limit the power of the army and the Roman Catholic Church.

Mexico's conservatives, who included most of the wealthy, the church leaders, and the army, opposed these reforms. In 1858, civil war broke out. Juárez, who had been elected president under the new constitution, was forced to flee. He set up a government in Veracruz.

In 1859, from Veracruz, Juárez issued a series of reform laws. These laws abolished the special privileges of the church and formally separated the roles of the church and state. This meant that the government replaced the church in administering the hospitals and in running the schools. The church's large estates were to be broken up, and the government was to seize all church property not used for worship.

In 1860, Juárez's armies defeated the conservatives, and the next year Juárez and liberal government returned to Mexico City.

The French Occupation. The years of fighting had exhausted Mexico's economy. After the civil war, Juárez stopped payment on the country's

Monument to Benito Juárez, Mexico City. Benito Juárez is honored by Mexicans as one of their greatest political figures. He upheld the civil laws and opposed the privileges of the clerics and the army.

debts to France, Great Britain, and Spain. The Europeans responded by sending troops to Mexico to force Juárez to pay. The British and Spanish troops did not stay long. However, in 1863, Mexican conservatives persuaded France to use its troops to overthrow Juárez. The French installed Archduke Maximilian of Austria as ruler of the newly created empire of Mexico.

Juárez who had been forced into exile, raised troops to battle against Maximilian. After the departure of French troops in 1867, Juárez's forces succeeded in capturing the emperor. Maximilian was executed and Juárez returned to Mexico City once again. Juárez governed as president of Mexico until 1872. His reform laws became part of the Mexican constitution.

The Dictatorship of Porfirio Díaz. In 1876, a mestizo general, Porfirio Díaz (poor-fee-REE-oh DEE-ahs), seized control of the government. He ruled Mexico as a dictator until 1910. Under Díaz, Mexico enjoyed a period of peace and prosperity. Mines, oilwells, and railroads were built. Foreign investments were encouraged. Mexico's economy began to grow.

However, the prosperity of the Díaz regime was not shared by all. The majority of Mexico's people lived in poverty and ignorance. Democracy also suffered as enemies of Díaz were killed, jailed, or exiled. The benefits of the Díaz rule went mainly to large landowners, the business people, and foreign investors.

122

The Revolution. In 1910, a young liberal named Francisco Madero (mah-DAY-roh) led the people in an armed revolt against Díaz. The following year, Díaz resigned, and Madero became president. Madero, however, could not stabilize the government. In 1913 he was assassinated by his own general, Victoriano Huerta (WEHR-tah), who established a dictatorship.

Revolts soon broke out all over the country as various armies and rebel bands struggled for power. Among the leaders were Francisco "Pancho" Villa (VEE-yah), a bandit chief who led an army of 10,000 in the north, and Emiliano Zapata (sah-PAH-tah), who led the peasant forces in the south. These colorful leaders demanded reforms, including the redistribution of land to the peasants and Indians. A doctor who traveled with Villa's army described Villa as follows:

> Villa . . . the eternal victim of all governments . . . the bandit that passes through the world armed with the blazing torch of an ideal: to rob the rich and give to the poor. . . . If General Villa takes a fancy to you, he'll give you a ranch on the spot. But if he doesn't, he'll shoot you down like a dog!

Leaders of the Mexican Revolution, "Pancho" Villa, seated in the center, and Emiliano Zapata, holding the large sombrero on his knee.

Fighting continued for several years. The victor was neither Villa nor Zapata, but a conservative follower of Madero named Venustiano Carranza (vay-noos-TYAH-noh kah-RAHN-sah). By 1916, Carranza was in control of the country.

In 1917, Carranza's government set forth a new liberal constitution. This constitution established freedom of religion and provided for **universal suffrage,** or the right of all adult males to vote. It established a minimum wage for workers and guaranteed the right to strike. It also called for the break-up of large estates and the **nationalization,** or government takeover, of natural resources. This constitution is still in force in Mexico today.

Economic and Social Change. Most of the presidents who came to power after 1917 worked to carry out the liberal provisions of the new constitution. General Álvaro Obregón (AHL-vahr-oh oh-bray-GOHN), was president from 1920 to 1924, and his successor Plutarco Elías Calles (ploo-TAHR-koh ay-LEE-ahs KAH-yays), served until 1933. They distributed some land among the peasants, built many schools in rural areas, began to provide education for the Indians, and supported the labor-union movement.

Serious problems arose when the government tried to enforce the constitutional provisions aimed at limiting the power of the church. In 1926, Calles closed all religious schools, deported foreign priests, and ordered all priests to register with the government. In protest, the priests closed their churches and refused to hold services. For three years, no mass was said in a Mexican church.

Upset by the closing of the churches, Catholics organized into rebel bands, called **Cristeros** because of their rallying cry, *Viva Cristo Rey!*— Long live Christ the King! The Cristeros burned schools, stoned teachers, and blew up trains. The army responded with equal violence. The religious revolt finally ended in 1929, when a compromise agreement enabled the churches to reopen.

At first, there were problems of peaceful succession of power under the constitution. Obregón had become president after a revolt overthrew and killed Carranza. In turn, Obregón was assassinated before he could begin a second term in office. The problem of succession ended in 1929, when Calles organized the Institutional Revolutionary Party (PRI). This organization became Mexico's chief political party. It has been powerful enough to control the Mexican political process ever since. Since its establishment, the PRI has won all state and national elections by large majorities.

The Cárdenas Era. In 1934, General Lázaro Cárdenas (LAH-sah-roh KAHR-day-nahs) was elected president. Cárdenas was a strong and idealistic leader. His program of social, economic, and educational reform made him the hero of the Indians and the Mexican working classes.

Under Cárdenas, the government distributed twice as much land among the peasants as had been done by all the previous presidents combined. His government supported labor unions, expanded educational opportunities, extended medical facilities, and improved communications and transportation. In a controversial move, in 1938 Cárdenas nationalized the Mexican oilfields. The American and British companies that owned the fields protested angrily, and eventually Mexico agreed to pay for the properties.

Mexico Today. In the half century since the Cárdenas era, Mexico has undergone a roller-coaster ride of economic ups and downs. During the 1970s the mood was one of optimism, due to the discovery of new oil fields at a time when world oil prices were at an all-time high. Mexico borrowed and spent as never before, running up huge debts to foreign countries and banks. In the 1980s the price of oil plunged, and Mexico found itself unable to pay back those debts. When Miguel de la Madrid Hurtado (day lah mah-DREED uhr-TAH-doh) became president in 1982, Mexico was deep in an economic crisis. De la Madrid made a number of reforms, including nationalizing the banks and cutting government spending. Yet inflation soared, as did unemployment.

In 1988 Carlos Salinas de Gortari (sah-LEE-nahs day gohr-TAH-ree) was elected president. Salinas initiated a series of more sweeping reforms. Focusing first on the business and industrial sectors, he abandoned policies that had been cherished since the early days of the revolution. First, government-owned businesses, such as banks and the telephone company, were sold to private investors. Then Salinas took steps to attract foreign investment into the country. This was accomplished mainly by promoting factories along the Rio Grande border called **maquiladoras** (mah-keel-ah-DOH-rahs). These were factories, owned mainly by large U.S. companies, in which Mexican workers assembled units whose pieces had been brought into the country free of import tax. After assembly, the manufactured goods were re-exported to the United States, paying only a small tax. In this way, Mexico gained jobs, and U.S. companies took advantage of Mexico's lower wage rates.

Between 1986 and 1991, the number of maquiladoras grew to over

President Carlos Salinas de Gortari of Mexico.

2,000. They employed more than 460,000 workers, about one-fifth of all manufacturing jobs in Mexico.

Late in 1991 Salinas turned to the agricultural sector. The small plots worked by farmers on the cooperatives called ejidos were no longer producing enough food for the ever-growing number of Mexicans. To increase productivity, Salinas proposed a constitutional amendment that would allow farmers to own, rent, or sell their plots of land. In this way, farmers could pool their resources to create farms with larger acreage. Passage of such a proposal would mark the official end of the land distribution program begun in 1917.

Although some political leaders criticized Salinas's sweeping reforms, a majority of Mexicans showed their approval at the polls. In the early 1990s, for the first time in almost two decades, inflation was down, employment was up, and the growth of the economy was finally outstripping population growth.

Relations with the United States. The Salinas government, together with a number of U.S. political and industrial leaders, worked to establish a **free-trade zone** throughout most of North America. Under such an agreement, goods would circulate freely among Mexico, Canada, and the

126

United States without imposition of **tariffs,** or import taxes. If achieved, this plan would create the largest free market in the world, with 360 million people and an annual output of $6 trillion.

A North American free-trade zone had opponents in both Mexico and the United States. In Mexico, some political leaders saw it as a sellout to *Yanqui* (Yankee) interests and a betrayal of the programs introduced after the revolution. In the United States, labor union leaders said that such an arrangement would expose American workers to unfair competition, erode the U.S. industrial base, and raise the trade deficit. Joining in protest were some environmentalists, who said that Mexico's lax enforcement of pollution laws would encourage U.S. companies to export their most polluting industries to Mexico. As proof, they pointed to the already polluted maquiladora region.

U.S. proponents, among them many economists, claimed that free trade would create thousands of new jobs for everyone, including U.S. workers. More workers would be needed in the United States, they claimed, to manufacture component parts and other high-tech products for export to the enlarged Mexican market. In response to concerns about the environment, they pointed to President Salinas's shutdown of several polluting factories and suggested that environmental safeguards could be built into any agreement.

Another benefit of a free-trade zone, some proponents suggested, might be to reduce the number of Mexican citizens crossing illegally from Mexico into the United States. As you have read, millions of Mexicans have entered the United States illegally in search of work. The United States has wanted to end this illegal immigration, but Mexico has argued that it is unable to absorb so many people without creating more economic problems at home. With the creation of more factories throughout Mexico, many of them U.S.-owned, workers would be able to stay at home without further damage to the Mexican economy.

Because of its location, size, population, and mineral wealth, Mexico has been a leader among Latin American nations. In the 1980s Mexico was instrumental in establishing the **Contadora** bloc of nations. Besides Mexico, members were Venezuela, Colombia, and Panama. The purpose of the Contadora bloc was to work for peace in Central America. The group opposed U.S. policies there, accusing the United States of wanting to use military force instead of negotiation to solve the area's problems.

Despite these problems, Mexico and the United States have much to offer each other. In addition, if the dream of a free-trade zone were to become a reality, a spirit of cooperation among good neighbors could be expected throughout North America.

127

Chapter 5:
CHECKUP

REVIEWING THE CHAPTER

I. Building Your Vocabulary

In your notebook, write the numbers from 1 to 5. After each number, write the word that matches the definition.

annex   ejido   tortilla
hacienda   maquiladora   nationalization

1. factory in border region where imported materials are used to manufacture items for re-export
2. small collective farm where land is owned and worked by the community
3. to bring land, resources, or industry under government control or ownership
4. to incorporate the territory of another country into one's own country
5. pancake made of corn flour

II. Understanding the Facts

In your notebook, write the numbers from 1 to 5. After each number, write the name of the Mexican leader who took the action that is described. (Use one name twice.)

Antonio Lopez de Santa Anna   Benito Juarez

Porfirio Carlos Salinas de Gortari   Emiliano Zapata

1. He sold government-owned businesses to private investors.
2. He abolished the special privileges of the Roman Catholic Church.
3. He led peasant forces in the Mexican Revolution.
4. He was an elected president who also ruled Mexico as a dictator.
5. He led the attack on Texans at the Alamo.

III. Thinking It Through

In your notebook, write the numbers from 1 to 5. After each number, write the letter of the correct answer to the question.

1. A key reason for the widespread poverty in Mexico is that
   a. most of the people are mestizos.
   b. a small proportion of the people controls much of the nation's wealth.
   c. the nation has no mineral resources of value.
   d. many people have gone to the United States to seek jobs.

2. Mexican agriculture has had trouble feeding the country's people because
   a. many farms, such as cooperatives, lack machinery and other resources.
   b. most of the land is owned by large commercial farmers or corporations.
   c. most rural people lack the skills to farm effectively.
   d. the country's climate is unsuited to growing fruits and vegetables.

3. Which of the following statements best sums up the history of Mexican relations with the United States?
   a. The two countries have always been friends and allies.
   b. The two countries have fought many wars and remain hostile to each other.
   c. The two countries have been at war in the past but are now active trading partners.
   d. The two countries have little in common and try to ignore each other as much as possible.

4. Which of the following was not called for in Mexico's Constitution of 1917?
   a. limiting the power of the Roman Catholic Church
   b. breaking up large estates
   c. giving women the right to vote
   d. nationalizing natural resources

5. Which of the following best describes Mexico's political system today?
   a. Mexico has a king who exercises absolute power.
   b. Mexico is a dictatorship.
   c. Mexico is a democracy like the United States, with two political parties alternating in power.
   d. Mexico is a democracy in which one political party is dominant.

DEVELOPING CRITICAL THINKING SKILLS

1. Explain how Mexico's environment has affected its economic development.

2. Describe the problems that the rapid growth of Mexico City has caused.

3. Discuss the contribution of the oil industry to Mexico's economy in recent years.

4. Explain the position of the Roman Catholic Church in Mexican life and politics.

INTERPRETING A MAP

Based on the map and the information in Chapter 5, answer the questions that follow.

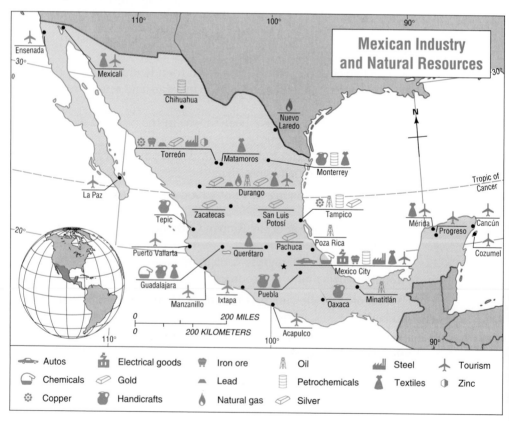

1. What are the major industries of Mexico City?
2. What cities are important tourist centers in Mexico?
3. Mexico's major oil industry is on which coast, the West Coast or the Gulf Coast?
4. What are the important minerals that Mexicans mine?
5. Where in Mexico are automobiles manufactured?
6. What are some of the major industries of Guadalajara?
7. In what cities is the steel industry centered?
8. Where in Mexico are textiles manufactured?

SUMMARIZING INFORMATION

Make a list of the leaders discussed in Chapter 5. Next to each name, write one or two sentences summarizing the leader's role in Mexican history.

ENRICHMENT AND EXPLORATION

1. Use an encyclopedia to gather statistics on Mexico's population from 1900 until today. Then use the statistics to make a line graph showing Mexico's population growth during the twentieth century.
2. Research the history of U.S.-Mexican relations. Choose one event or incident from that history. Write two accounts of the event you have chosen—one from the point of view of a Mexican citizen, the other from the point of view of a U.S. citizen.
3. Using pictures from magazines and travel booklets, make a bulletin board display comparing life in urban and rural Mexico. Be sure to include pictures reflecting the cosmopolitan atmosphere of Mexico City as well as the simpler existence in the countryside.
4. Two of the most colorful figures in Mexico's history are Francisco "Pancho" Villa and Emiliano Zapata. Select one of those men and find out more about his life and career. Then share your findings with the class. If possible, ask your teacher or school librarian if the class might obtain and watch the classic film Viva Zapata, based on the life of the Mexican hero.

THE CARIBBEAN AND THE WORLD

1492–Today

1492	Columbus lands at San Salvador.
1508	Ponce de León establishes first stable European settlement in Puerto Rico.
1511	European settlement begins in Cuba.
1655	British capture Jamaica.
1776	*U.S. Declaration of Independence*
1830s	Jamaican slaves freed.
1861–1865	*U.S. Civil War*
1868–1878	Cuba defeated in war with Spain.
1895	Cuban rebellion again ends in defeat.
1898	Spanish-American War; U.S. wins Cuba and Puerto Rico.
1902	Cuba independent; U.S. forces withdraw.
1914–1918	*World War I*
1917	U.S. Congress provides for election of Puerto Rican legislature.
1933	Fulgencio Batista comes to power in Cuba.
1939–1945	*World War II*
1952	New constitution establishes Puerto Rico commonwealth.
1958	Federation of West Indies formed.
1959	Castro overthrows Batista.
1961–1991	Soviet Union provides economic and military aid to Cuba.
1961	Bay of Pigs invasion
1962	Cuban Missile Crisis
	Jamaica becomes independent.
1980s	Cuba backs Sandinistas in Nicaragua.
1991	Soviet Union announces end of aid to Cuba.

6 *Caribbean America*

Caribbean America is an **archipelago** [ar-kuh-PEL-uh-goh] made up of thousands of islands. (*Archipelago* is the geographers' name for a large group of islands.) These islands, extending from Florida to the northern coast of South America, are called the West Indies. The West Indies archipelago can be divided into three main island groups—the Greater Antilles, the Lesser Antilles, and the Bahamas. A few of the islands are large, but most are quite small.

The islands of the West Indies share a colorful, often violent, history. The common thread is colonialism and slavery. Most of the colonial powers held land in the Caribbean at one time or another. Spain, France, the Netherlands, Great Britain, and the United States—all had claims in the area.

The colonists established large sugar plantations. Most of the Indians who were forced to work these plantations soon died of disease or hardship, and the colonists imported millions of Africans to work as slaves. Today, the populations of the islands are mostly a mix of the descendants of the African slaves and Europeans and, in some cases, of Asians and Europeans.

In recent years, many changes have taken place in the Caribbean. In 1960, there were only three independent nations in the region. Today there are 13.

In the Greater Antilles are Cuba, Jamaica, the Dominican Republic, and Haiti. Of these, Cuba and the Dominican Republic are former Spanish colonies, Haiti belonged to France, and Jamaica to Great Britain. Haiti and the Dominican Republic share the island of Hispaniola. The two countries are quite different and have fought each other many times.

In the Lesser Antilles, the independent nations are Antigua and Barbuda, Barbados, Dominica, Grenada, St. Christopher and

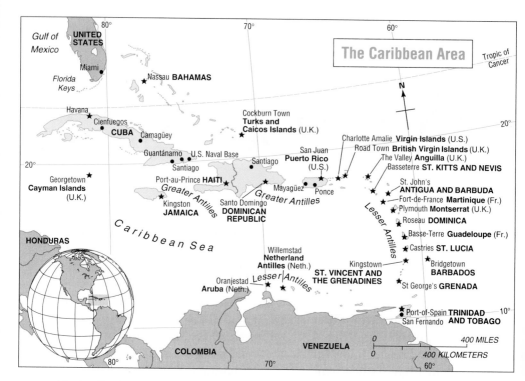

Nevis, St. Lucia, St. Vincent and the Grenadines, and Trinidad and Tobago. The remaining independent nation of the Caribbean is the Bahamas, made up of several hundred islands. The Bahamas and all of the nations of the Lesser Antilles are former British colonies, and British cultural influence is strong here.

There are also many nonindependent islands in the Caribbean. They belong to either Great Britain, France, the Netherlands, or the United States.

The islands of the Caribbean are generally mountainous and volcanic. Mangrove swamps and lagoons dot the coastlines. The climate is warm and pleasant, but there are frequent hurricanes. While some of the islands are economically better off than others, all are poor. These young countries also have many political problems, and all face serious challenges in the near future.

In this chapter, we will examine three of the islands of the Caribbean. First, we will look at Cuba, an independent Spanish-speaking nation. Then we will read about Puerto Rico, a Spanish-speaking commonwealth of the United States. Finally, we will learn about one of the area's few English-speaking nations, the island of Jamaica.

CUBA

The republic of Cuba is the largest nation in the West Indies. Because of its great beauty and pleasant climate, it is often called the "Pearl of the Antilles."

The Land.   Cuba is a long, narrow island, about 700 miles long but averaging only about 60 miles wide. It lies at the entrance to the Gulf of Mexico, some 90 miles south of Florida.

Most of Cuba is a low plain. However, there are also several mountain ranges. The highest and most rugged is the Sierra Maestra (see-AY-rah mah-AY-strah), in the southeast. Cuba has a long coastline with many fine natural harbors, including Havana, Santiago de Cuba, and Guantánamo (gwan-TAHN-uh-moh). Of the many rivers, only the Cauto (KOW-toh), in the southeast, is important.

Cuba lies completely within the tropics. However, the climate is moderated by the surrounding water and by the trade winds (as you remember, winds that blow steadily toward the equator). As a result, temperatures are pleasant throughout the year. Rainfall is abundant, and violent hurricanes are common, particularly during August, September, and October.

A view of the city of Havana. One of the oldest cities in the Americas, Havana is Cuba's largest city and the chief port in the West Indies. It consists partly of an old city with narrow streets and fine examples of colonial architecture. The modern section of the city has wide boulevards, impressive public buildings, and many cultural facilities.

Cuban teenagers in the uniform of the Young Pioneers, a Communist youth group. Cuba has a racially diverse population.

Because of Cuba's warm, even climate, adequate rainfall, and fertile soil, thousands of varieties of tropical fruits and flowers thrive there. The wetter mountains are covered by valuable forests of mahogany, cedar, and royal palm trees.

The People.   After the arrival of the Spanish in the 1500s, Cuba's small American Indian population died out as a result of disease introduced by the Europeans, harsh treatment by the colonists, and fighting. Seeking a cheap labor supply, the Spanish began to import slaves from Africa. By 1865, 750,000 enslaved Africans had been brought to Cuba, and Africans and mulattoes outnumbered the white population of the island. However, this trend was soon reversed. With the abolition of slavery in the 1880s and the arrival of large numbers of Spanish immigrants in the early 1900s, the proportion of whites began to increase. Following the revolution of 1959, about which you will read later, another population shift occurred, as large numbers of whites fled the country.

Today, there are over 10 million people in Cuba. Of these, between 30 and 40 percent are of African descent. Almost all Cubans speak Spanish, although some people, especially in the cities, also speak English. A part of the population speaks Yoruba, an African language.

The Economy.   For over 200 years, Cuba's economy has been based on the production of a single crop—sugar cane. Efforts to diversify agriculture resulted in the growth of the world's best tobacco. Coffee, cacao, and vegetables of all kinds are also grown throughout the country.

136

Sugar cane is still Cuba's most important crop, and many Cubans earn a living growing and processing it. Only Brazil and, in some years, India produce more sugar cane. In addition to refined sugar, important sugar products include molasses, rum, and alcohol.

Before the revolution, sugar was raised under the *colono* system. Under this system, a large company owned the land. The company rented the land to the farmer, and the farmer hired laborers to work the land. The farmers were paid by the company for the cane they delivered to the mill. After 1959, many sugar plantations were taken over by the government. The original plan was to divide the land among the farmers who worked on it. However, the government kept control of the land. Now, instead of working for the company, farmers work for the government on state-owned farms.

Tobacco is Cuba's second most important crop. Some of the world's best tobacco comes from farms in the western part of the island. Other important crops are rice, corn, bananas, and citrus fruits. Cattle, sheep, pigs, horses, and goats are the principal livestock, and many Cubans keep bees. The forests provide mahogany, rosewood, and ebony. There is excellent fishing all year round, and sponge fishing is an important industry off the southern coast.

Unlike most Caribbean countries, Cuba has fairly rich mineral resources. The Sierra Maestra has deposits of copper, manganese, chromium, coal, gold, and silver. Cuba's nickel deposits are the third largest in the world.

Early History.   There were three Indian groups who inhabited the island of Cuba—the Guanajatabeyes, the Ciboneys, and the Tainos. Although the Guanajatabeyes were the earliest inhabitants, the Tainos were the dominant group. Members of the Arawak tribe, the Tainos had come to Cuba from the Amazon region of South America in the 1400s.

Columbus landed in Cuba on October 28, 1492, and claimed it for Spain. European settlement did not begin, however, until 1511, when Diego Velásquez (vuh-LAS-kuhs), a Spanish conquistador, arrived with 300 soldiers. By 1514, Spanish conquest of the island was complete, and Velásquez began the establishment of numerous settlements. Because of Cuba's excellent harbors and central location, other Spanish adventurers began to use the island as a base for exploration and colonization of the New World.

Most of the Spanish who settled Cuba took up farming. They grew sugar cane and tobacco on large plantations, and Cuba was soon one of the richest colonies in the West Indies. During the 1600s and 1700s,

buccaneers, or pirates, were attracted by the island's great wealth and frequently raided along the coast.

The island continued to prosper, however, and by the late 1800s its sugar economy was the basis of one of the world's fashionable societies. Cubans amassed great fortunes and spent money lavishly. They built elegant palaces and held large and extravagant balls. Havana, the capital, was the liveliest city of the Caribbean. It had beautiful shops, theaters, and stately **plazas,** or town squares. Its many terraced cafes were always full of people sipping coffee and sharing stories. In the evenings, a concert often took place in the main plaza. Upper-class women, however, were rarely seen in public places.

Prosperity was not shared equally, however. The majority of the population lived a life of poverty and disease. Only about one-fifth of the school-age population attended school. Beggars roamed the streets of the cities. Smugglers were common in the port of Havana, and the newspapers were full of stories of harbor crime.

First Attempts at Independence.   Cuba did not join in the liberation movements that sprang up throughout much of Latin America in the early 1800s. One reason for this may have been the fact that Cuba could be reached more easily by Spanish military forces than most of Spain's other American colonies.

Then, in 1868, Cuba exploded in rebellion against Spain. Led by a wealthy planter named Carlos Manuel de Céspedes [SAYS-pay-thays], the Cubans demanded independence and the abolition of slavery. Although fighting lasted for ten years, the Cubans were not successful, and Cuba remained a Spanish colony. Spain, however, did make some concessions to the rebels, including an agreement to abolish slavery.

In 1895, another revolt against Spanish rule broke out in Cuba. One of the leaders, the poet José Martí [mar-TEE], became a national hero for his role in the rebellion. However, like the Ten Years' War, this rebellion also ended in defeat for the Cubans.

The Spanish-American War.   The Spanish government treated the *insurrectos,* or revolutionaries, ruthlessly. They herded the Cubans into prison camps where many died from hunger and neglect. The United States government protested this treatment, with no success.

There was much support in the United States for the cause of Cuban independence, and in 1898 events came to a head. In February, the U.S. battleship *Maine* was mysteriously blown up while on a visit in Havana harbor. The United States blamed Spain for the explosion, and in April, the Congress declared war on Spain. The Spanish-American

War lasted only a few months. The United States was victorious. As part of the peace treaty, Spain agreed to give up Cuba.

Although the treaty recognized Cuban independence, Cuba was placed under a U.S. military government. The presence of American forces angered many Cubans. However, during the occupation, much was done to rebuild the war-torn country. Under the leadership of General Leonard Wood, American soldiers repaired roads and public buildings, built sanitation facilities, and distributed food. Perhaps most spectacular was the conquest of yellow fever, a deadly disease that had long plagued the Cuban people.

Independence. Finally, in 1902, the United States withdrew its forces, and Cuba became an independent republic. Its first elected president was Tomás Estrada Palma (toh-MAHS eh-STRAH-thah PAL-mah).

The United States, however, had not given up all interest in Cuba. The new Cuban constitution, adopted in 1901, contained a set of provisions known as the Platt Amendment. The Platt Amendment limited Cuban independence by giving the United States the right to intervene in Cuban affairs. It also allowed the United States to buy or lease land for military bases on the island. (In 1903, the United States received a permanent lease on Guantánamo Bay and began to build a naval base there; this base is still under U.S. control in the 1990s.) Many Cubans opposed the Platt Amendment, but the United States insisted on it.

Independence did not bring stability to Cuba. Political life was characterized by disputes between rival factions, violence, and corruption. In 1924, the Cuban people elected General Gerardo Machado (mah-CHAH-thoh) as president. During his campaign, Machado had attacked the Platt Amendment and had promised reforms. However, after being elected, he took the powers of a dictator. Finally, in 1933, an army revolt forced the unpopular Machado to flee the country. Two months later, an army sergeant named Fulgencio Batista (fool-HEN-see-oh bah-TEE-stah) seized control of the government. From that time until 1959, all real power in Cuba was held by Batista.

The Batista Years. Batista worked to gain U.S. support. In 1934, the United States and Cuba signed a treaty that canceled the Platt Amendment, except for the provision concerning the leasing of Guantánamo. During World War II, Cuba under Batista acted in close cooperation with the United States. Cuba prospered as it leased bases to the United States, found a willing market for its sugar crop, and expanded the production of its important mineral resources.

In 1940, Cuba adopted a new constitution and elected Batista president. However, the constitution prevented Batista from seeking reelection. In 1952, on the eve of a presidential election, Batista seized power through a military coup. Under Batista, Cuba enjoyed a period of great economic prosperity. However, the majority of the people did not share in the benefits of this prosperity. Foreign investors controlled much of the island's economy, and organized crime and corruption were accepted facts of life. Further, Batista began a period of political oppression. Those who opposed him were imprisoned, killed, or exiled. Many people considered Cuba in 1959 the most corrupt nation in the Caribbean. Movements soon arose to oust Batista from office.

The Rise of Fidel Castro.   Among those who detested Batista's tactics was a young lawyer named Fidel Castro (fee-DEL KAS-troh). On July 26, 1953, Castro tried to start a revolution against Batista by leading a raid against the Moncado Army Barracks near Santiago. Many of the rebels died in the raid. Others, including Castro and his brother Raúl (rah-OOL) escaped to the nearby mountains. When he received assurances from the Roman Catholic bishop of Santiago that he would receive a fair trial, Castro surrendered to the government.

At his trial, Castro accused the Batista regime of betraying the Cuban people. He proclaimed the objectives of his revolutionary movement, now named the "26th of July Movement," after the date of the unsuccessful revolt. He promised social justice for farm workers and the unemployed, and industrial progress for the nation as a whole. Castro received a sentence of 15 years in prison. However, he was freed a year and a half later, in 1955, when Batista declared an **amnesty,** or pardon for political prisoners.

The Revolution.   Following his release from prison, Castro went to Mexico, where he began to recruit and train a force to invade Cuba. On December 2, 1956, Castro and 82 of his followers landed on the east coast of Cuba. Most of the rebels were soon killed. Only Castro and 11 others, including an Argentine-born physician named Ernesto "Ché" Guevara (CHAY gay-VAH-rah), escaped to the mountains, the Sierra Maestra.

In the mountain camp, Castro began to build a band of **guerrillas** to attack the Batista regime. (Guerrillas are members of an irregular, usually small, military force trained to move quickly and to attack without warning over difficult terrain.)

In 1957, Castro's rebels began to attack. They derailed trains, blew up bridges, and destroyed electric power plants. The morale of the

Fidel Castro speaking before a group of American journalists in the 1950s. Castro came to power in Cuba in 1959.

government troops sagged lower and lower. On the other hand, Castro's hit-and-run victories increased the people's support of the rebels. In January 1959, Batista fled the country, and Castro's forces took over the government. Castro proclaimed himself premier. It was the first time in Latin American history that a group of guerrillas had successfully overthrown a military regime.

Cuba under Castro. In his first days in power, Castro gave no clear indication of what he planned to do. Soon, however, there were reports of large-scale trials and executions, first of Batista supporters, then of Castro's other political opponents.

In 1959 and early 1960, the Castro government seized sugar estates and cattle ranches owned by American citizens. Relations with the United States began to deteriorate. In mid-1960, Castro took over American oil refineries in Cuba. In response, the United States stopped buying Cuban sugar, leaving Cuba without a customer for the product that was the basis of its economy. Castro then took over all remaining U.S. businesses in Cuba. He also offered to sell sugar to the Soviet Union in return for arms. In January 1961, the United States broke off diplomatic relations with Cuba.

The Bay of Pigs Invasion. On April 17, 1961, a force of 1,800 Cuban exiles landed at the Bay of Pigs on Cuba's southern coast. Their goal was to overthrow the Castro government. They were sponsored by the

United States, which hoped to replace Castro with a government more sympathetic to the interests of the United States. The advantage first gained by surprise was quickly lost. Within a few days, Castro's forces captured or killed most of the exiles. The invasion failed.

The Cuban Missile Crisis.   Tension between the United States and Cuba continued to mount. In December 1961, Castro announced he was a Communist and dissolved all political parties except the Communist party. He censored the press, and his land reform program put land in the hands of the state, not the farmers. Castro, fearful that the United States was planning to invade Cuba, asked the Soviet Union for more military aid. In October 1962, U.S. intelligence services discovered Soviet nuclear missiles in Cuba and learned that the Soviet Union was shipping materials for building missile launch sites there. President John F. Kennedy ordered the U.S. Navy to **blockade,** or prevent ships from reaching, Cuba. He demanded that the Soviet Union remove all missiles and missile bases from the island. For several days, the world waited tensely for the Soviet response. Even nuclear war seemed possible. Finally, the Soviets agreed to Kennedy's demands; in return the United States pledged not to invade Cuba.

Foreign Relations.   Isolated after the Cuban Missile Crisis, Castro tried to spread revolution throughout Latin America. However, the guerrilla groups that he supported in several Latin American countries were not successful. The Organization of American States (OAS), an organization formed after World War II by the nations of the Western Hemisphere to promote inter-American cooperation, condemned Castro's actions. In addition, the OAS expelled Cuba from its membership and **boycotted,** or refused to buy, its goods.

During the 1970s, Cuba became more cautious in its approach to revolutionary activities and reduced its aid to rebels in other Latin American countries. It continued, however, to send troops to Angola and Ethiopia, in Africa, to aid Communist-backed governments involved in civil wars there.

In the 1980s, Cuba backed the revolutionary Sandinista government in Nicaragua, and the guerrilla movement trying to overthrow the government of El Salvador (You will read about these in Chapter 7.) Generally, however, Castro tried to improve relations with the democratic nations of Latin America. Several Latin American nations, including Peru and Argentina, resumed diplomatic relations with Cuba.

Cuba Today.   Cuba in 1960 and Cuba today are very different countries. In the early 1960s, about half the people lived in the countryside. By the late 1980s, the urban population made up about 70 percent of the population. In 1965, slightly more than one of every three Cuban workers were employed in agriculture. Today, that figure is closer to one out of five.

Distinctions based on race, class, sex, or occupation have been eliminated or greatly reduced. Enormous strides have been made in providing housing, medical care, and education for the Cuban people. For example, better health care, particularly for the very poor, has resulted in a dramatic decline in the infant mortality rate, the number of infants who die before reaching the age of one. Basic social services are free for everybody. Official corruption and violent crime have been brought under control. A special campaign against illiteracy has had great effects. Before the revolution, about half of Cuban children between the ages of 6 and 14 did not attend school. Approximately 42 percent of people living in the countryside were illiterate. Today, many more children attend school, and only 3 percent of the population is illiterate, one of the lowest illiteracy rates in Latin America.

Politically, revolutionary Cuba has done less to fulfill Castro's promises. Castro rules as a dictator and, with a small handful of loyal supporters, makes all major decisions. The Communist party is the only legal political party. **Civil rights**, the political rights of a nation's citizens, are denied. Among these are the right to a free press and the right to oppose the government. The government controls the arts, and much of their content is shaped to suit government policy. Many political prisoners are held in jail without trial.

A Cuban record shop.

CASE STUDY:

Going to School in Cuba

Following the Cuban revolution, education in Cuba underwent enormous changes. In the following excerpt, a Cuban boy describes his experiences at school.

> My name is Gregory. . . . I live in Cuba. I want to talk about the *beca* where I study. The *beca* is a kind of school where children live. They sleep and eat and study and play and do everything at the school. My school is a sports *beca*. It is very strict, something like the army. We have a schedule for sports and everything else. Every day we work out in whatever sport we're in. That's so the children will be strong, and when they're grown up they'll be prepared physically as well as mentally.
>
> This year I'm the Pioneer Correspondent for my *beca*. One of my jobs is to do political work with children who have a bad attitude. For example, there's a boy who sleeps in the same room I do. I've done a lot of work with him, showing him the correct way to treat other people, how to act in class, and in school.
>
> There's a kind of love that exists among the children at the *becas*. It's called *compañerismo*, or comradeship. We share everything. I feel like the *compañeros* are my brothers.
>
> Let's see, what else can I say? Well, in the *beca* I feel great, but it's only natural that sometimes I want to be in a better *beca* or have something special, more toys, etc. But I've got to keep on learning that I can't have special things or more toys because here in Cuba the Revolution gives the same number of toys to everyone.

Karen Wald. *Children of Ché: Childcare and Education in Cuba* (Palo Alto, Ramparts Press, 1978), pp. 44-45.

1. Based on Gregory's account, what things are stressed in Cuban schools?

2. Why can't Gregory have more toys? How does he feel about this?

3. How does Cuba's government use education to promote its goals?

Some conditions of daily life also present problems in Cuba today. Electric power outages occur often in Havana and other large cities. The production of rice and beans, two staples of the Cuban diet, has not kept pace with population growth. Consequently, food is scarce and must be rationed. Each household receives a ration book and must buy its food in a government store. Many Cubans have expressed dissatisfaction with the lack of consumer goods. There are long lines and high prices for appliances such as irons and refrigerators. Some blame the government's centralized economic control, poor management, and heavy spending on the military. Others blame the American trade embargo. Between 1980 and 1986, the Cuban government tried to quiet these complaints by allowing farmers to sell their products in private markets.

Cuba's relationship with the Soviet Union remained important into the 1990s. For many years after 1960, Soviet aid increased steadily. From 1961 to 1989, the Soviet Union granted more than $63 billion in economic aid and more than $10 billion in military aid to Cuba. In the 1980s, more than 84 percent of Cuba's foreign trade was with Communist countries. Two-thirds of this total was with the Soviet Union. Without Soviet aid, the Cuban economy would have been in serious trouble.

Much of the assistance from the Soviet Union was in the form of **subsidies** on Cuban products. A subsidy, in this case, is the payment for a product at a price greater than the current market value. For example, in 1989 the world market price for a pound of sugar was about 9 cents. However, the Soviet Union paid 40 cents per pound, or more than four times the market price. The Soviet Union also bought Cuban nickel with similar trade subsidies, and it sold Soviet oil to Cuba at a lower-than-world-market price.

The Soviet Union also played an important role in maintaining Cuba's military forces. The Soviet Union has provided modern military equipment, including over 200 jet fighters, to Castro without cost. The Soviets also maintained a force in Cuba of about 6,000 soldiers, 3,500 military advisers, and 2,000 civilian advisers.

Despite its ties with the Soviet Union, the Castro government had at times indicated interest in resuming normal trade relations with the West, especially the United States. As you have read, the United States began a boycott of Cuban goods in the 1960s. There was some improvement in relations in the 1970s, including a U.S.-Cuban fishing treaty and the lifting of a U.S. ban on travel to Cuba. However, during the administrations of Ronald Reagan, from 1981 to 1989, and George Bush, which began in 1989, relations between Cuba and the United States reached their lowest point since the 1960s.

Beginning in 1990, the Soviet Union, which was in severe financial difficulty, began to cut back its subsidies to Cuba. The price paid for sugar, for example, was cut from 40 cents to 25 cents a pound. Then, in 1991, the Communist Party fell from power in the Soviet Union. Soon thereafter, Soviet President Gorbachev announced that all subsidies to Cuba would end and that all Soviet military forces would be withdrawn.

Cuba has made great advances since its 1959 revolution. It has also sustained major losses. Social justice has been achieved for many people, but often at the cost of personal liberty. In Cuba, feelings about the revolution have been mixed. Many Cubans have shown their dislike of Castro's Cuba by fleeing the country. Many others, however, continue to support the revolution

Economically, Cuba remained a poor country, even in those years when its economy was heavily subsidized by the Soviet Union. The withdrawal of Soviet aid, announced in 1991, seemed sure to create huge problems. At a time when many other Communist governments were collapsing, first in eastern Europe and then in the Soviet Union itself, Castro vowed that Communism would stay in place in Cuba. Whether Castro would be able to keep that vow remained a major question for the 1990s.

PUERTO RICO

In language, customs, and traditions, Puerto Rico belongs to the Spanish culture of Latin America. Politically, it is part of the United States. Thus, Puerto Rico links the Western Hemisphere's British influenced north with its Spanish-influenced south.

The Land. Puerto Rico is the easternmost island of the Greater Antilles. It includes the main island of Puerto Rico and several smaller islands.

Puerto Rico is relatively small, only 100 miles long and 35 miles wide. Rising up out of the Caribbean Sea and the Atlantic Ocean, it is formed by the high peaks of two mountain chains whose bases are buried beneath the sea. Most of the terrain is mountainous, but fertile lowlands rim the coast and form valleys between the mountain ranges.

Major Cities. San Juan (SAN WAHN) is the capital, chief port, and commercial and industrial center of Puerto Rico. It is located on a small rocky island north of the main island, to which it is connected by bridges and a causeway. The Spanish explorer Juan Ponce de León (WAHN

El Morro, a fortress in San Juan, Puerto Rico.

PAHNS duh lee-UHN) founded the city in 1521. Today, it is a mixture of the old and the new, with modern luxury hotels and high-rise apartment buildings standing alongside historic towers and churches. Tourism is an important industry. Aside from a pleasant climate and beautiful beaches, the major attractions include the narrow colonial streets of "Old San Juan" and the imposing stone walls of El Morro, a fortress built at the entrance to San Juan harbor more than 300 years ago.

Ponce (POHN-say), on the Caribbean Sea, is Puerto Rico's second largest city. It is an important port and manufacturing and shipping center. Mayagüez (meye-uh-GWEZ), on the west coast, is also important.

The People.   Puerto Rico has a population of about 3.3 million people. Nearly three-fourths of the people are of Spanish descent. The remaining one-fourth are mostly of African descent or mulatto. Spanish is the language spoken by most Puerto Ricans. However, the law requires schools to teach English a minimum of 70 minutes each day. The overwhelming majority of the people are Roman Catholics.

147

Puerto Rico's **population density**, or number of people per square mile, is one of the highest in the world. Overcrowding is a serious problem. For many years, large numbers of Puerto Ricans moved to the mainland United States in search of jobs. Between the end of World War II and 1953, nearly 74,000 people left Puerto Rico for the United States each year. Migration then slowed down, dwindling to almost zero in the early 1960s and 1970s. With the onset of an economic depression in the late 1970s, emigration picked up again. Between 1980 and 1983, 90,000 Puerto Ricans arrived on the "mainland." Unemployment is a major factor in the rate of emigration. In the mid-1980s, it was estimated that about 21 percent of Puerto Rico's total population were migrants. There were about 2 million Puerto Ricans living in the United States, mainly in New York, New Jersey, Illinois, Florida, and California.

Many of the migrants return to Puerto Rico after a few years. Because of this moving back and forth, they sometimes face cultural difficulties. While living in New York City, for example, many lose fluency in Spanish. They also pick up new customs. Returning to Puerto Rico, they may find themselves rejected as "Newyoricans."

Education and Culture.   All children between the ages of 6 and 14 must attend the public schools. The curriculum is similar to that of schools in the United States and includes both academic and vocational subjects. The University of Puerto Rico, the main center of higher learning, grants degrees in many fields, from medicine to the arts.

The basic culture of Puerto Rico is Spanish. Thus, sports such as cockfighting are popular. However, U.S. culture has also left its mark. Puerto Ricans adore baseball; they not only play the game, but are staunch supporters of their local teams. The former major league star Roberto Clemente is a national hero. Clemente, a rightfielder for the Pittsburgh Pirates for 18 years, died at the age of 38 while airlifting supplies to earthquake victims in Nicaragua. In an essay written after Clemente's death, one Puerto Rican schoolchild wrote that "Clemente was so great that the earth could not hold him; so he had to be buried at sea."

Puerto Rican young people enjoy the latest trends in American dancing and music, as well as the rhythms of their Spanish and African heritage. People enjoy long sessions in cafés, the *paseo*, or evening walk, and political debate. Gambling is popular, and there are numerous lotteries held daily.

Like other Latin Americans, Puerto Ricans like fiestas, or festivals. Their religious processions are brilliant and colorful pageants.

College students registering for courses at the University of Puerto Rico.

Puerto Rico boasts numerous internationally known artists, musicians, and writers. Foremost among today's novelists is Luis Rafael Sánchez, whose book *Macho Camacho's Beat* portrays life in modern San Juan with humor and wit. Puerto Rico also has a symphony orchestra. The annual Casals Festival is named after the celebrated Spanish cellist (CHEL-uhst) Pablo Casals, who for many years made his home in Puerto Rico. The festival attracts the world's finest musicians.

Early History. Columbus landed in Puervo Rico in 1493 and claimed it for Spain. The first stable European settlement on the island was established 15 years later, in 1508, by Juan Ponce de León, who gave the island its name, Puerto Rico, Spanish for "rich port."

Upon their arrival, the Spanish found the island occupied by a tribe of Arawak Indians, a peaceful, agricultural people. They tried to force the Indians to work for them. In 1511, the Indians revolted but were quickly suppressed by the Spanish. Most of the Indians died from overwork and disease, and the colonists began importing enslaved Africans, as they had elsewhere.

The early settlers farmed and mined gold, but the gold deposits were not very large, and the Spanish colony did not prosper. However, because of its location, the island became important as a military base guarding Spain's other Latin American colonies.

At first, Spanish laws prohibited Puerto Rico from trading with other countries. The laws also set limits on immigration. Eventually, under pressure from the settlers, Spain instituted reforms and relaxed immigration and trade laws. Nevertheless, in the 1850s, a movement for self-government in Puerto Rico began to grow. There were several unsuccessful uprisings against Spain. Finally, in 1897, Spain granted Puerto Rico a charter that permitted some degree of self-rule.

149

The United States in Puerto Rico.   The new government had little chance to operate. As you have read, one year later, in 1898, the Spanish-American War broke out. By the treaty ending this war, Spain ceded Puerto Rico to the United States.

For two years, a U. S. military government ruled Puerto Rico. Then, in 1900, Congress established a local administration with an appointed governor and upper house of the legislature and an elected lower house. However, Congress reserved the right to review all legislation. Soon, Puerto Ricans began to pressure for greater participation. In 1917 the U.S. Congress passed an act providing for election of both houses of the legislature. (The governor would still be appointed by the U.S. president.) It also made Puerto Ricans citizens of the United States.

Under United States rule, many improvements were made in Puerto Rico. Aqueducts, hydroelectric plants, railroads, highways, government buildings, public schools, and hospitals were constructed. However, the rate of progress did not keep up with the rate of population increase. Although better off than many of their Latin American neighbors, most Puerto Ricans were still very poor, and many were without jobs.

Operation Bootstrap.   In 1940, Puerto Rico was an impoverished island with a one-crop agricultural economy and very few natural resources. Dependent for centuries on its sugar crop, Puerto Rico produced only half the food needed for its steadily growing population. Per capita income, the average income of each person in a place, was $120 per year. Life expectancy, the average number of years that people in a place usually live, was only 35 years. Illiteracy and unemployment were commonplace.

In 1948, Puerto Rico's governor, Luis Muñoz Marín (loo-EES moon-YOHS mah-REEN), launched a series of economic reform programs designed to increase jobs and improve living conditions. Describing his plans. Muñoz Marín said that Puerto Ricans were going to "pull ourselves up by our own bootstraps." His programs thus became known as Operation Bootstrap.

Operation Bootstrap brought many improvements to Puerto Rico. A land-reform program distributed small plots of land to thousands of families. To diversify agriculture, tobacco, coffee, pineapples, and other fruits were planted on the island's limited farmland. Muñoz Marín and his advisers launched an extensive program to attract investors to bring industry to the island. New factories were built. Roads, public health, and schools were improved. Waterfront shacks and slum neighborhoods gave way to neat housing projects and the latest in resort hotels.

Operation Bootstrap was a tremendous success. Per capita income soared—to $250 a year in 1950 and a remarkable $1,800 a year in 1973. In the 1990s, per capita income in Puerto Rico was over $3,000 a year. This was the highest in Spanish-speaking Latin America. Thousands of manufacturing plants sprang up, producing shoes, textiles, baby garments, and chemical and electrical goods. Tourism boomed. Tropical disease and illiteracy were just about wiped out, and life expectancy was raised to 75 years—about the same as on the U.S. mainland.

The Commonwealth. In 1952, with the approval of the U.S. government, Puerto Rico drew up a new constitution. Under this constitution, Puerto Rico became a **commonwealth** of the United States. The word "commonwealth" as applied to Puerto Rico describes a political unit somewhat like a state of the United States. Like a state, the Commonwealth of Puerto Rico has an elected governor and legislature, and a representative in Congress. However, unlike the people in a state, residents of the Commonwealth of Puerto Rico may not vote for the U.S. president. Furthermore, the Puerto Rican representative in Congress does not have a vote. Finally, Puerto Ricans do not pay income taxes to the United States federal government. In 1967, Puerto Ricans voted to continue commonwealth status.

This arrangement satisfies some, but not all, Puerto Ricans. Many believe Puerto Rico should become the fifty-first state of the United States. Others favor total independence for Puerto Rico. Some of the more radical independence groups have resorted to violence. (In the 1950s, one such group attempted to assassinate President Harry S Truman.) The Puerto Ricans who desire statehood have united into the Statehood Republican Party, the second most powerful political group on the island.

Puerto Rico Today. Puerto Rico's period of spectacular economic growth came to a sudden halt in 1973, when world oil prices leaped sky-high. Puerto Rico, with no oil resources of its own, was hit particularly hard. Because of their need for oil and petroleum products, all of the heavy industries closed down. Thousands of people lost their jobs; in 1985, it was estimated that close to 40 percent of the island's population was unemployed. Even the tourist trade declined. The island has become totally dependent on help from the U.S. federal government. In 1985, the United States was spending $10 million a day in democratic Puerto Rico; this is three times as much per person as the Soviet Union spent on economic aid to the Cuban dictatorship. For example, most residents of Puerto Rico receive **food stamps,** coupons from the government that enable them to obtain free food.

Several other factors contribute to the economic slump. Economic funds often go for consumer needs rather than into productive use. Almost all consumer goods must be imported—Puerto Rico is the fourth largest customer for United States goods in Latin America. In addition, Puerto Rico's government is the largest employer on the island. The number of public employees increased dramatically in the 1970s. Since industry could not create enough jobs, the government expanded its payroll to keep up with the growing labor force.

When Puerto Rico's Operation Bootstrap got underway, it attracted much attention. Other developing countries thought the program might become a model for their economies. However, the serious economic problems of the 1970s and 1980s have led many people in developing countries to seek other solutions to their problems.

JAMAICA

The island of Jamaica lies south of Cuba. Today an independent country, for more than 300 years Jamaica was a colony of Great Britain and part of what was known as the British West Indies.

The Land.   Jamaica, the third largest island in the Caribbean, is a land of rugged mountains and high plateaus. The plateaus are formed of limestone made up of the skeletons of thousands of coral. The principal mountains, located in the east, are usually covered with a bluish mist. The highest point, Blue Mountain Peak, rises more than 7,400 feet above sea level. There are many good harbors along the island's long coastline. Kingston, the capital of Jamaica, has the seventh largest harbor in the world.

The climate is tropical, although constant breezes keep the temperature even. The coastal area is hot and humid, with an average temperature of 80°F. The highlands are cooler and pleasant, and rainfall is abundant.

People and Culture.   The overwhelming majority of Jamaica's 2.5 million people are of African or mixed African-European descent. There are small Middle Eastern and Asian minorities, descendants of people from Lebanon, Syria, India, and China. Jamaica's national motto is

Christopher Columbus, upon reaching Jamaica in 1494, called it "the fairest isle that eyes have beheld." Today the island's beauty has made tourism an important source of income.

"Out of many, one people." This motto refers to the multiethnic mix that characterizes its population.

English is the official language, but *patois* (pa-TWAH), a **dialect** of English, is spoken by most of the people. (A dialect is a form of a language spoken in a particular region or by a particular group. It differs in vocabulary, grammar, and pronunciation from other dialects of the language.) The people follow many British customs, and most of the political institutions reflect British influence.

As in most Caribbean countries, work is often difficult to find in Jamaica. As a result, over the years large numbers of Jamaicans left their island homeland to find jobs in other lands. Between the 1880s and 1920, Jamaicans went to Panama to help build the Panama Canal, to Cuba to cut sugar cane, and to other Central American countries where laborers were needed. During the 1950s and 1960s, many Jamaicans emigrated to the United States and England; since 1967 most migrants have gone to the United States and Canada. Today, over one million Jamaicans—equal to almost half the island population—live overseas.

The majority of the population is Protestant, but many Jamaicans belong to religious groups that combine Christian and African beliefs and practices. About 70,000 Jamaicans of African descent belong to the **Rastafarian movement**. Members of this religious group worship former Emperor Haile Selassie I of Ethiopia as a god. (Ras Tafari was Haile Selassie's name before he became emperor.)

Rastafarians adopted many of the beliefs of Marcus Garvey. Garvey was a Jamaican who preached that all people of African descent should consider Africa their home and return there to live. They believe Africans are superior to other Jamaicans. The music and dance of the Rastafarians, called **reggae**, was made popular throughout the world by Bob Marley. Marley, who died in 1981 at the age of 36, is a national hero in Jamaica for his efforts in fighting for social change.

Music is an important part of Jamaican culture. Much of Jamaica's musical tradition can be traced back to slave days. Since slaves were not allowed to talk while they worked, they communicated by chanting their messages. Today, work songs based on slave chants are sung by Jamaican laborers of all kinds.

Another form of music is **John Canoe**—often written and pronounced by Jamaicans as *junkanoo*. This is performed in the streets at Christmas time. The participants, dressed in costumes and masks, go from house to house collecting money and leading songs and dances created for the occasion.

Daily Life.   Meals in Jamaica are fairly simple events, with the main meal usually eaten in the afternoon. Jamaican dishes are known for their spiciness. This results from a generous use of allspice, ginger, and peppers. A popular dish is salt fish and ackee, a fruit that was originally imported from West Africa. To make the dish, the pulp of the ackee is cooked with onions and peppers and then served with codfish cakes.

Education and Health Care.   Jamaica's educational system is based on British school programs. During the colonial era, most Jamaicans completed only a primary education. There were few secondary schools on the island. Students who qualified for higher education usually were sent to study in England. Following independence in 1962, many secondary schools were established in Jamaica, and the numbers of Jamaicans attending secondary school increased. Many Jamaicans still go abroad for university training. Jamaica has a high level of literacy, over 90 percent.

Throughout Jamaica, medical facilities provide health care. Since

A performance of a Jamaican play.

the 1940s, there has been a marked decline in deaths from infectious diseases. One of the most severe problems is a shortage of trained doctors and dentists. Many medical professionals leave for jobs in England or the United States, where the average salary is considerably higher than in Jamaica.

The Economy. Tourism, mining, and manufacturing are the dominant factors in Jamaica's economy. Since its discovery in the 1950s, **bauxite,** used to make aluminum, has been of major importance. Jamaica is the world's second largest producer of bauxite. However, in the 1980s, the bauxite industry was severely threatened by a dramatic drop in world bauxite prices. Many workers lost their jobs, and production fell by more than 50 percent. Several foreign aluminum corporations announced plans to pull out of Jamaica and close down operations.

More than one-third of Jamaica's workers are farmers raising a wide variety of crops. The most important are sugar cane, bananas, and citrus fruits. Jamaica is one of the few producers of allspice, a spice made from the berries of the pimento tree. However, farm production has not kept up with population growth, and large quantities of food must be imported. Little modern equipment is available, and the majority of farmers continue to use primitive hand tools.

Early History. Christopher Columbus landed in Jamaica in 1494 and claimed it for Spain. The Spanish used Jamaica mainly as a supply base for ships, and they did little to settle or develop the island. In 1655, the

English captured the island, and for the next 50 years English pirates in the Caribbean used Jamaica as a base to attack Spanish ships and ports.

In the 1700s, British settlers began to develop large sugar plantations on the island. They imported thousands of slaves from Africa to work in the fields, and the island prospered. But Jamaica was primarily a place where British investors hoped to get rich. Many considered England their home and made little effort to develop Jamaican institutions or culture.

The slave trade ended in 1804. Then, in the 1830s, after much struggle, Jamaican slaves were freed. Faced with a severe labor shortage, the sugar economy began to decline. Economic hardship soon resulted in unrest among the population. The most notable incident was the Morant Bay Rebellion in 1865. Paul Bogle, a Jamaican farmer, led a revolt of former slaves against white rule. The British suppressed the uprising, and Bogle was captured and hanged.

A Crown Colony.   After the Morant Bay Rebellion, Britain made Jamaica a **crown colony** and forced the local legislature to resign. As a crown colony its laws were made by the British government, symbolized by the crown. The governor of the colony was appointed by the British and was responsible only to them. Members of the British minority dominated the government and business. Most Jamaicans had little chance to participate in either.

Independence.   After World War I, resentment against British rule began to grow in Jamaica. During the 1930s, a wave of strikes and riots swept the island. Jamaican leaders urged the British Parliament to give the people more political power. In 1944, Britain granted all adult Jamaicans the right to vote. A new constitution provided for some self-government, and Jamaicans were allowed a larger role in island politics. As political conditions on the island improved, foreign investments began to pour in. After bauxite deposits were discovered, the island began to prosper once more.

In 1958, Jamaica joined with nine other British colonies in the Caribbean to form the Federation of the West Indies. The Federation did not last long, however. Jamaica, believing it was not benefiting enough from membership, withdrew from the Federation in 1961. In 1962, Jamaica became fully independent. It also became a member of the **Commonwealth of Nations**, an organization made up of Great Britain and many of its former colonies.

Jamaica Today.   Since Jamaica became independent in 1962, it has faced many problems, including inflation, unemployment, and poverty. However, its political system is one of the most stable in Latin America. Elections are held regularly, and power has been transferred from one party to another several times.

Jamaica's two major political parties offered different solutions to the country's serious economic problems. The People's National Party (PNP) favored a policy of democratic socialism, based on a mixture of state-owned and private enterprises. The PNP's rival, the Jamaica Labor Party (JLP) was, despite its name, a conservative organization that believed strongly in private enterprise.

In 1972, Michael Manley of the PNP was elected prime minister and launched a program that involved nationalization of certain industries, increased expenditure for welfare, and agricultural reform. In foreign affairs, he sided with other "Third World" nations in not aligning Jamaica with either of the two superpowers, the United States or the Soviet Union. He established close ties with Communist Cuba.

Reelected in 1976, Manley's government could not withstand the severe effects on Jamaica of the world recession. The economy deteriorated further, and in 1980 the country overwhelmingly voted Edward Seaga (say-AH-gah) and the JLP into office.

Seaga's policies were designed to help private businesses and to improve relations with the United States and other Western powers. However, Seaga's administration was no more successful in curing Jamaica's ills than Manley's had been. High unemployment, street demonstrations, a general strike in 1985, and drug-related violence marked the years of Seaga's leadership. Such instability led to a sharp drop-off in tourism, a major source of income for the country. Many Jamaicans sought to escape the island's poverty by emigrating to the United States, Great Britain, and Canada. In 1989, Manley was returned to office and introduced policies more moderate than his earlier ones.

What has happened in Jamaica is characteristic of today's Caribbean nations. Inadequate housing, low wages, and limited resources are common problems. Economic growth is limited by dependence on earnings from export of a single agricultural or mineral product. However, exports from the region were expected to increase as a result of a 1990 U.S. law allowing more goods to enter the United States duty free. In addition, the Caribbean Development Bank and the Caribbean Community and Common Market (CARICOM) help stimulate economic growth in the region. In a number of Caribbean nations, a new generation of leaders has emerged who want their countries to be more self-reliant.

REVIEWING THE CHAPTER

I. Building Your Vocabulary

In your notebook, write the numbers from 1 to 5. After each number, write the word that best completes the sentence.

dialect	blockade	subsidy
buccaneer	boycott	archipelago

1. In refusing to buy Cuban products, the OAS was declaring a trade _____.

2. A large group of islands is called a (an) _____.

3. A language spoken in a particular region or by a particular group is called a (an) _____.

4. By buying Cuban sugar at a price that exceeded the world market price, the Soviet Union was granting Cuba a (an) _____.

5. In order to stop Soviet ships from reaching Cuba with more missiles, President Kennedy established a (an) _____.

II. Understanding the Facts

In your notebook, write the numbers from 1 to 5. After each number, write **true** or **false** for the statement. Rewrite each false statement so that it is true.

1. Before the Cuban revolution of 1959, Cuba was a prosperous democracy that had close relations with the United States.

2. As communism crumbled in Eastern Europe and the Soviet Union, Fidel Castro announced that Cuba would remain a Communist state.

3. The per capita income of Puerto Rico is the highest in Spanish-speaking Latin America.

4. Puerto Rico is linked to the United States by a common language and a common culture as well as by political ties.

5. Jamaica's legacy as a former French colony is indicated by the high number of Jamaican students who go to Paris for university training.

III. Thinking It Through

In your notebook, write the numbers from 1 to 4. After each number, write the letter that corresponds to the correct answer to the question.

1. The islands of the Caribbean are united by the fact that all of them
   a. are former colonies of Great Britain.
   b. gained their independence in the 1960s.
   c. have economies based on the cultivation of sugarcane.
   d. share a history of slavery and colonial rule.

2. Since the start of the twentieth century, relations between Cuba and the United States have been deeply affected by
   a. Communist rule over Cuba.
   b. Cuban gratitude for U.S. help in throwing off Spanish colonial rule.
   c. Cuban resentment about U.S. interference in Cuban affairs.
   d. American resentment about Cuban efforts to undermine U.S. influence throughout Latin America.

3. Because they reside in a commonwealth of the United States, Puerto Ricans
   a. have the same voting rights and pay the same taxes as other Americans.
   b. are exempt from paying U.S. income taxes.
   c. can vote in U.S. presidential elections but have no representation in Congress.
   d. have no voice in choosing the island's governor.

4. One reason for Jamaica's economic difficulties in recent years has been the island's
   a. heavy dependence on the export of a few major raw materials, such as bauxite.
   b. unstable political system.
   c. failure to attract foreign investment.
   d. lack of significant natural resources.

INTERPRETING A CHART

Use the information in the chart and in Chapter 6 to answer the questions on page 162.

	COLONIZING POWER	DATE OF INDEPENDENCE	GOVERNMENT
Antigua and Barbuda	Great Britain	1981	(FR) Parliamentary democracy
Bahamas	Great Britain	1973	(FR) Representative democracy
Barbados	Great Britain	1966	(FR) Parliamentary democracy
Cuba	Spain	1902	(NF) Communist republic
Dominica	Great Britain/ France	1978	(FR) Parliamentary democracy
Dominican Republic	Spain/France	1844	(FR) Representative democracy
Grenada	Great Britain/ France	1974	(FR) Parliamentary democracy
Haiti	France	1804	(PF) Republic
Jamaica	Spain/Great Britain	1962	(FR) Representative democracy
St. Christopher and Nevis	Great Britain	1983	(FR) Constitutional monarchy
St. Lucia	Great Britain	1979	(FR) Parliamentary democracy
Trinidad and Tobago	Great Britain	1962	(FR) Parliamentary democracy
St. Vincent and the Grenadines	France/ Great Britain	1979	(FR) Constitutional monarchy

POPULATION	MAIN CROPS	MAJOR INDUSTRIES	INFANT MORTALITY RATE (PER 1000 LIVE BIRTHS)
64,000	Cotton; sugarcane.	Agriculture; tourism.	23
246,000	Fruits; vegetables.	Tourism; rum.	21
263,000	Sugarcane; corn.	Rum; molasses; tourism.	16
10,582,000	Sugarcane; tobacco; coffee; citrus and tropical fruits.	Refined sugar; metals.	12
85,000	Bananas; citrus fruits; coconuts.	Agriculture; tourism; soap; cigars.	13
7,241,000	Sugarcane; cocoa; coffee; tobacco; rice.	Sugar refining; cement; textiles.	62
84,000	Nutmeg; cocoa; bananas; mace.	Agriculture; tourism; garments; processed foods.	30
6,142,000	Coffee; sisal; cotton; sugarcane; bananas; cocoa; tobacco; rice.	Rum; molasses; tourism.	107
2,441,000	Sugarcane; bananas, citrus fruits, coffee; allspice.	Bauxite; rum; molasses; cement; paper.	16
43,000	Sugarcane.	Sugar.	40
153,000	Bananas; cocoa; coconuts; citrus fruits; livestock.	Agriculture; tourism; manufacture (garments).	18
1,270,000	Bananas; arrowroot; coconuts.	Agriculture; tourism.	32
114,000	Sugarcane; cocoa; citrus fruits; coffee; bananas.	Oil products; rum; cement; tourism.	10

161

1. Which country in the Caribbean region was the first to gain its independence?
2. Which country in the Caribbean region gained its independence most recently?
3. What country was the colonizing power in the Dominican Republic?
4. Which country has the highest infant mortality rate in the Caribbean region? The lowest?
5. Which country has the largest population in the Caribbean region?

DEVELOPING CRITICAL THINKING SKILLS

1. Discuss the reasons for widespread poverty in the Caribbean islands and what might be done to overcome that poverty.
2. Explain why some Cubans have been strong supporters of Fidel Castro while others have vigorously opposed his rule.

RECOGNIZING CAUSE AND EFFECT

Study the time box on page 132. Take two pairs of events in the time box and write a paragraph about each pair. In your paragraph, demonstrate a cause-and-effect relationship between the earlier event and the later one.

ENRICHMENT AND EXPLORATION

1. Imagine that you have been hired by a U.S. business firm to evaluate a proposal to build a factory in Cuba, Puerto Rico, or Jamaica. Make a list of at least five questions you would want to answer in the course of your research. Suggest how you would answer the questions for each of the islands named.
2. Organize a debate on the following topic: Should Puerto Rico become a state, remain a commonwealth, or become an independent nation? One or two students can represent each point of view. Another student can act as moderator.
3. Ask your school librarian to help you find a book written about young Puerto Ricans or Cubans living in the United States. Read the book, and write a short report on its contents.

162

7 *Central America*

As you learned in Chapter 1, Central America is the long, narrow bridge of land that connects the continents of North and South America. It is made up of the republics of Belize, Costa Rica, El Salvador, Guatemala, Honduras, Nicaragua, and Panama. The entire region is about 200,000 square miles, roughly the size of the state of Texas. Except for Belize, which belonged to Great Britain until 1981, all of the Central American nations were colonies of Spain before independence.

THE REGION

The combined population of the seven countries of Central America is about 27 million people. In Costa Rica, most of the population is of Spanish ancestry. In Guatemala, more than 90 percent of the population are descendants of the Maya Indians. Mestizos, people of mixed Spanish and Indian background, predominate in El Salvador, Honduras, Nicaragua, and Panama. In Belize, the majority of the people are descendants of Africans imported as plantation laborers during colonial times. Spanish is the official language in all of Central America except Belize, where English is the official language. In Guatemala, a number of Indian languages are spoken, and some of the people do not understand Spanish. Throughout the region, the vast majority of the population is Roman Catholic.

Early History.   As you have read, Central America was the home of the great Maya civilization, which was at its height from A.D. 300 to 800. Europeans first arrived in the area in the early 1500s. In 1502, Christopher Columbus explored the Caribbean coast from Honduras to

163

CENTRAL AMERICA AND THE WORLD

1502–Today

1502	Columbus explores Caribbean coast, Honduras, and Panama.
1525	Spanish complete conquest of Central America.
1776	*U.S. Declaration of Independence*
1821	Central American provinces declare independence.
1822	Central America joins Mexico.
1838	Central American nations once again become independent.
1840	Coffee cultivation introduced to El Salvador.
1861–1865	*U.S. Civil War*
1903	Panama becomes independent from Colombia.
1912–1933	U.S. Marines stationed in Nicaragua.
1914–1918	*World War I*
1920s	Sandino emerges in Nicaragua.
1932	Salvadoran Marxists stage revolution.
1934	Somoza seizes and murders Sandino.
1939–1945	*World War II*
1944	Military dictator ousted in El Salvador.
1948	New constitution abolishes army in Costa Rica
1954	U.S. secretly backs Guatemalan rebellion
1979	Sandinistas take control in Nicaragua. El Salvador distributes land to peasants. Belize gains independence.
1982	Contras begin guerrilla war against Sandinistas.
1989	Six Jesuit priests murdered in El Salvador.
1990	Violetta Chamorro elected Nicaraguan president.

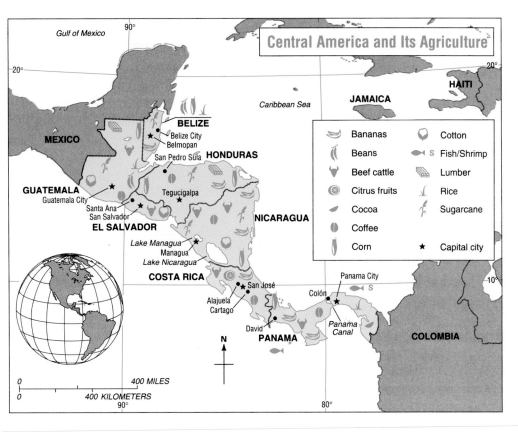

Central America and Its Agriculture

Gulf of Mexico

90°

20°

Caribbean Sea

JAMAICA

HAITI

MEXICO

BELIZE

Belize City
Belmopan

San Pedro Súla HONDURAS

GUATEMALA

Guatemala City

Tegucigalpa

Santa Ana
San Salvador

EL SALVADOR

NICARAGUA

Lake Managua

Managua

Lake Nicaragua

COSTA RICA

San José

Panama City

Colón

Alajuela

Cartago

David

Panama
Canal

PANAMA

COLOMBIA

10°

80°

N

Bananas		Cotton
Beans	S Fish/Shrimp	
Beef cattle	Lumber	
Citrus fruits	Rice	
Cocoa	Sugarcane	
Coffee		
Corn	★ Capital city	

0   400 MILES

0   400 KILOMETERS

90°

Panama. As elsewhere in Latin America, Spanish conquistadors in search of gold soon followed. In some places the Spanish established settlements. The original Indian population was almost entirely destroyed. They died as a result of the harsh conditions of slavery and from disease introduced by the Europeans. By 1525, Spanish conquest of Central America was complete. The entire region, except for Panama and present-day Belize, became part of the Viceroyalty of New Spain.

In 1821, the five Central American provinces from Guatemala to Costa Rica declared their independence from Spain. In 1822, they became part of the Mexican empire of Agustín Iturbide. However, the union with Mexico was unpopular, and in 1823 the five Central American lands joined in the **United Provinces of Central America**. This federation began to break up in 1838. During the next 10 years, its members became the independent republics of Costa Rica, El Salvador, Guatemala, Honduras, and Nicaragua. Panama, which was part of Colombia, became independent in 1903. Belize, which had been a colony called British Honduras, gained independence in 1981.

CASE STUDY:

Two Cultures Meet

Rigoberta Menchú, a Quiché Indian woman, was born in the tiny village of Chimel in Guatemala. She learned Spanish at the age of 20. The following is an excerpt from a tape recording in which she recounted the events of her life.

> My first visit to the capital was a big step in my life. I was my father's favorite. I went with him everywhere.
>
> It was the first time that I'd been in a truck with windows. We were used to traveling in closed trucks, as if we were in an oven with all the people and animals. It was the first time I'd ever sat on a seat in a truck—*and* one with windows.
>
> I hardly slept at all looking at the countryside we passed through . . . . It impressed me very much, it was wonderful to see everything along the way—towns, mountains, houses very different from our own. It made me very happy, but also a bit frightened because I thought, as the truck pulled away, that we would go over into the ditch.
>
> When we reached the capital, I saw cars for the first time. I thought they were animals just going along. It didn't occur to me they were cars. I asked my father: "What are they?" "They're the same as the big trucks, only smaller," he said, "and they're for people who only want to carry small loads."
>
> When I first saw them, I thought that the cars would all bump into each other, but they hardly did at all. When one stopped, they all had to stop. It was all so amazing to me. I remember when I got home telling my brothers and sisters what the cars were like, how they were driven, and that they didn't crash into one another or kill anyone, and a whole load of other things as well. I had a long tale to tell at home.

Elisabeth Burgos-Debray, editor. *I. . . Rigoberta Menchú: An Indian Woman in Guatemala* (United Kingdom: Verso, 1984).

1. Describe Rigoberta's feelings about her journey to the capital.

2. Based on this story, what can you infer about life in Rigoberta's village?

A Guatemalan Indian weaving. Many of Guatemala's Indians have adopted modern ways. Others have intermarried with Spanish-speaking people. Those who have kept their traditions often suffer from discrimination and violence from both army troops and left-wing guerrillas.

Banana Republics. The United States dominated Central America for many years. Beginning in the late 1800s, giant U.S.-based corporations owned or leased most of the fertile land. These corporations built and owned the railroads. They decided who should run for president, fixed elections, and bribed officials in return for favors. Bananas were one of the products that brought these U.S. companies enormous profits. In the United States, the nations of Central America came to be known as **banana republics**. This nickname implied U. S. superiority and poked not-so-good-natured fun at these exploited neighbors to the south.

The United States also interfered militarily in Central America. In the early 1900s, the United States wanted to build a canal through Panama, which was then part of Colombia. The canal would connect the Atlantic and Pacific oceans. Colombia would not agree to the U.S. plan, and in 1903 the United States encouraged Panama to declare its independence from Colombia. With only a brief interruption, U.S. Marines were stationed in Nicaragua from 1912 to 1933. In 1954, the United States secretly backed a rebellion that overthrew the government in Guatemala.

While U.S. corporations grew wealthy from the products of Central American soil, the Central American nations remained poor and backward. Political and social life was controlled by a small privileged group, who stayed in power with the help of the military. The economy was dependent on income from two crops, bananas and coffee. Profits from these crops went to large plantation owners. Meanwhile, the majority of the people worked for the large corporations for low wages or struggled to feed themselves by farming small plots of scrubby land with primitive implements.

A Period of Growth. Beginning in 1959, Central America underwent a period of rapid economic growth. Per capita income (as you remember, the average income of each person in a place) doubled. New products such as cotton, sugar, and beef began to be exported, and dependence on bananas and coffee decreased.

Economic growth was accompanied by many social and political changes. New roads and expanded bus service improved communications in the region. The adult literacy rate jumped from 44 percent in 1960 to 72 percent in 1976. Many people moved to the cities, and demands for jobs and services increased.

Soon a middle class began to emerge. People became better informed and more interested in politics. By the early 1970s, the new middle class began to look for ways to reduce the power of the ruling class and the military. Political parties appeared, and elections were held. However, those in power frequently arranged for cheating at the polls or used violence to scare voters—or even candidates. Except in Costa Rica, repressive military governments continued in power.

Contemporary Problems. The economic boom came to a sudden end in the 1970s. Like the rest of the world, in 1973 the nations of Central America were hit by a severe economic depression. This was caused by an increase in the international price of oil. Prices of export goods fell, and the cost of living rose. Many Central American nations faced serious difficulties in feeding their rapidly growing populations. In many countries, the situation became very tense. Violence was not unusual.

Today, Central America is an area undergoing great political, social, and economic changes. Each of the tiny nations faces different problems and different challenges. Each must find its own solutions. In this chapter we will take a closer look at three of these nations: Costa Rica, historically prosperous and politically stable; and Nicaragua and El Salvador, scenes of continuing unrest that has focused world attention on Central America.

COSTA RICA

Costa Rica is unique in Central America. It is one of Latin America's most stable countries and has a long democratic tradition. Unlike its neighbors, it has a prosperous economy, a large middle class, a high literacy rate, and no army.

The Land.   Costa Rica is a small, mountainous country, about the size of West Virginia. It is bordered by Nicaragua on the north, the Caribbean Sea and Panama on the east, and the Pacific Ocean on the south and west. A chain of volcanic mountains, called **cordilleras** (kordl-YER-uhs), stretches across the center of the country from northwest to southeast. Some of the volcanoes are still active.

The mountains divide Costa Rica into three land regions. On the east and west are heavily forested coastal lowlands with hot, humid climates. Within the mountains is the central plateau, known as the **meseta** (may-SAY-tah). With its springlike climate, the meseta is the heart of the country. Most of the people live here, and the nation's capital, San José, is located in the meseta. The meseta's rich volcanic soil makes it an important agricultural area.

The People.   Costa Rica has a population of about 2.7 million people. It is the only Central American nation whose population is mostly of European descent. Mestizos make up only about 20 percent of the total. Costa Rica also has two small minority groups: about 30,000 Africans and about 20,000 Indians. The Africans are descendants of people from the island of Jamaica who came to work on Costa Rica's banana plantations in the late 1800s. They live along the Pacific coast. Many still speak English as their first language. Nearly all other Costa Ricans speak Spanish, and the overwhelming majority is Roman Catholic. Costa Ricans call themselves *Ticos*.

Unlike other Latin American nations, Costa Rica developed as a country of small owner-operated farms. When the Spanish first arrived in Costa Rica, they were welcomed by the Indians. However, when the Spanish tried to enslave them, the Indians resisted fiercely or fled into the rain forest. Those who did remain died of disease introduced by the Europeans or from the harsh conditions of slavery. Before long, there were almost no Indians remaining in Costa Rica.

Without forced labor, the Costa Ricans had to do their own work. Unlike the colonists in other Latin American countries, they could not build up huge estates based on slave labor. Instead, they developed small family farms. A spirit of equality arose. This was something like the spirit among pioneers of the North American West.

Today, Costa Rica does not have the rigid two-class system in which a few wealthy people own most of the land and control the government. Distribution of wealth is more equal than in any other Central American nation. There is a wealthy upper class. But there is also a large middle class. People in the lower class earn decent wages as plantation workers. The large urban slums common in many Latin American nations are rare in Costa Rica.

A Costa Rican farmhouse. What are Costa Rica's most important crops?

The Economy.   Coffee cultivation was introduced to Costa Rica in the early part of the nineteenth century. The country's soil and weather made it possible to produce coffee beans that are still regarded as among the best in the world.

Today, agriculture remains Costa Rica's principal economic activity, and the country relies heavily on foreign trade of its agricultural products. Coffee is the most important crop, followed by bananas. Other important export crops are sugar and cattle. The country has also begun to develop manufacturing industries. The leading manufactured goods include furniture, leather goods, processed foods, medicines, and textiles.

Costa Rica's economy is one of the most successful in Latin America, and compared to other Latin Americans, Ticos enjoy a high standard of living. They are well dressed and well fed. Excellent roads and prosperous coffee farms fill the rolling countryside.

However, like many other nations, Costa Rica depends on imported oil. The worldwide energy shortage of the 1970s caused serious economic problems. Per capita income dropped sharply, from $1,650 in 1980 to $1,020 in 1984. Inflation rose, and unemployment reached over 16 percent. The most serious problem was the foreign debt, which skyrocketed from $270 million in 1970 to $3.6 *billion* in 1985. Of every four dollars Costa Rica earns in exports, it must pay out three dollars in interest to foreign banks. By 1986, however, the economy began to improve. U. S. aid had greatly increased. Moreover, the prices the rest of the world paid for coffee went up, and the cost of imported oil went down. Per capita income rose to $1,760 in 1988, and unemployment was reduced to 5.6 percent.

History and Political Development.   As you have read, Costa Rica became an independent republic after the United Provinces of Central America collapsed in 1838. The years following independence were relatively peaceful and prosperous. Coffee and bananas were introduced as cash crops. Free compulsory education was established. A pattern of orderly, democratic government was begun.

This pattern has been disrupted twice. In 1917, Federico Tinoco (tee-NOH-koh) overthrew the elected president. He ruled as a dictator until 1919. Then, with help from the United States, he was deposed. In 1948, there was a second breakdown of the political system. President Teodoro Picado (pee-KAH-doh) attempted to change election results to keep himself in power. A six-week civil war followed. Picado was forced into exile, his opponent became the president, and a new constitution was adopted. The army was abolished.

San José, Costa Rica. The government spends most of its budget on health care, education, roads, and social security and welfare payments. The average income per person is almost three times as much as in El Salvador or Nicaragua.

In 1960, Costa Rica joined the **Central American Common Market**. This organization works toward promoting economic cooperation in Central America. Unfortunately, progress has been severely hindered by regional conflicts. Costa Rica has tried to remain **neutral,** or not take sides, in these struggles. However, it has allowed forces opposed to the Nicaraguan government to establish bases on Costa Rican soil. Many Costa Ricans fear that guerrilla activity may spread from nearby nations into their own country.

NICARAGUA

Although Nicaragua and Costa Rica share a common border, the contrast between these two Central American nations is enormous. Costa Rica has a long history of political stability and democracy. Nicaragua has a history of oppression and dictatorship and has been torn by civil war.

172

Costa Rica is prosperous, and the people live comfortably. Nicaragua is poor, and while a few people live extremely well, the majority lives in poverty. In the late 1980s, Nicaragua was a major trouble spot of the Western Hemisphere.

The Land.   With a land area of 50,000 square miles, Nicaragua is the largest nation in Central America. Shaped like a triangle, the country is divided into three main land regions. The Central Highlands have peaks as high as 8,000 feet. Along the Caribbean, a wide lowland belt is home to thousands of Indians. In the south along the Caribbean is the steamy Mosquito Coast, named for the Miskito Indians who inhabited the area. Most of Nicaragua's population lives in a low-lying area along the Pacific coast. Several volcanoes, some of them active, are located here. Central America's two largest inland bodies of water— Lake Managua and Lake Nicaragua—are located in Nicaragua.

The People.   Nicaragua has 3.3 million people. The great majority are mestizos. They live along the Pacific Ocean. Several thousand Indians live on the Caribbean coast. Most Nicaraguans speak Spanish. Roman Catholicism is the predominant religion. However, there is a group of English-speaking Protestants of African descent on the eastern coast. Their ancestors are mostly from Jamaica.

The Economy.   Agriculture is the basis of Nicaragua's economy. Exported farm products provide most of the country's income. In most years, cotton is the most valuable crop. It is raised in the low Pacific areas. Coffee is the other major crop. Sugar cane, bananas, and rice are also exported. Corn and beans are the main crops grown as food for the Nicaraguans themselves. Cattle raising in the Central Highlands yields beef for export. Food processing, textiles, and chemicals are important industries. Nicaragua has valuable tropical hardwood forests.

Early History.   After becoming an independent republic in 1838, Nicaragua was torn by internal political struggles. In one six-year period, the new nation had fifteen presidents! Among these was an American named William Walker. In 1855, the liberals had asked Walker to assist their cause. Instead, Walker arrived with a band of followers and seized control of the government. The following year, the liberals and conservatives combined forces and drove Walker from the country.

The United States had an early interest in Nicaragua. For many years it seemed the best place to build a canal to link the Atlantic and

Pacific oceans. However, because the nation's government was very unstable, the United States decided to build the canal in Panama instead. The United States remained interested in Nicaragua, however. This was partly because its location made it important for the defense of the Panama Canal. In 1912, U.S. Marines were sent to Nicaragua at the request of the Nicaraguan government to protect United States interests there.

During the 1920s, a Nicaraguan rebel leader emerged who became popular with Latin Americans everywhere. His name was Augusto César Sandino (sahn-DEE-noh). Sandino strongly opposed U.S. interference in Nicaragua. From a hideout in the mountains, he led guerrilla raids against the corrupt Nicaraguan government. He also attacked the U. S. Marines stationed in Nicaragua.

In 1929, the Nicaraguan government established a new national police force, called the Guardia. The Guardia was trained and led by American officers. In 1933, the U.S. Marines were withdrawn from Nicaragua. The Guardia replaced them as the nation's security force. At the same time, the Nicaraguan government declared an amnesty for Sandino and his forces. (As you recall, an amnesty is a pardon.) In return, Sandino pledged to lay down his arms. A year later, in 1934, Sandino was seized by the commander of the Guardia and murdered. The name of the Guardia commander was Anastasio Somoza (soh-MOH-sah).

Nicaragua under the Somozas. Anastasio Somoza forced the Nicaraguan president to resign in 1936. The next year, after an election in which he was the only candidate, Somoza became president. For the next 43 years, Nicaragua was ruled by a Somoza. When Anastasio Somoza was assassinated in 1956 his elder son, Luis Somoza, became president. When Luis died in 1967, another brother, Anastasio Somoza Debayle (thay-BEYE-lay), took over the government.

The Somozas ruled as dictators, maintaining enormous political and economic power. Under their rule, less than 5 percent of the population controlled 75 percent of the nation's wealth. The Somoza family used the nation's economy for its own gain. Sometimes it was almost impossible to distinguish the property of the Somozas from the property of Nicaragua. In general, the Somozas had close ties with the United States. The U.S. government considered them an important anti-Communist force in Central America.

Shortly after Anastasio Somoza Debayle took office in 1967, he encountered opposition from a group of guerrillas hiding in the mountains. The guerrillas called themselves **Sandinistas** (sahn-dih-NEES-tahs), in honor of the murdered rebel Augusto Sandino. Somoza believed the guerrillas were nothing more than a minor band of Communist outlaws, and he sent his troops to get rid of them.

The Sandinistas Gain Power.   However, the Sandinistas gathered tremendous popular support among the people of Nicaragua. Many business people, professional groups, and church leaders began to oppose Somoza. In the late 1970s, widespread protests broke out against Somoza. Somoza realized his power was coming to an end, and in 1979 he fled to Miami. The Sandinistas took over the government.

The majority of Nicaraguans favored the overthrow of the Somoza regime. However, the Sandinista victory was achieved at a high price. More than 30,000 people lost their lives in the years of fighting. Also, the nation's economy was almost destroyed.

Sandinista soldiers. The armed forces of Nicaragua are about 12 times as large as they were under the Somoza dictatorship. To pay for this huge defense buildup, many social and economic programs have been reduced or ended.

At first, the United States made an effort to establish good relations with the Sandinista government. However, after 1981, when Ronald Reagan became president of the United States, relations between the two countries became increasingly strained. The United States accused the Nicaraguans of helping the Communist guerrillas in nearby El Salvador. It also attacked Nicaragua for its close relations with Communist countries, particularly the Soviet Union and Cuba.

In late 1981, the United States approved a secret plan to support military actions against the Sandinista government. The U.S.-backed opposition groups were known as the **contras,** a shortened term for antirevolutionaries in Spanish. They were composed of former Somoza supporters and one-time Sandinista leaders who no longer supported the government. Their forces numbered about 10,000 men.

The contras began to wage a guerrilla war against the Sandinista government in 1982. From 1982 to 1984, these rebels received over $80 million in aid from the United States. In 1984, Nicaragua accused the United States of secretly helping the contras mine its ports. The International Court of Justice ruled that the United States should stop any blockading or mining of Nicaraguan ports. Meanwhile, the Soviet Union had provided the Sandinista government with tanks and helicopter gunships. The Soviet Union and Communist Eastern European countries also sent Nicaragua about 475 military advisers. Cubans, North Koreans, and East Germans serve as advisors for the Sandinista police force.

Nicaraguan officials estimated that about 7,000 people had been killed as a result of clashes with the contras. Among the targets of the contras were the coffee farmers in the mountains. The contras terrorized and sometimes kidnapped farmers suspected of being Sandinista supporters. As a result, the coffee crop was cut by about 25 percent in 1984.

Faced with increasing guerrilla activity and fearing an invasion by the United States, the Sandinista government built up a large army. For the first time in Nicaraguan history, all males were required to register for military service. Fifteen-year-old boys could be drafted. The Nicaraguan army became the largest in Central America, numbering over 60,000. Approximately 50 percent of Nicaragua's budget was used to fight the contras.

By 1990, Nicaragua faced an economic disaster. In 1985 the United States had imposed an economic **embargo** on Nicaragua; that is, it prohibited all trade between the United States and Nicaragua. The loss of money from exports, combined with the cost of the war, brought the country near to collapse. To end the war and resume exports, the Sandinistas recognized that they needed to allow a free election.

The election, which took place early in 1990, was closely supervised by outside observers, including teams from the United Nations and the Organization of American States. All agreed that it was a free and fair contest, unquestionably the fairest election in Nicaragua's history. The winner of the election was an anti-Sandinista coalition called the UNO, made up of 13 parties united by little else than their opposition to the Sandinistas. Soon after the election, the UNO's candidate, Violeta Chamorro (chah-MOHR-oh), was inaugurated as president.

Nicaragua Today. As a result of the election of 1990, the condition of Nicaragua began to improve. Soon after she became president, Chamorro worked out a peace agreement with the contras. Within two months the contras, under United Nations supervision, had voluntarily turned in their weapons and disbanded. Within another two months, the size of the Nicaraguan army was reduced by almost a third, to 41,000. An agreement was reached with the Sandinistas, still the largest party although now out of office, concerning the leadership of the army. Trade resumed with the United States, as did U.S. aid.

The new government took steps to return Nicaragua to a market economy. It would take time, however, for these reforms to begin to improve the lives of the people. Sandinista-led strikes threatened to disrupt the reforms, and tensions developed among the different groups that made up the UNO coalition. Meanwhile Nicaragua remained the poorest country in Latin America.

EL SALVADOR

El Salvador is the smallest and most densely populated of the Central American republics. In recent years, it has experienced civil war.

The Land. With a territory of only 8,164 square miles, El Salvador is about the size of the state of Massachusetts. It is sandwiched between Guatemala on the northwest and Honduras on the northeast. It occupies a narrow strip of land along the Pacific Ocean. The capital and largest city is San Salvador.

El Salvador is a land of rugged mountains, cone-shaped volcanoes, green valleys, and scenic lakes. Ash from the many once-active volcanoes gives El Salvador a very fertile soil. Dense forests once covered much of the land, but most of the trees were cut down for fuel. As a result, soil erosion is a serious problem.

The People.   About 95 percent of the population are mestizos. Although there was once a large Indian population, very few Indians remain today. Many of the nation's Indians were killed by the army in the 1930s as part of an effort to wipe out Communist influence in the country. There are also practically no Africans in El Salvador. Although Africans were imported as slaves during the colonial era, most of them intermarried with the Europeans or Indians.

In the early 1990s, 5.3 million people lived in tiny El Salvador. The population density of 641 persons per square mile was one of the highest in Latin America. (However, that is still much less than the 1,000 persons per square mile in the state of New Jersey.) It was estimated that the population of El Salvador would double within 30 years.

Because of its small size, population growth is one of El Salvador's most serious problems. It is difficult for this tiny nation to support its rapidly expanding population. More than 80 percent of the people live in poverty. Many families do not earn enough to eat a minimum basic diet. In rural areas, 73 percent of the children suffer from malnutrition. For every 1,000 infants born, 60 die before they reach their first birthday.

Conditions are worst in rural areas, where more than half of the population lives. Almost one-half of the peasants have no land. Children often do not attend school, and almost one-half of the rural population cannot read or write. Over one-third of the rural families live in one-room dwellings.

Wealth is very unevenly distributed in El Salvador. Although a small urban middle class began to develop in the 1950s, most of the population is very poor. A few upper-class families control most of the land and wealth. Per capita income is one of the lowest in Latin America. Anger about these economic conditions has been one of the major causes of the unrest and violence in El Salvador in recent years.

Cities.   The capital and largest city is San Salvador. It is located in a high valley in an area of volcanoes. San Salvador is small, with muddy roads and tin-roofed houses. It is not unusual to see people cooking in the street. Except for the four main avenues, the streets have no formal names. However, the residents are familiar with the city and can usually find their destination without the use of street addresses.

The Economy.   Agriculture is the basis of El Salvador's economy. Coffee is the most important crop, accounting for over 80 percent of the nation's exports. It is raised on large plantations on the slopes of the volcanoes and in the highlands. Cotton, rice, and sugar cane are also

178

Life in a coffee plantation village in El Salvador. The workers' families are preparing supper. The smoke is from wood cooking fires.

important. Efforts have been made in recent years to expand the country's manufacturing industries. Textiles are the major manufactured export. The nation's small-farm owners cultivate tiny plots for their families. The principal crops are beans, corn, and rice.

Early History. In the years following independence, several developments occurred in El Salvador that set the pattern for its history over the next century and a half.

The Indians of El Salvador, like many American Indian groups, believed in **communal ownership** of land. Under this system, land cannot be held as personal property. Instead, it belongs to the entire community. Before the arrival of Europeans, the land belonged to everyone.

In 1840, coffee cultivation was introduced into El Salvador. This crop was ideally suited to El Salvador's rich volcanic soil and mountain climate. It soon became the basis of the nation's economy. The government wished to expand the coffee-growing lands. Therefore, it did away with communal ownership of land. Many peasants were thrown off their property. Within a few years, the country's most fertile land had become concentrated in the hands of a few wealthy families. This privileged group was often referred to as the "Fourteen Families." They owned most of the land, controlled the economy, and governed the country.

Military Rule.   During the Great Depression of the 1930s, the world price of coffee nosedived. Economic conditions in El Salvador became very bad. The peasants began to call for strikes and demonstrations. Taking advantage of the discontent, in 1931, General Maximiliano Hernandez Martínez (mahr-TEE-nez) seized the government. He established a military dictatorship that lasted until 1944.

One of the most violent events in El Salvador's history occurred during Martínez's rule. In 1932, Salvadoran Marxists decided to stage a revolution. They were led by Augustin Farabundo Martí, the mestizo son of a wealthy landowner. The revolutionaries called on the Indians and mestizos to take the land from the wealthy landowners. They told soldiers to kill their officers rather than attack the peasants who would be seizing the land.

General Martínez quickly sent the army to put down the rebellion. The results were tragic. Over 30,000 peasants were killed. Martí was captured and shot. Few of the peasants, however, had taken any direct action against the government or the wealthy. Most were guilty of nothing further than wanting reform.

Martínez was ousted in 1944. However, military rule, often repressive, continued. Considerable economic progress was made during the 1950s. In the 1960s the military regime began to allow some opposition groups to function. Labor unions were legalized, and women were granted the right to vote.

For many years, there had been friction over various issues between El Salvador and neighboring Honduras. In July 1969, a tense soccer game between the two nations turned into a full-scale war. Although the "soccer war" lasted only four days, El Salvador spent one-fifth of its annual budget to fight it. Further, it lost a profitable trade with Honduras, and diplomatic relations between the nations were suspended for ten years.

Civil War.   During the 1970s, tensions were rising throughout Central America. In El Salvador, people protested the long years of corrupt

180

military governments, electoral cheating, and economic unfairness. Several attempts at political and economic reform were made. In 1979, the government undertook an ambitious U.S.-backed program to distribute land to the peasants. The Salvadoran army took over 472 privately owned plantations. They turned them into cooperatives. On the cooperatives, the farmers shared the ownership of the lands, crops, and cattle.

The attempt at reform divided the population. Landowners and many members of the military opposed reform. The poor formed mass organizations to support reform. The Catholic Church was divided in its response. Terrorist groups were formed, and the nation was soon involved in a civil war.

El Salvador Today.   Since 1980, El Salvador has been one of the most troubled countries of Latin America. Murders, disappearances, torture, and gunfights have been everyday occurrences. Right-wing death squads have killed those who favored social change. Left-wing guerrillas have waged war on government forces from hideouts in the mountains. From 1980 to 1989, more than 70,000 people were killed, and more than 500,000 people, over 10 percent of the population, became homeless.

Despite the fighting, neither side was able to gain a military advantage. A political moderate, José Napoleón Duarte (doo-AHR-tay), was elected president in 1984 and served until 1989. Duarte tried to negotiate an end to the civil war, but both sides stubbornly refused to accept a settlement. Meanwhile, the extreme right wing continued its terror campaign, which resulted in the assassination of the Catholic archbishop and many clergy, trade unionists, and political activists. In 1989, another moderate, Alfredo Cristiani, succeeded Duarte. Cristiani was no more successful than Duarte in ending the civil war.

In November 1989, six Jesuit priests were murdered. The following January, Cristiani announced that a number of army officers and enlisted men had been arrested in the slayings. However, for months no trial of the accused was begun. The reason commonly accepted was that going ahead with the prosecution would risk a military coup.

The civil war had a devastating effect on El Salvador's economy. More than 40 percent of the work force was unemployed or underemployed. Land reform programs ran into serious trouble as farmers were unable to repay loans they had taken to buy land. Left-wing groups sabotaged coffee crops and disrupted public transport and power transmission. El Salvador became greatly dependent on economic aid from the United States, which provided $4 billion in assistance between 1980 and 1990.

Preparing coffee to be brought from San Salvador to a Pacific port city. San Salvador is El Salvador's leading financial, trading, and industrial center.

In 1989, Cristiani launched a program of returning such state-owned enterprises as sugar refineries, textile mills, and banks, nationalized since 1980, to private ownership. As with much else in El Salvador, the success of this effort depended on ending the civil war.

Central America Today. Central America faces the task of feeding, housing, and employing its rapidly expanding population, at a time when the world economy has ceased to grow. Central American nations borrowed billions of dollars to finance their development and have had trouble repaying their loans as their export markets shrank. Political instability has diminished somewhat in the 1990s, although the sharp differences in wealth between business owners and landowners on the one hand and workers and peasants on the other remained an ever-present source of tension.

182

REVIEWING THE CHAPTER

I. Building Your Vocabulary

In your notebook, write the numbers from 1 to 5. After each number, write the word that matches the definition.

cordillera	neutral	collective
Sandinistas	contras	meseta

1. a farm on which many farmers share ownership of land and equipment

2. opposition fighters who tried to overthrow Nicaragua's government in the 1980s

3. chain of mountains

4. guerrilla group that fought against the Somoza dictatorship

5. area of high, level land

II. Understanding the Facts

In your notebook, write the numbers from 1 to 5. After each number write the letter of the correct ending of the sentence.

1. All of the following belonged to the United Provinces of Central America except
   a. Costa Rica and Honduras.   **b.** Panama and Belize.
   c. Guatemala and Nicaragua.

2. In 1954, the United States helped to overthrow the government of
   a. Nicaragua.   **b.** Costa Rica.   **c.** Guatemala.

3. Costa Rica is different from Nicaragua and El Salvador in that
   a. none of its people are mestizos.   **b.** it has never been under military rule.   **c.** it has no army.

4. The name "Sandinista" is taken from
   a. a rebel leader who was murdered by a security officer.
   b. a patriotic poet.   **c.** a popular dictator.

5. Two major problems facing El Salvador are
   a. rapid population growth and uneven distribution of wealth.
   b. poor soil and a lack of good harbors.   **c.** weak governments and the lack of a ruling class.

III. Thinking It Through

In your notebook, write the numbers from 1 to 4. After each number, write the number of the correct answer to the question.

1. U.S. domination over Central America in the first part of the twentieth century resulted from
   a. military conquest during the Spanish-American War.
   b. the intervention of U.S. troops led by William Walker.
   c. a combination of economic investment and military intervention.
   d. the desire of Central Americans to copy the U.S. political system.

2. Except in Belize, Central America contains few people of African ancestry because
   a. slavery was never practiced in the region.
   b. most Africans brought to the region died under the harsh conditions.
   c. much of the region is mountainous and so slave labor could not be employed profitably.
   d. Africans held under slavery in the region escaped and fled.

3. Peace returned to Nicaragua after 1990 because
   a. opponents of the government won an election and took control.
   b. the United States switched sides and quit backing the contras.
   c. the contras won a clear military victory over the old government.
   d. the United Nations sent a peacekeeping force to maintain order.

4. Which of the following statements best describes El Salvador's experience since the 1970s?
   a. Only when a strong government came to power was it possible to carry out land reform and remove social tensions.
   b. A series of military governments caused so much terror that the people rose up and overthrew the old order.
   c. Efforts to carry out social reforms divided the people and led to years of civil war.
   d. Despite civil war, El Salvador's businesses prospered and the standard of living rose.

DEVELOPING CRITICAL THINKING SKILLS

1. Show how the Indians' belief in communal ownership of land caused problems in their relations with the Europeans.

2. Explain the difficulties that Central Americans have encountered in their attempts to establish political and economic unity for the region.

3. Compare and contrast the political systems of Costa Rica, Nicaragua, and El Salvador.

4. Describe the relations between the military forces and the upper classes in Central American countries.

ANALYZING SOURCES

As you have read, beginning in the late 1800s several U.S. corporations gained great power in Central America. One of those corporations was the United Fruit Company, which owned vast banana and sugar plantations in the region. In the following poem (Source A), the Chilean poet and Nobel Prize winner Pablo Neruda expresses his feelings about the United Fruit Company. Read the poem, and then read Source B. Source B presents a very different point of view. After reading both selections, answer the questions that follow them.

Source A

When the trumpets had sounded and all
was in readiness on the face of the earth,
Jehovah divided his universe. . .
the most succulent [juicy] item of all,
The United Fruit Company Incorporated
reserved for itself; the heartland
and coasts of my country,
the delectable [delicious] waist of America

They rechristened their properties
the "Banana Republics" . . .
they . . . unleashed all the covetous [greedy], and
contrived the tyrannical Reign of the Flies—
Trujillo* the fly, and Tacho* the fly

the flies called Carias,* Martinez*,
Ubico*—all of them flies. . .
. . . flies buzzing drunkenly
on the populous middens [garbage dumps]. . .
Then in the bloody domain [kingdom] of the flies
The United Fruit Company Incorporated
unloaded with a booty of coffee and fruits
brimming its cargo boats, gliding
like trays with the spoils
of our drowning dominions.

And all the while, somewhere, in the sugary
hells of our seaports,
smothered by gases, an Indian
fell in the morning:
a body spun off, an anonymous
chattel [slave], some numeral tumbling,
a branch with its death running out of it
in the vat of the carrion [dead flesh], fruit laden and foul

---

*Names of Central American dictators.
   Excerpts from Pablo Neruda, "The United Fruit Co." From Selected Poems of Pablo
Neruda, edited and translated by Ben Belitt, Grove Press, New York, 1961.

Source B

People's attitudes about social responsibility changed, and the United
Fruit Company began to treat its Central American workers more fairly.
It provided schooling and medical treatment. It worked with newly
formed labor unions to establish wages. Today, in Honduras, the United
Fruit Company pays higher wages than do nonunionized local producers. Indeed, workers for the company are entitled to vacations with double pay. In addition, the company now gives a large portion of its profits
to the governments of of the countries in which it operates.

Information compiled from news reports, including The Wall Street Journal, September
   17, 1985.

1. What was Neruda's attitude toward the United Fruit Company?

2. According to Neruda, what parts of Latin America did the United
   Fruit Company take for itself?

3. To what do you think Neruda was referring when he used the phrase
   "the delectable waist of America"?

4. How did Neruda describe the relationship between the United Fruit Company and the dictators of Central America?

5. (a) How did the poet use vivid description to make his point? (b) Do you think all Latin Americans would like this poem, or agree with its point of view? Why, or why not?

FINDING SUPPORTING FACTS

List the facts in the chapter that support the following statement: The distribution of wealth is more equal in Costa Rica than elsewhere in Central America.

MAKING A CHART

Use the information in this chapter to make a chart for Costa Rica, Nicaragua, and El Salvador. The chart should include the name of each country, its capital, principal population groups, languages spoken, and major products.

ENRICHMENT AND EXPLORATION

1. Imagine you are a government soldier or a guerrilla in the recent civil wars of either Nicaragua or El Salvador. Write a diary entry telling of your fears and hopes and describing a day's activities. Write a minimum of one page.

2. A number of volunteer organizations and religious groups have organized work camps in Central America, where U.S. teenagers and adults can help Central Americans to rebuild after recent devastation. Contact such organizations in your area and find out what opportunities are available. If possible, interview a young volunteer who has participated in such a program. Make a written or oral report on your findings.

3. Imagine you are a young person from Central America visiting the community in which your school is located. Write a letter back home, describing your experiences. Make comparisons to life in Central America.

4. Use an encyclopedia to research the Central American nations not covered in detail in Chapter 7: Belize, Guatemala, Honduras, and Panama. Use the information you find to add those countries to the chart you began in "Making a Chart," above.

SOUTH AMERICA AND THE WORLD

1500–Today

1500s–1600s	Brazil colonized by Portuguese.
1549	Bahia (Salvador) is first capital of Brazil.
1580	Spanish establish colony at Buenos Aires.
1776	Spain establishes Viceroyalty of La Plata.
	U.S. Declaration of Independence
1810	New Grenada declares independence.
1816	José de San Martín leads rebellion in Argentina, defeating Spanish.
1819	Simón Bolívar defeats Spanish near Bogotá.
1822	Brazil wins independence from Portugal.
1828	War between Brazil and Uruguay
1830	Venezuela and Ecuador break away from Grán Colombia.
1841–1889	Pedro II is emperor of Brazil.
1861–1865	*U.S. Civil War*
1889	Brazil proclaimed a republic.
1899–1902	War of a Thousand Days
1903	Panama breaks away from Colombia.
1914–1918	*World War I*
1934	Brazil adopts new constitution.
1939–1945	*World War II*
1940s–1950s	La Violencia in Colombia.
1946–1955	Juan Domingo Perón President of Argentina
1952	Eva Perón dies.
1957	National Front formed in Colombia.
1964–1985	Brazil under military rule
1977–1983	Argentina under military rule.
1982	Argentina defeated in Falkland Islands.
1989	U.S. assists Colombia in war on cocaine.

8 *South America*

South America is a vast and diverse continent. It includes every kind of terrain, from hot, steamy jungles to snow-covered mountains. It has rich soils and large mineral deposits. It has varied populations and a rich cultural heritage. However, it is also an area of great political, social, and economic inequality. Poverty, suffering, and discontent exist side by side with wealth, prosperity, and opportunity.

South America is made up of 12 independent nations—Argentina, Bolivia, Brazil, Chile, Colombia, Ecuador, Guyana, Paraguay, Peru, Suriname, Uruguay, and Venezuela—and one overseas department and region of France called French Guiana. In this chapter, we will take a close look at three of these nations: Brazil, Colombia, and Argentina.

BRAZIL

With an area of over 3 million square miles, Brazil is the largest country in South America. It occupies nearly one-half of the continent and borders on every South American country except Chile and Ecuador. On the east, it bulges into the Atlantic Ocean with a coastline that stretches 4,500 miles.

The Land.   Brazil has a varied landscape. The world's largest tropical rain forest stretches across much of the north. This rain forest is watered by the mighty Amazon River and its many tributaries. Desertlike plains extend across the northeast. Rich farmlands and lush grazing areas occupy the plateaus of the center and south. Beautiful beaches line the long Atlantic coast. The climate varies from humid and hot in the Amazon Basin to temperate in the southern and west-central regions.

The beaches around Rio de Janeiro are among the most beautiful and popular in the world.

Most of the people live along the coast. (For details on the land and climate of Brazil, see Chapter 1.)

The People.   Brazil's population, about 154 million people, is the largest in South America. Brazilians are a blend of many nationalities. People of European, mainly Portuguese, descent form the largest group, followed by those of mixed origin. About 6 percent are people of African descent. Brazil is also home to the world's largest Japanese community outside of Japan. The region's original Indian population was almost totally wiped out after the arrival of the Europeans. The few remaining Indians live mostly in the rain forests of the Amazon Basin.

More than 90 percent of Brazilians are Roman Catholic. However, the influence of the church is not as strong as in most other South American nations. Many Brazilians practice Candomblé. This religion combines African spiritual beliefs and Roman Catholicism. Almost everyone in the country speaks Portuguese.

Regional Diversity and Cities.   Because Brazil is so vast, the various regions of the country developed largely in isolation from each other.

As a result, no region is typical of the entire country. Instead, each region has its own distinct ethnic and cultural heritage. Economic conditions and standards of living also vary greatly from region to region. Regional rivalries and competition are traditionally very strong.

As recently as 1965, only about half of Brazil's people lived in urban areas. By the late 1980s, almost 75 percent of the population was urban. Unlike most countries of Latin America, Brazil has many major cities. In 1960, only six of Brazil's cities had a population of over 500,000. Today, there are fourteen. Six cities have a population of over 1 million inhabitants. Each of Brazil's cities has a distinct cultural, ethnic, and economic character that reflects the region in which it is located.

Brasília (brah-ZEEL-yah) is the capital of Brazil. It was built in the interior of the country in the 1950s as part of an effort to promote economic development in that area. It officially replaced Rio de Janeiro as the capital in 1960. Brasília is Brazil's fastest-growing city.

Rio de Janeiro (REE-oh duh zhuh-NAYR-oh), often called Rio, was the capital of Brazil from 1763 to 1960. It is located on Guanabara Bay, one of the world's most beautiful natural harbors, and is a center of international tourism. It is also the cultural center of Brazil. Rio is probably most celebrated for Carnival, held every February. During this four-day fiesta, people in fabulous costumes dance in the streets to celebrate the approach of Lent. The people of Rio are called *cariocas*.

São Paulo (sow POW-loo) is the largest city in South America. It is also Latin America's major industrial center. São Paulo produces almost half of Brazil's industrial income. However, the city, which has over 18 million inhabitants, is plagued by pollution and traffic jams. The people of São Paulo are known as *Paulistas*.

The northeast is Brazil's poorest and most backward region. Per capita income is 40 percent lower than in the more prosperous south. Illiteracy rates are 40 percentage points higher. Infant mortality rates are twice as high. Two large cities are located in the northeast. *Salvador*, founded in 1549 as Bahia (bah-EE-ah), was Brazil's first capital. Today, it is the only Brazilian city with a predominantly African population. It is built on two levels. Elevators carry people from one level to another. The other northeastern city, *Recife* (ruh-SEE-fuh), is the area's principal port. Recife is the scene of many colorful and bustling street markets.

One of the most out-of-the-way cities in Brazil is *Manaus* (mah-NOWS). It is located so deep in the Amazon region that it takes five days to reach it by boat from the Atlantic coast. Founded in 1850, this jungle outpost was a thriving center for Brazil's rubber industry in the late 1800s and early 1900s centuries. A $2 million Opera House remains as a monument to the rubber boom that built this city. Today, the rubber industry is dead, and Manaus survives mainly as a tourist center for the Amazon region.

One of the most pressing needs of Brazil's cities is adequate housing. Brazil's population is growing rapidly; experts estimate that it will double over the next 30 years. As the population grows, increasing numbers of people leave the poor rural areas. They crowd into the cities in search of jobs and better opportunities for themselves and their children. These people become residents of the **favelas,** shantytowns erected on empty lots or the sides of hills. The shacks that make up the favelas are built of boards, stone, corrugated tin, and even cardboard. The favela population in Rio de Janeiro numbers about 1.8 million. In recent years, the Brazilian government has begun to construct low-cost apartment houses in the urban centers in order to provide better homes for the poor.

With such contrasts, it is clear that there is not one typical description of daily life in Brazil. Not only are there contrasts between different regions of Brazil. There are also great contrasts between city life and rural life. Most city dwellings have electricity, but only one out of five rural homes has electricity. Most city people have safe drinking water. Less than half the rural areas do. About four out of ten Brazilian households have adequate sewage facilities. What kind of appliances do people use in daily life? For the country as a whole, about one out of three households has a car. One out of six households has a telephone, but three out of four have TVs. There is thus a big contrast between the haves and have-nots in Brazil.

Education.   Brazil is a young country. Some 48 percent of the population is under 20 years old. In recent years, the government has made tremendous progress in combating illiteracy. The literacy rate jumped from 50 percent in 1950 to 76 percent in 1989. However, despite these efforts, many children of school age do not attend school, especially in rural areas.

The Economy.   Historically, Brazil had a one-crop agricultural economy based on the growth and export of coffee. Today, thanks to rich natural resources and rapid industrial growth, Brazil has the richest and most varied economy in Latin America. Its **gross national product** (GNP), the total value of goods and services produced in a country yearly, is the highest in Latin America and the ninth highest in the world.

192

Favelados *are the residents of the* favelas, *the shantytowns of Brazil's cities. Based on this picture and this chapter, what do you think are some of the problems faced by the people of the* favelas?

However, Brazil faces serious economic problems. Although the economy is strong, wealth is concentrated in the hands of a few. Most Brazilians are very poor. Brazil has the largest foreign debt of any Latin American country. Its rate of **inflation** was over 100 percent in the early 1980s. Inflation is an economic condition in which there is a rise in prices and a decrease in the value of money. These problems pose a serious threat to the continued growth of the nation's economy.

Manufacturing has grown rapidly in Brazil since 1945. Brazil now ranks among the world's leading industrial nations. Manufactured goods account for about 60 percent of all the nation's exports. Brazil is the tenth largest automobile producer in the world. Since the 1970s it has also been an important manufacturer of military equipment. Other important manufactured products include paper, textiles, shoes, plastics, and telephones and communications equipment.

Agriculture is also important in Brazil. The introduction of modern agricultural methods in recent years has helped increase production. Brazil now grows enough food for itself with enough left over for export. Only the United States exports more food products.

193

Coffee, once the basis of the nation's economy, is still a major export. Brazil produces over one-fourth of the world's coffee crop. However, in recent years Brazil has begun to **diversify,** or vary, its agricultural production. Perhaps the most spectacular growth occurred in soybean production. Between 1970 and 1975, Brazilian soybeans jumped from 3 percent of the world market to 75 percent. Brazil is also an important exporter of grains such as rice and wheat, tobacco, and oranges. It ranks among the world leaders in raising cattle, hogs, horses, and sheep and in growing sugar-cane, corn, and cacao (kuh-KOW). Cacao is the plant from whose beans are made cocoa powder and chocolate. Corn and manioc are grown primarily for domestic use. Traditionally, Brazil is an important exporter of agricultural products such as coffee, soy, meat, oranges, cotton, sugar, and cacao. However, world market prices for these raw goods tend to vary widely and unpredictably. As a result, in recent years the government has encouraged a shift to processed agricultural products such as yarn and fabric.

The expansion of Brazilian agriculture has created some unexpected problems. In the desire to find new land to cultivate, the country's small landowning class has begun to develop the remote Amazon region. Ownership is often unclear, and competition for the land is fierce and sometimes violent. Many helpless peasants have been driven off their land by hired gunmen. Now, without either land or permanent jobs, these peasants are forced to work as seasonal laborers.

Brazil has rich and varied *natural resources.* Its forests are among the richest in the world. Forest products include nuts, tung oil, carnauba wax, and fine quality timber. Brazil is the fifth largest plywood producer in the world.

Brazil has vast mineral wealth. By the mid-1980s, only the Soviet Union and China produced more iron ore. Much of this iron ore is used to manufacture steel, and Brazil is one of the world's leading steel traders. Brazil has the largest reserves of manganese in the Western Hemisphere. It also has substantial deposits of gold, quartz, tungsten, bauxite, nickel, mica, lead, zinc, silver, coal, chrome ore, tin, and uranium. A wide variety of precious and semiprecious stones is found in Brazil. In the 1980s, the government began an extensive program to develop the untapped mineral wealth of the Amazon region. Vast oil reserves have been discovered off the southeast coast. In all of Latin America, only Mexico and Venezuela now produce more oil.

Hydroelectricity, or water power, provides most of Brazil's electricity. The Itaipú Dam, on the Paraná River, is the world's largest hydroelectric project. It was built in cooperation with Paraguay. Brazil has also invested in nuclear power, producing its first reactor in 1982.

Brazil in the 1970s depended on foreign oil for 70 percent of the oil it needed to provide power for its industries. It imported oil from the nations of the Middle East. When world oil prices rose sharply in the 1970s, Brazil's economy was badly hurt. Today Brazil is seeking to develop substitutes for imported oil. It now imports only about 40 percent of its oil needs. Under one program, sugar cane is used to make alcohol. The alcohol is then mixed with gasoline to form **gasohol,** which can be used as automobile fuel in place of pure gasoline. Almost all of the country's new cars now run on gasohol.

Brazil's Economic Problems. Like many other Latin American countries, Brazil must cope with the huge gap between its rich and poor people. In recent years, this gap has been widening. About half of the national income goes to only a tenth of the population. The poorest half of the nation receives only about 15 percent of the national income. The result is that almost three quarters of the people live in over-crowded, substandard housing and suffer from malnutrition. In the *favelas,* or slums, of the cities, in which about 30 percent of the people live, homes are no more than shacks made of cardboard, metal, or wood that lack sewers and running water.

Another major problem is the foreign debt. In the 1960s and 1970s, Brazil borrowed billions of dollars from foreign banks to finance the development of mineral resources and the building of hydroelectric plants. When finished, the power plant at Itaipú on the Paraneá River will be one of the world's largest. However, the burden of repaying these loans, added to sharply rising prices of imported oil, resulted in extremely high inflation. To curb inflation,. which in 1988 was over 1700 percent, and help pay its foreign debts, in 1990 the government introduced an austerity program. The government eliminated many of its agencies, froze bank accounts, and cut back subsidies to private industries. This program reduced inflation, but it also resulted in a severe recession that idled a large part of Brazil's industry and made thousands of workers jobless.

Early History. As you read in Chapter 3, Brazil was colonized in the 1500s and 1600s by the Portuguese, who established a system of sugar plantations there. It won its independence from Portugal in 1822 without bloodshed and became an empire ruled by Pedro I. (For details on Brazilian colonization and independence, see Chapter 3.)

Although Pedro I had helped Brazil win independence, he was not very popular. Opposition increased after Brazil lost the territory that is

CASE STUDY:
Dreaming of Riches in Brazil

Jorge Amado was born in 1912 in the Brazilian state of Bahia. His novels reflect his sympathy for the common people. In the following excerpt from *The Violent Land*, a Bahian peasant describes his reasons for leaving the safety of his village to make a dangerous journey to an unknown land.

> Antonio Victor thought back to the Estancia bridge, where the moon is lovely and life is at peace. . . . It was on those moonlit nights, feet dangling in the water of the river, that he had planned his departure for the Ilhéos country.
>
> Men had written back, men who had gone there, saying that money was easy to get. They said, also, that it was easy to get hold of a piece of land and plant it with a tree called cacao, a tree that bore a golden-colored fruit worth more than gold itself. The land was there waiting for those who would come and take it; it belonged to no one as yet. It would be his who should have the courage to plunge into the wilderness, clear the forest, plant cacao, grain, and sweet potatoes, and live for a few years on meal and wild game until the cacao began to bear fruit. Then there would be riches, more money than a man could spend. . . .
>
> From time to time, on the other hand, there would come word of someone who had died from a bullet or a snake-bite, or who had been stabbed in a quarrel. . . . But what was a mere life when so much wealth was to be had?
>
> In Antonio Victor's home town, life had been poverty-stricken and had held no hope for the future. The men, almost all of them, would leave, most of them never to return. But those who did come back came back rich, with rings on their fingers. . . .

Jorge Amado. *The Violent Land* (New York: Alfred A. Knopf, 1965), pp. 10-11.

1. Why does Antonio Victor want to leave his home town?
2. How does Antonio Victor plan to become rich?
3. What does he mean when he says that the "golden-colored cacao fruit [is] worth more than gold itself"?

now the country of Uruguay during a war in 1828. In 1831, Pedro was forced to **abdicate,** or give up the throne. He left his throne to his son, Pedro II, who was five years old at the time.

Pedro II officially became emperor of Brazil in 1840, at the age of fifteen. His reign, which lasted forty-nine years, was one of great progress. He increased Brazil's foreign trade and encouraged immigration. He built railroads and promoted the expansion of industry and agriculture. During Pedro's reign, Brazil became the world's leading producer of coffee.

As you read earlier, slaves were important to the plantation economy of Brazil. In 1888, while Pedro was visiting Europe, the government passed a law abolishing slavery. Naturally, the plantation owners were unhappy about this. Other Brazilians were also discontented. Some people, known as **republicans,** believed Brazil should abolish the empire and become a republic. There was also strong opposition to Pedro in the army. These groups joined together and overthrew the emperor. On November 18, 1889, Brazil was proclaimed a republic.

In the years following the creation of the republic, Brazil prospered. A boom in wild rubber from the Amazon and an expanding market for Brazilian coffee brought the country great wealth. The rubber boom ended in the early 1900s, when rubber plantations were developed in East Asia. However, during World War I, Brazil became an important supplier of manufactured goods for the Allies. The resulting industrial growth kept the economy strong.

Following the war, foreign demand for Brazil's goods dropped sharply. At the same time, the price of coffee fell rapidly. Thousands of workers lost their jobs. Political and economic unrest developed. During the 1920s, the economic slump worsened and unemployment continued to rise. Finally, in 1930, a group of army officers overthrew the republic. Getúlio Vargas (zhuh-TOO-lyo VAHR-guhs), a popular politician and leader of the revolt, became president.

Brazil under Getúlio Vargas.   Vargas ruled Brazil for over 20 years. He was a **caudillo** (kow-THEE-yoh), or "strong man," a type of leader that is a particular feature of Latin American politics. The caudillo, usually a military figure, comes to power by the use of force and rules as a dictator. Caudillo rule is known for bringing order and stability. Although stern and even harsh, the caudillo is usually greatly loved by the people. This affection is very personal, however. The influence of the caudillo does not often last after his death or removal from office.

Brazil began to recover under Vargas. A new constitution was adopted

197

in 1934. It increased wages, shortened work hours, and expanded the power of labor unions. All adult citizens—including women for the first time—were given the right to vote. Vargas also did much to modernize Brazil's economy by encouraging industrialization and the diversification of agriculture.

Many of Vargas's programs involved active government participation in the economy. This aroused strong opposition among some Brazilians. Vargas claimed that the country was in danger. In 1937, he adopted a new constitution that gave him the powers of a dictator. Economic progress continued, but political freedom was lost. Elections were canceled, political parties were forbidden, the press was censored, and the government took over the labor unions.

In 1945, following World War II, a group of army officers forced Vargas to resign. However, Vargas was reelected in 1950. His second administration was plagued by severe economic problems. Among the most serious problems were inflation and political corruption. In 1954, a movement arose to force Vargas from office. Upon learning of the plot, Vargas resigned and then committed suicide.

Recent Governments.   In 1955, Juscelino Kubitschek (zhoo-suh-LEE-noh KOO-buh-chek) was elected president. In an attempt to encourage development of the country's interior, Kubitschek built the new capital city, Brasília, 600 miles from the Atlantic coast. Under Kubitschek, Brazil's economy, particularly its manufacturing industries, experienced rapid growth. However, inflation continued to be a problem.

Brazil's next president, Jânio Quadros (ZHA-nyoo KWAH-droos), was elected in 1960 by the greatest popular majority in Brazilian history. This was to be Brazil's last election for 25 years. Despite his initial popularity, Quadros's economic programs aroused great opposition. He resigned after only seven months in office.

Quadros was succeeded by Vice-President Joao Goulart (zhow goo-LAHR). Brazilian military leaders feared that Goulart's economic policies would lead to a Communist takeover of Brazil. In 1964, military troops, led by General Humberto Castelo Branco, forced Goulart from office.

For two decades, between 1964 and 1985, Brazil's military ran the government. Control was complete; criticism of the government was not permitted. Censorship, arrest, and torture of those who opposed the regime were common.

Brazil Today.   Gradually, the military regime began to prepare for a return to democracy and civilian rule. In 1985, Tancredo Neves (NEV-uhs) was chosen as Brazil's first civilian president since 1964. However, he became gravely ill on the eve of his inauguration and died soon after. The vice-president-elect, José Sarney, was then sworn in as president. Sarney was succeeded by Fernando Collor de Mello (koh-LOHR) in 1990. Collor announced a reform program for Brazil's economy. However, he was hampered by lack of support in parliament, and by late 1991 the future of Collor's government was in question.

COLOMBIA

Colombia, located in the northwest corner of South America, is the only country on the continent with coastlines on both the Atlantic Ocean and the Pacific Ocean. It was named in honor of Christopher Columbus.

The Land. With an area of 440,000 square miles, Colombia is about as large as Texas, New Mexico, and Arkansas combined. It has three main regions: The Central Highlands, the Eastern Plains, and the Coastal Lowlands. The Central Highlands are part of the Andes Mountains. In their cool, high valleys and basins are located most of Colombia's major cities: Bogotá (boh-guh-TAH), the capital; Medellín (may-thuh-YEEN); and Cali (KAHL-ee). Near these population centers are rich mines, fertile farms, and coffee plantations.

The vast eastern plains are sparsely settled. Rain forests of the Amazon basin cover much of the southern part of this region, while the northern llanos support cattle ranching. The Coastal Lowlands bordering the Caribbean Sea contain the country's major port cities, Barranquilla (bahr-uhn-KEE-yuh) and Cartagena (kart-uh-GAY-nuh). Inland are plantations that produce such tropical crops as bananas and sugar cane.

The People. Colombia has more than 33 million people, making it the fourth most populous country in Latin America. Income distribution is uneven. A small number of Colombians, most of them descendants of Spanish settlers, are very rich. Their wealth comes mainly from land that they have inherited. The middle class of business and professional people is growing, but the number of Colombians who live below the poverty line is huge.

Since 1950 there has been a widespread movement of people from the country to the city. They migrate in search of a better life, but their hopes usually are dashed when the only housing most can afford is in crowded slums on the outskirts of cities. These neighborhoods, which

Colombian novelist Gabriel García Márquez, right, being interviewed after winning the Nobel Prize for Literature in 1982.

often lack water, electricity, and sewers, become breeding grounds of crime and social discontent.

Great disparities between rich and poor exist in education. Many rural schools have only two or three grades, while in the cities there are more than 40 universities. In spite of these differences, about 85 percent of all Colombians can read and write. Almost all speak Spanish, in a variety of the language that they consider to be purer than that spoken in other Latin American countries. Colombia has a long tradition of literary excellence. One Colombian writer, Gabriel José García Márquez (see page 95), won the Nobel Prize for Literature in 1982.

Ethnically, Colombians reflect Indian, Spanish, and African heritages. During colonial times, slaves were brought to work the plantations along the coast. In time, some of the Spanish intermarried with Indians and Africans, producing today's mestizos (58 percent of the population) and mulattoes (14 percent). People of combined Indian and African descent are 3 percent of the population, and those of fully African descent are 4 percent. Only one percent of Colombians are fully Indian, while 20 percent are of fully European descent.

The Economy.   Although Colombia is rich in resources, it has not become a fully developed industrial economy. Agriculture is the most important sector of the economy, employing one-fourth of all workers. Most of them are laborers on large estates or are tenant farmers who produce barely enough to feed their families. Agricultural products account for one-half of all exports, of which the most valuable is coffee. Colombia is the world's second largest producer of coffee, after Brazil.

Colombia's most important exports after coffee are petroleum and coal. Oil fields near the Venezuelan border have long produced enough petroleum for Colombia itself. After the discovery of new fields in the northeast in the 1980s, a 500-mile pipeline was rapidly built, and Colombia became a net exporter of oil almost overnight. In another stroke of luck, coal was recently discovered on a peninsula that juts into the Caribbean. Its high quality plus its nearness to ports have helped to make it a major export commodity.

In addition to energy resources, Colombia has rich deposits of gold, platinum, nickel, and iron. It is the source of 90 percent of the world's emeralds.

The majority of Colombians live and work in cities. About two-thirds of city dwellers work in shops and offices. Another third works in factories, most of which are small, family-run operations that produce a limited range of such items as textiles, processed foods, and paper.

Early History. Before Columbus opened the New World to European settlers, various Indian groups inhabited the area now known as Colombia. The most advanced of these, the Chibcha (see page 36), lived in the Andean Highlands. In 1549 the Spanish invaded this area and established a colony. Its capital, Bogotá (named after the Chibcha chief, Bacatá), became the administrative center for the Viceroyalty of New Granada, an area encompassing modern Colombia, Venezuela, Ecuador, and Panama.

In 1810, after a French invasion of Spain, New Granada took advantage of the mother country's weakness to declare its independence. Three years later, Spain sent troops to South America to put down the colonial uprising. In 1819 a fierce battle took place north of Bogotá, in which the Venezuelan general Simón Bolívar defeated the Spanish. Bolívar became the first president of the Republic of Gran Colombia (see pages 70-72).

The Republic. Bolívar's republic did not hold together for long. Venezuela and Ecuador broke away in 1830. Panama remained until 1903, when the United States helped it to break away from Colombia. Colombia had rejected a U.S. request to build a canal across Panama. The new government of Panama gave its approval for the canal.

Unlike many South American countries, Colombia was able to establish a tradition of democracy, based on civilian government and regular free elections. Two political parties took shape early in the republic's history. One, the Conservative Party, believed in a strong central government, the union of church and state, and limited suffrage. The other, the Liberal Party, believed in strong regional government, the separation of church and state, and wider voting privileges. One or the other of these parties has been in control for most of the republic's history.

In spite of its democratic institutions, clashes between the two parties have been marked by violence and bloodshed. During the War of a Thousand Days (1899-1902), more than 100,000 people lost their lives. Widespread banditry and warfare also occurred during a period known as La Violencia (The Violence), which lasted through the 1940s and 1950s. La Violencia claimed the lives of 200,000 to 300,000 Colombians.

The National Front and Beyond.   In 1957 the leaders of the two parties met in order to find a solution to this unbearable situation. They devised a system in which the presidency alternated between the parties every four years. This coalition, known as the National Front, brought an end to the bloodshed and set the nation on a course of social and economic reforms. The National Front continued until the late 1970s, when it was gradually phased out.

No sooner had political strife ended, however, than new troubles began. Gangster organizations known as **drug cartels** established an illegal but highly profitable trade in drugs. Operating at first out of Medellín and later out of Cali, the cartels gained a virtual monopoly of the world supply of cocaine. Through bribery of politicians, murders, bombings, and alliances with leftist guerrilla movements, the drug cartels achieved a degree of power that threatened the entire fabric of the country.

Colombia Today.   Illicit narcotics **trafficking,** as drug smuggling is called, has continued to be a major problem. In 1989 the U.S. government supplied the Colombian government with military equipment and advisers to help in the war against the cocaine traffic. In return, the United States asked that heads of drug cartels be **extradited** to the United States—that is, turned over to stand trial. When the Colombian government complied, the drug cartels responded by stepping up terrorism. As a result, the government discontinued extradition.

The cocaine war accounted for only part of Colombia's instability. Old-style political violence also returned. In 1989, more than 7,000 deaths were attributed to politically inspired violence.

Conditions on the economic front were also gloomy. Foreign investment dropped by half because of violence and political chaos. The world price for coffee plummeted, so that this export no longer brought in as much revenue as before. For a while it seemed that oil revenues might offset the loss, but guerrillas repeatedly bombed the pipeline, and operations came to a standstill. One of the few bright spots in the economic picture was the rise in coal exports, but even coal production fell off because of repeated strikes.

In 1991 most observers agreed that Colombia stood at a crossroads. It needed to address the fundamental problems of social and economic injustice. Only then could Colombia emerge from its crisis and begin to realize the peace and prosperity that its rich resources and democratic tradition should make possible.

ARGENTINA

With an area of over 1 million square miles, Argentina is the second largest country in South America. It is a long country, shaped like a triangle. The narrowest part is in the south. Its Atlantic coastline measures 2,500 miles. Argentina is bordered by Bolivia and Paraguay on the north, Chile on the west, and Uruguay and Brazil on the east.

Argentina was given its name, from the Latin *argentum*, meaning silver, by early Spanish explorers who hoped to find mineral treasures there. This hope for mineral wealth was disappointed. However, Argentina turned out to possess other riches that have enabled it to become one of the wealthiest nations of Latin America. Perhaps most notable was its fertile black soil. Politically, Argentina has been less successful. Its history has been one of repeated civil wars and revolutions as it has struggled to achieve a democratic form of government.

The Land.   Most of Argentina is completely flat. It can be divided into six natural regions. Patagonia, in the extreme south, is bleak and forlorn. Although it occupies more than one-fourth of the nation's land, it is almost unpopulated. The Andean region, in the west, occupies another quarter of the national territory. A high, dry plateau, it, too, is mostly unoccupied. The northern half of Argentina is composed of three regions. From west to east, they are the puna, a high, level area; the Gran Chaco, a forested lowland; and Mesopotamia, a heavily forested swampy area. Finally, there are the pampas, Argentina's richest and most populated region. The pampas are a vast fertile plain that stretches for miles. The pampas support most of the country's agriculture and industry and are home to more than one-half of its population. (For details on the land and climate of Argentina, see Chapter 1.)

The People.   Argentina has a total of about 31 million inhabitants. Its population is more European than that of any other nation of Latin America. More than three-fourths of all Argentinians are descendants either of the early Spanish settlers or of the 6 million Italian and Spanish immigrants who arrived during the late 1800s and early 1900s. Mestizos make up only about 10 percent of the population. There are also about 50,000 Indians, who are concentrated in the northwest.

The tradition of immigration continued in the mid-twentieth century. More than half of the people who immigrated to Latin America from Europe after World War II settled in Argentina. Many Jews sought refuge here, and today Argentina has the largest Jewish population in Latin America. In the 1970s and 1980s, the trend was reversed. Many Argentinians began to migrate to the United States, Venezuela, Brazil, and several European countries. A major reason for this outward migration was the repressive political regime, which you will read about later, that gained control of the country in 1976.

Urban Life.   Argentina is one of the most urbanized countries in the world. More than four-fifths of the population live in cities. One-third of the people live in Buenos Aires (BWAY-nehs EHR-eez). Buenos Aires is Argentina's capital and the second largest city in South America. It is an imposing metropolis. Here one finds beautiful parks, magnificent avenues, hundreds of bookstores. Large modern apartment houses mix with older mansions. The city boasts the finest opera house in Latin America. Argentina's immigrant heritage is evident in the architecture, language, and customs of this cosmopolitan city. Argentina's other principal cities are Córdoba, a leading industrial center, and Rosario, a major port and transportation center.

Rural Life.   Rural life in Argentina is centered around vast cattle ranches called **estancias.** These estancias represent 75 percent of all farmland in Argentina. Since almost all of this land is used for grazing, settlements are far apart. Paved roads are practically nonexistent, and isolation is common.

Each estancia is managed from a central headquarters. The wealthy owners usually live in Buenos Aires or in Europe. They visit the estancia only during the summer or on weekends. A hired staff tends to the daily chores of the estancia. These laborers differ from other rural Latin Americans. They are not peasants who cultivate a single, small plot of land. Rather, they often move from one estancia to another. Most live with their families in neat brick homes with thatched roofs. Much of the everyday living is carried on outdoors.

Education. In 1868, a schoolteacher named Domingo Faustino Sarmiento (sahr-MYAYN-toh) was elected president of Argentina. Under Sarmiento, Argentina established a system of free, compulsory education. Today, 94 percent of Argentinians can read and write. This is one of the highest literacy rates in the world.

The Economy. One of Argentina's principal natural resources is its rich farming and grazing land. As a result, by the nineteenth century Argentina had become a major world supplier of meat and grains. It engaged in a thriving foreign trade with the industrialized nations of Europe. In exchange for its agricultural commodities, it received manufactured goods. Its economy grew rapidly. By the 1930s Argentina's per capita income was the eighth highest in the world.

However, following World War II, Argentina's economy faced several serious problems: inflation, government mismanagement, and a record foreign debt. These problems first appeared in the 1950s. All efforts to solve them have been unsuccessful, and they continue to plague Argentina today. In the early 1980s, the annual inflation rate reached nearly 700 percent. A cup of coffee that cost one peso (Argentina's unit of money) in 1973 cost 30,000 pesos in 1983! Unemployment was at a high of 15 percent. And Argentina's foreign debt, owed to U.S. and other Western banks, had reached $45 billion. This was the third largest foreign debt in the world.

Agriculture, particularly grains and livestock, have long been the backbone of Argentina's economy. The first Argentine cattle, raised by the colonists in the sixteenth century, were lean, bony animals that yielded tough meat. After a new breed was introduced in the nineteenth century, Argentina became one of the world's major exporters of beef.

Argentinians eat more beef than do the people of any other nation in the world. However, since World War II, the country's cattle industry has been faced with hard times. There is not always enough beef to meet both domestic and export demands. In the past 20 years, the government has frequently been forced to decree *vedas,* or meatless days. On vedas, it is prohibited to sell meat to the local populace.

Argentina is the second leading exporter of corn in the world, and the fifth leading exporter of wheat. In a shift away from traditional trading patterns, in the 1980s Argentina began shipping large quantities of wheat to the Soviet Union. Other important crops are sorghum, potatoes, sugar, wine, barley, and oats. Large quantities of fruit are produced both for domestic markets and for export. Argentina ranks fourth in the world in wool production.

Along with Mexico and Brazil, Argentina has one of the most developed *manufacturing* sectors in Latin America. Traditional industries such as food processing and textile manufacture are important. In recent years, however, emphasis has shifted to the manufacture of goods such as automobiles, machinery, chemicals, steel, and agricultural equipment. Other important industries include the manufacture of cigarettes, paper, industrial plastics, and cement. However, with the sharp decline in the economy in the 1970s and 1980s, manufacturing has suffered tremendous losses.

Early History.   The Spanish first arrived in the area that is now Argentina in the early 1500s. After an earlier settlement was destroyed by Indians, the Spanish succeeded in establishing a colonial city at Buenos Aires in 1580.

At first, Argentina was ruled as part of the Viceroyalty of Peru. Buenos Aires was maintained solely as a military fort for defense against the Portuguese in neighboring Brazil. However, in the eighteenth century, silver production began to decline in the Peruvian viceroyalty, and Spain turned its attention to the region of Argentina. The colonists there had introduced livestock and wheat, and the markets for these agricultural products were growing. In 1776, Spain established this region as a new colony. It was called the Viceroyalty of La Plata, and Buenos Aires was the capital.

As you have read, the people of Buenos Aires began demanding independence from Spain in the early 1800s. Led by José de San Martín, a colonial force defeated the Spanish in 1816. The people of present-day Argentina formed a new country called the United Provinces of La Plata. They made Buenos Aires its capital. (For details on colonial life and independence, see Chapter 3.)

The years following independence were dominated by internal struggle. As in most of the new South American republics, there was no central authority. The people of Buenos Aires wanted a strong central government run from their province. People in the rural provinces, however, insisted on maintaining local power. These conditions led to frequent civil wars.

Each province was ruled by a local caudillo, a military dictator. The caudillo often recruited **gauchos** to act as supporting armies. The gaucho, or Argentine cowboy, was a frontiersman who roamed the pampas on horseback, herding cattle. Part Indian, part Spanish, the gaucho was known for his independent spirit and individualistic way of life. According to legend, the gaucho lived on his horse, ate nothing but meat, slept under the stars, and drank *maté* from a gourd. He was easily recognized by his clothes. The gaucho wore loose, full trousers, cowhide boots, flat broad-brimmed hats, and a poncho. Argentinians today honor the gaucho as a symbol of their national character.

In 1829, one of the caudillos, Juan Manuel de Rosas (hwan mahn-WEL day ROH-sahs), seized power by force. He established a dictatorship that lasted over 20 years. Finally, in 1852, an army revolt overthrew the government. Rosas fled to England.

A National Government Is Established.   In 1853, a national constitution was drawn up. It was modeled on that of the United States. The constitution established a **federal system** of government—a system in which power is divided between the national government and the various provincial governments. The capital was at Paraná. At first, Buenos Aires refused to join, and fighting broke out. After several years of struggle, Buenos Aires joined the confederation. The country was renamed Argentina, and Buenos Aires became its capital. Bartolomé Mitre (bahr-toh-loh-MAY MEE-tray), a Buenos Aires general, became the first constitutional president.

Under Mitre and his successor, Domingo Sarmiento, Argentina enjoyed a period of stability and prosperity. Large numbers of immigrants came from Europe. Schools and railroads were built. Mail and telegraph services were started. Foreign trade and investment grew. By the 1900s, Argentina was the wealthiest nation in Latin America.

Until the late 1800s, Argentina was ruled by a privileged group of estate owners, bankers, and merchants. As the economy expanded, a new middle class began to demand greater political participation. In 1912, the legislature passed the Saenz Peña (SAH-ayns PAY-nyah) Electoral Law. For the first time, every man over the age of 18 was allowed to vote. The Radical party, which had been founded in 1890 by merchants, factory workers, and tenant farmers, came to power. The Radicals ruled Argentina from 1916 until 1930, when they were overthrown by the military.

The 1930 military **coup,** or overthrow of the government, marked the beginning of over 50 years of political chaos and economic decline in Argentina. Since 1930, no elected Argentine president has completed his term in office. Although elections were occasionally held, they were often accompanied by fraud. Sometimes the results were simply ignored. Military governments came and went. No group was capable of ending the political crisis that plagued the nation.

The Peróns. During World War II, an army colonel named Juan Domingo Perón (pay-ROHN) rose to power. Perón had served as minister of labor during the early 1940s. In this position, he won the loyalty of the nation's millions of urban workers by pushing for higher wages and social reforms. Backed by the *descamisados,* or "shirtless ones," as these workers were called, as well as by the army, Perón was elected president in 1946 and again in 1952. With huge popular support, he established a highly authoritarian regime. He suppressed all opposition.

One of Perón's greatest assets was his wife, Eva Duarte Perón. She served as his principal aide. Evita, as she was lovingly called, was an actress from a lower-class background. She was idolized by the Argentinians. Evita's popularity kept the regime in power even when its policies were bringing the nation near economic collapse. Evita also supported women's causes and was responsible for gaining the vote for Argentina's women. In 1952, however, Eva Perón, only 33 years old, suddenly became ill and died. Over 2 million Argentinians lined the route along her funeral procession.

Juan and Eva Perón at the height of their power.

Eva Perón's death was a great blow to the popularity of the regime. Perón was already experiencing serious economic difficulties. He now found himself faced with open opposition from many groups, including the Roman Catholic church, the landowning classes, and the army. In 1955, the army overthrew Perón, who fled to Spain.

During the next 18 years, a series of dictatorships tried unsuccessfully to solve Argentina's economic problems. Many Argentinians continued to believe only Perón could help them. In 1972, Juan Perón was allowed to return to Argentina. There, at the age of 78, he was elected once more to the presidency. His new wife, Isabel, was elected vice-president. Perón, who was old and sick, died only months later, and Isabel became the first woman president in the Americas. The economic and political situation continued to worsen, however. In 1976, Isabel Perón was removed by the military.

Military Rule.   When the military seized power in 1976, inflation was soaring and guerrilla groups were terrorizing the country. Several former national leaders had been kidnapped and killed. The new government mounted a program of state terrorism against the guerrillas. In what came to be known as the "dirty war," the armed forces arrested, tortured, and killed between 6,000 and 10,000 people. Twenty thousand other Argentinians simply "disappeared."

Argentina's military government was led by General Leopoldo Galtieri (lay-oh-POEL-doh gahl-TYEHR-ee). In 1982, Galtieri stunned the world by invading the Falkland Islands. These islands, off the southeast Argentine coast, have been controlled by the British since 1833. However, they are claimed by the Argentinians, who call them the Malvinas (mahl-VEE-nahs).

Galtieri had hoped to gain popular support for his government by a quick victory in the Falklands. He did not expect Britain to resist the Argentinian takeover. Much to his surprise, however, the British fought back, sending their fleet halfway around the world to defend the Falklands. The outnumbered Argentinian troops were easily encircled. Ten weeks after the invasion, Argentina, with 1,900 dead, decided to surrender. Following this humiliating defeat, public opinion turned against the regime. Galtieri was forced to resign, and the military government promised a return to civilian rule.

Argentina Today.   In 1983, after eight years of military rule, political repression, and economic decline, presidential elections were held. A

The Plaza de Mayo in Buenos Aires. Open spaces, fine shops, theaters, and a cosmopolitan atmosphere make Buenos Aires the cultural center of Argentina.

democratic government was ushered into power. It was headed by moderate Republican Raul Alfonsín (rah-OOL al-fon-SEEN).

Immediately after taking office, Alfonsín took steps to restore confidence. He promised to control the actions of the military and to control human rights abuses. In an unusual move, Alfonsín ordered trials for leaders of the military who had been responsible for the repression. Alfonsín's biggest challenge, however, remained the rebuilding of the Argentine economy. In that effort he was largely unsuccessful, and in 1989 the voters replaced him with Carlos Saúl Menem (MEN-uhm), a Peronist. Menem immediately introduced an emergency program that, by late 1991, seemed to be making progress in bringing Argentina's economic problems under control.

REVIEWING THE CHAPTER

I. Building Your Vocabulary

In your notebook, write the numbers from 1 to 5. After each number, write the word that matches the definition.

gauchos	favelas	estancias
vedas	pampas	cariocas

1. shantytowns
2. large cattle ranches
3. the cowboys of Argentina
4. the vast, fertile plains of northern Argentina
5. the people of Rio de Janeiro

II. Understanding the Facts

In your notebook, write the numbers from 1 to 5. Identify the country to which each sentence refers, and write the country's name after the number.

1. Its coastline touches both the Atlantic and the Pacific Oceans.
2. Its official language is Portuguese.
3. It fought a war with Great Britain over the Falkland Islands.
4. It has the largest population of any country in South America.
5. It is the source of most of the world's emeralds.

III. Thinking It Through

In your notebook, write the numbers from 1 to 5. Write the letter of the correct answer to each question next to its number.

1. The practice of Candomblé is rooted in Roman Catholicism and
   a. Judaism.
   b. African spiritual beliefs.

c. the traditional Portuguese respect for nature.

d. ancestor worship.

2. One result of the reign of Emperor Pedro II was that Brazil
   a. became the world's leading producer of coffee.
   b. lost the territory that is now Uruguay.
   c. built a new capital city, Brasília, in the interior.
   d. gave all citizens over 18 the right to vote.

3. What important role has the United States played in Colombian history?
   a. It helped Colombia gain independence from Gran Colombia.
   b. It sponsored the talks that led to the creation of the National Front.
   c. It freed Colombia from Spanish rule during the Spanish-American War.
   d. It encouraged Panama to break away from Colombia.

4. Which of the following was favored by the Colombian Liberal Party?
   a. a strong national government
   b. close cooperation between church and state
   c. reestablishment of Gran Colombia
   d. limited suffrage

5. How are the histories of Brazil and Argentina alike?
   a. Both were settled by Portuguese colonists.
   b. Both were freed from colonial rule by José de San Martín.
   c. Both were often ruled by military governments.
   d. Both depended on coffee export earnings for government revenue.

DEVELOPING CRITICAL THINKING SKILLS

1. Explain how Brazil has become a leading world economic power.

2. Show how Colombia has attempted to solve the problems of political violence and terrorism in the twentieth century.

3. Describe the role played by Juan Perón in Argentinean history.

4. Discuss the reasons why the caudillo is a particular feature of Latin American politics.

ENRICHMENT AND EXPLORATION

1. South American countries are frequently in the news. Select one of these countries, and collect clippings about it from newspapers and magazines: Bolivia, Chile, Ecuador, Guyana, Paraguay, Peru, Suriname, Uruguay, or Venezuela. Use your clippings to make a scrapbook about the country. Organize the scrapbook into categories, such as economy, politics, travel, human rights, daily life, and so on.

2. A major problem facing many South American countries is an overwhelming foreign debt. Select one of the countries in this chapter and research its foreign debt. Find out how big the debt is, to whom it is owed, how it developed, and the steps being taken to repay it. Report your findings to the class.

LATIN AMERICA AND THE WORLD

1810–Today

1826	Bolívar calls conference in attempt to unite Latin American governments.
1861–1865	*U.S. Civil War*
1879–1883	Chile fights Peru and Bolivia.
1889–1890	Pan American Union established.
1898	U.S. victory in Spanish-American War; Puerto Rico annexed; Platt Amendment.
1903	Panama gains independence from Colombia.
1904	Roosevelt Corollary issued.
1914–1918	*World War I*
1916	Pancho Villa invades Texas and New Mexico.
1930s	Bolivia and Paraguay fight over Gran Chaco.
1933	Franklin Roosevelt announces Good Neighbor Policy.
1939–1945	*World War II*
1948	Organization of American States is formed.
1954	U.S.-backed rebels overthrow president of Guatemala.
1959	Cuban revolution brings Castro to power.
1961	Alliance for Progress established.
1965	U.S. Marines set up new government in Dominican Republic.
1978	Panama Canal treaties ratified.
1982	Mexico, Brazil, and Argentina default on foreign debt payments.
1983	U.S. invades Grenada.
1983	Contadora group first meets.
1990	U.S. invades Panama ousts Noriega.

9 *Latin America and the World*

Because of its vast size and population, its cultural diversity, and its varied political experience, Latin America is a highly complex region. Each nation has adopted its own policies toward its close neighbors, its hemisphere, and the world. In this chapter, we will examine recent trends in these policies to discover where Latin America is headed today.

RELATIONS WITH THE UNITED STATES

Latin America and the United States have a special relationship. They are geographically close. They share a common past as European colonies. However, most Latin Americans see the relationship as unequal. They believe that the United States has long determined what happens "south of the border." According to the Mexican poet, Octavio Paz:

> [North Americans] are always among us, even when they ignore us or turn their back on us. Their shadow covers the whole hemisphere. It is the shadow of a giant.

U.S. policy toward Latin America cannot be easily defined or summarized in a single sentence. The United States never formally created one particular document that can be called its statement of its Latin American policy. Rather, a series of U.S. policies has developed over the years, changing according to the times and circumstances.

The Monroe Doctrine. As you know, the countries of Latin America first began to fight for independence from their European colonial rulers in the early nineteenth century. At that time, Napoleon, the emperor of France, was trying to conquer all of Europe. The European nations were too busy with their own problems to pay much attention to Latin America. However, in 1815 Napoleon was defeated. The same year, some European nations joined in an **alliance** that threatened to put down colonial revolutions. (An alliance is a close relationship formed among nations to achieve a common goal.)

The United States had won its own independence from Britain only a short while earlier. The new nation was very sympathetic and encouraging toward the independence movements of its southern neighbors. The people of the United States became alarmed at rumors that the European nations were planning to help Spain recover its Latin American colonies. In 1823, U.S. President James Monroe responded to this situation in a message to Congress. The policy he announced came to be known as the Monroe Doctrine.

The **Monroe Doctrine** was the first official U.S. declaration of policy regarding Latin America. President Monroe declared that the United States would not interfere in any of Europe's remaining colonies in the Western Hemisphere. However, the United States would oppose any attempt by a European nation to reestablish a lost colony. Efforts to form new colonies or to interfere with any of the American governments would also meet U.S. opposition.

The Monroe Doctrine had far-reaching effects. For many years, the United States used it to keep out any influence but its own in the Western Hemisphere. By the end of the nineteenth century, the Monroe Doctrine had been used numerous times, against three nations. These were France, Spain, and Great Britain. France had been interfering in Mexico. Spain had been trying to retake the Dominican Republic. And Great Britain had become involved in a boundary dispute with Venezuela. Among Latin Americans, the Monroe Doctrine was greatly resented. In their eyes, it was a U.S. tool to dominate the region.

U.S. relations with Latin America were also affected by the theory of **Manifest Destiny**. The idea became popular in the United States in the 1840s. According to the theory's supporters the United States had a Manifest Destiny—or historic duty—to expand its territory to the Pacific Ocean. This belief became the justification for annexing Texas from Mexico. The Mexican War came soon after. It ended with even a greater loss of territory for that Latin American nation (see Chapter 5).

The Roosevelt Corollary. The next period of U.S. policy in Latin America was marked by a bold display of power. The U.S. victory in the Spanish-American War of 1898 had two major results. The United States annexed Puerto Rico. At the same time, the United States gained the right to establish a naval base in Cuba. Through the Platt Amendment to the new Cuban constitution the United States then gained the right to interfere in Cuban internal affairs.

Since the late 1800s, the United States had wanted to build a canal connecting the Atlantic and Pacific oceans. The United States had negotiated for many years with Colombia to obtain land on which to build such a canal. However, the negotiations were not successful. Finally, in 1903, the United States supported—perhaps began—a revolution for independence in the small Colombian state of Panama. When the revolution was over, the new Panamanian prime minister promptly signed a treaty granting the United States a 10-mile-wide strip of land, "forever." The treaty granted all the rights necessary to build a canal across the land. President Theodore Roosevelt boasted: "I took Panama."

The Panama Canal was very important to the United States. Even before the canal was completed, the United States realized that it would need protection from European powers, who might threaten this U.S. possession. Thus, in 1904, President Theodore Roosevelt announced a new policy toward Latin America. In his annual message to Congress, Roosevelt said that if the independence of any country in the Western Hemisphere was threatened in any way, the United States would act as an "international police power" to prevent a foreign country from stepping in. This statement became known as the **Roosevelt Corollary** to the Monroe Doctrine.

The Roosevelt Corollary was called into use several times during the next years. The United States used this policy to justify varying degrees of interference in a number of Latin American countries. Most of these were in the Caribbean and Central America. On and off over the next thirty years, U.S. Marines occupied Cuba, the Dominican Republic, Haiti, and Nicaragua. Three of these nations—Cuba, the Dominican Republic, and Haiti—were made **protectorates** of the United States for varying periods of time. (A protectorate is a region controlled by a foreign power, although the local ruler remains head of the government.) In Mexico, during an incident in 1914, several American sailors were arrested. In response, President Wilson ordered American marines and sailors to occupy the town of Veracruz. The occupying troops were soon withdrawn. In 1916 Mexican groups were involved in fighting, with Pancho Villa's forces opposing those of the Mexican president. (See Chapter 5.) Villa tried to provoke American

THE BIG STICK IN THE CARIBBEAN SEA

President Theodore Roosevelt provided political cartoonists with a good theme when he declared that the United States should "speak softly and carry a big stick" when dealing with other countries.

intervention by killing eighteen American mining engineers. He next crossed the border into Texas and New Mexico and killed seventeen Americans. To prevent further raids, 15,000 American troops entered Mexico. They chased Villa through northern Mexico. After failing to catch Villa, they were ordered home in 1917.

Latin Americans began to fear the power of the United States. They called it the "Colossus of the North." Many suspected that the United States was trying to control the entire hemisphere. The United States claimed that it was protecting its weaker neighbors from European interference. Many Latin Americans, however, felt that this policy was an insult to their national pride.

The Good Neighbor Policy. During the 1920s, the United States began to modify some of its attitudes toward Latin America. The relations between the regions began to improve. However, the greatest change came in the 1930s with Franklin D. Roosevelt. Roosevelt was first inaugurated as U.S. president in 1933. Soon after taking office, he announced the **Good Neighbor Policy.** This was the policy of "the neighbor who resolutely respects himself and because he does so, respects the rights of others." The United States joined the nations of Latin America in signing the

Montevideo Pact. The pact declared, "No state has the right to intervene in the internal or external affairs of another state."

The Good Neighbor Policy was more than mere words. Roosevelt canceled the Platt Amendment. U.S. Marines came home from the Caribbean on his orders. The United States also signed a number of trade agreements with Latin American countries. As a result, commerce between the regions expanded greatly. A new program exchanged teachers, students, cultural leaders, scholars, and professional men and women between the regions. To help Latin Americans improve their agriculture, industries, educational systems, and health services, the United States sent teams of technical experts. A climate of cooperation gradually developed. During World War II most of the nations of Latin America united behind the United States.

Post-World War II.   In the years immediately following World War II, the spread of communism in Eastern Europe and in Asia became the major concern of U.S. foreign policy. The United States shifted its attention away from Latin America. However, in the mid-1950s, many nations in Latin America began to experience political and economic upheavals. Radical political movements emerged.

The United States had major commercial interests in Latin America. The U.S. government believed that the radicals posed a threat to the U.S. investments in the region. Therefore the U.S. government was determined to prevent any of these groups from gaining power.

The first incident occurred in Guatemala. In 1944, Guatemala had elected a reform government. Ten years later, in 1954, the government, led by Jacobo Arbenz Guzmán, passed a land reform law that allowed it to take over and distribute unused land. Most of the land was owned by the United Fruit Company, a U.S. corporation. Arbenz also permitted Communists to participate in his government.

The United States decided to intervene. It believed that the Guatemalan government was controlled by Communists. Under the orders of President Dwight D. Eisenhower, the United States secretly armed a rebel group that overthrew the Guatemalan president. Many of the nations of Latin America resented this interference. They condemned the United States for overthrowing an elected government.

The United States was also worried about the rise of communism in other Central American and Caribbean countries. As a consequence, the U.S. government openly supported many Latin American dictators. They were often corrupt, repressive, and extremely unpopular among the people they ruled. But their anti-Communist stands won them U.S.

support. One of these dictators was Fulgencio Batista in Cuba. Another was Rafael Trujillo in the Dominican Republic. The Somoza family ruled in Nicaragua. The U.S. policy of supporting such rulers gave rise to much anti-United States sentiment in Latin America. On a goodwill visit in 1958, U.S. Vice-President Richard Nixon was cursed and spat at by angry crowds in several South American countries.

Recent Years. In the late 1960s, the relations between Latin America and the United States entered a new phase. As you read in Chapter 6, in 1959 Fidel Castro led a revolution that brought him to power in Cuba. Once installed as dictator, Castro challenged the accepted idea that the Western Hemisphere was a U. S. **sphere of influence**. (A sphere of influence is a region in which one nation has special economic and political privileges.) Castro called for major social and economic changes. However, more important to the United States, he aligned Cuba with the Soviet Union and other Communist countries. Revolutionary groups in other Latin American nations began to look to Cuba as a leader in the Western Hemisphere.

U.S. Vice-President Richard Nixon was greeted by protestors in Caracas, Venezuela, in 1958.

The U.S. president at the time, John F. Kennedy, responded to Castro's challenge in several ways. One way was to use force. As you have read, Kennedy tried to eliminate the Castro government by means of the Bay of Pigs invasion. As you know, this attempt was unsuccessful.

Kennedy also tried "peaceful revolution." In 1961, he announced the establishment of the **Alliance for Progress**. This was a ten-year program to improve Latin American housing, education, sanitation, and public services. It was also intended to promote tax and land reform. The United States and 19 Latin American nations (all but Cuba) participated in the program. Underlying the program was an important idea. It was the belief that ending widespread poverty would prove the most effective weapon against the spread of communism in the Western Hemisphere .

Although the Alliance made some progress, its results were generally disappointing. Most of the money it raised was used to help business interests and military forces. The masses of poor people benefited little from it.

Several years later, Latin Americans became even more disillusioned with the United States. In the spring of 1965, a group of army officers overthrew a newly formed government in the Dominican Republic. The government was civilian, but Communist-supported. Heavy fighting broke out. President Lyndon Johnson ordered 400 U.S. Marines into the Dominican capital of Santo Domingo to aid the military. He said that they were needed to protect the lives of American citizens. During the next two weeks, however, an additional 20,000 troops landed, and 10,000 more stood by in navy vessels offshore. U.S. troops remained in the Dominican Republic until August. These events were observed closely in Latin America. To Latin American leaders in other countries, the U.S. action sent an unpleasant message. Some believed that if the United States did not like their policies, it would support revolutions to overthrow them.

In the 1970s, the administration of President Richard Nixon abandoned the social and economic aims of the Alliance for Progress. President Nixon also made another change. He made it clear that the United States would not accept the seizure of property belonging to U.S. businesses in Latin America.

In 1970, Salvador Allende Gossens was elected president of Chile. He was a Marxist. The United States had provided financial assistance to Chilean forces seeking to prevent Allende from gaining power. Once in office, Allende angered the United States by reorganizing Chilean control of the copper mines. These had once been foreign-owned. To bring down the Allende government, the United States tried to create economic chaos in Chile. Many American banks and businesses held back from further investments in Chile. Finally, in 1973, the Allende government was overthrown in a bloody military revolt. A repressive military government came to power. Many people believed that the United States had helped finance the forces that overthrew Allende, though the U.S. government denied this.

One of the most significant developments in U.S.-Latin American relations during the administration of President Jimmy Carter, from 1977 to 1981, was the Panama Canal treaties. Upon ratification of the treaties in 1978, Panama gained control of the Panama Canal Zone. (Until then it had been under the jurisdiction of the United States.) Under another clause, by the year 2000 the United States will withdraw all troops from the Canal Zone. Panama will then have complete control of the canal.

President Carter also took a strong stand on behalf of human rights. As president, Carter declared the following in a speech before the United Nations: "No member of the United Nations can claim that mistreatment of its citizens is solely its own business." Soon the United

U.S. President Jimmy Carter and Panamanian President Omar Torrijos signed the Panama Canal treaties in 1977. The U.S. Senate ratified the treaties in 1978.

States cut back aid to Argentina, Brazil, Uruguay, and Chile. At that time, there were human rights violations in those countries. Carter's human rights stand met with both praise and blame. Many Latin Americans hoped that this policy would lead to the end of dictatorships in their countries. On the other hand, some complained that their countries were being singled out for punishment. These people pointed out that the United States continued to carry on normal relations with other nations where human rights were not respected.

As you read in Chapter 7, when Ronald Reagan became U.S. president in 1981, many Central American countries were experiencing political upheavals. Reagan saw these upheavals as part of a power struggle between the Soviet Union and the United States. His principal objective was to avoid the creation of a new Communist state in the Western Hemisphere, particularly in Central America and the Caribbean. To do this, he increased U.S. military activity in the region. Guerrillas were trying to overthrow the leftist government in Nicaragua. Reagan provided backing for them. The moderate government in El Salvador was under fire from leftist guerrillas. So he increased military aid to El Salvador.

A more dramatic action came in 1983 in Grenada (gruh-NAY-duh). A small island-nation in the Caribbean, Grenada had had a Marxist government since 1979. It had leaned increasingly toward friendship with Communist Cuba and the Soviet Union. After the assassination of Grenada's prime minister in 1983, the United States feared that instability would follow. Claiming a need to protect U.S. medical students, the United States sent troops to Grenada. Some Caribbean nations assisted the United States. The invasion succeeded in removing Grenada's Marxist government.

A similar invasion took place in Panama in 1989. In Panama the problem was General Manuel Antonio Noriega, a dictator who had recently prevented the legally elected President Guillermo Endara from taking office. Noriega also was said to be involved in drug smuggling. For two years, the United States had applied economic pressure to Panama, but Noriega remained in control. In December 1989, President George Bush sent 12,000 troops to Panama. Noriega's government was replaced one led by Endara. Noriega was captured and brought to the United States to stand trial for drug trafficking.

In the 1980s, democracy made many gains in South America. The dictatorship in Argentina ended. In 1985 Brazil transferred power from the military to civilians. In 1989, General Alfredo Stroessner (STRESS-nuhr), the dictator who had long ruled Paraguay, was overthrown. His successor was constitutionally elected, but it remained to be seen whether democracy would take root in Paraguay. The last country in South American to return to constitutional government was Chile. There, a military dictatorship gave way to an elected president in 1990. However, the former dictator, General Augusto Pinochet (peen-oh-SHAY), remained as head of the army, a position he was guaranteed until 1998.

By the early 1990s, the prospects for democracy in the Caribbean and Central America had also improved, although problem areas remained. In Haiti, a president was freely elected for the first time in many years, but in 1991 he was overthrown by the army. In Nicaragua, however, a freely elected government took office in 1990. Elections continued to be held in El Salvador despite the turmoil there.

RELATIONS WITH EACH OTHER

Simón Bolívar, the "Liberator," dreamed of a unified Latin America. In 1826, he called a conference to unite all the new Latin American nations under one government. But the nations could not agree. National jealousies and rivalries hindered all attempts at cooperation. Bolívar was disillusioned. Before his death in 1830, he wrote:

> America is ungovernable. Those who have served the revolution have plowed the sea.

It was another 60 years before the republics of Latin America made their first successful move toward international cooperation.

Organizations for Cooperation.   In 1889 to 1890, delegates from the nations of Latin America and the United States met in Washington, D.C. At the meeting, they established the first inter-American organization, the *Pan American Union*. Its purpose was to create closer economic, cultural, and political ties among the nations of the Americas. In the early 1900s, the Union held several meetings to discuss common problems. It worked to promote trade among member nations and settle disputes. The Union also aimed to encourage cultural understanding and exchanges.

In 1948, the members of the Pan American Union created a new organization. This was called the *Organization of American States (OAS)*. Its purpose was to promote peace and justice in the Western Hemisphere.

Member nations agreed to work for the peaceful settlement of disputes among the American republics. The OAS also agreed to provide for the defense of its members against outside attack. In addition, the OAS established a number of economic councils. The goal was to assist economic development in the poorer nations of the Americas.

The OAS has handled many conflicts in the Americas since its establishment. In 1955, it condemned Anastasio Somoza of Nicaragua. (Somoza had been aiding in the attempted overthrow of the government of neighboring Costa Rica.) Between 1949 and 1961, the OAS helped resolve disputes that arose at various times between the Dominican dictator Rafael Trujillo and the nations of Cuba, Guatemala, Haiti, and Venezuela. In 1964, the OAS worked toward the solution of a dispute between the United States and Panama over control of the Panama Canal. And the OAS played an important role in ending the so-called soccer war between Honduras and El Salvador in 1969.

The OAS found itself faced with a difficult problem in 1959. Cuba was a charter member of the organization. But Fidel Castro established a Communist government there that year. In 1962 the OAS voted to expel Cuba from the organization. This was its most serious action against a member state. Two years later, a trade boycott was imposed. Cuba was charged with trying to promote communism and revolutionary activity in other OAS countries. More than twenty-nine years later, Cuba has still not been allowed back into the OAS. Several South American countries have acted on their own, however, and reestablished relations with Cuba.

Many Latin Americans are not completely satisfied with the OAS. They feel that the United States uses the organization to accomplish its own political purposes, rather than for the good of the region as a whole. Over the years, there have been attempts to establish a new organization for Latin American unity that would exclude the United States. However, none of these efforts have been successful.

Dissatisfied with the OAS and unable to create a replacement, Latin Americans have begun to look outside the Western Hemisphere for help. In 1985, Nicaragua took its problems to the International Court of Justice. The Court, which meets in the Netherlands, is the main judicial body of the United Nations. Nicaragua complained that the United States was using military force against Nicaragua and was interfering in its internal affairs. The Court ruled in Nicaragua's favor. However, the United States refused to accept the ruling. It claimed that the Court had no power in the case.

In recent years, Latin American nations have set up regional orga-

CASE STUDY:
A Call for Understanding

Gabriel García Márquez, a Colombian author, won the Nobel Prize for Literature in 1982. Following is an excerpt from the speech García Márquez delivered when accepting the prize.

Latin America neither wants, nor has any reason, to be a puppet without a will of its own.

Why do the Western nations respect our originality in literature but mistrust our originality in our attempts at social change? Why do they think the social justice sought by progressive Europeans is not also the goal of Latin Americans? Why don't they understand that since the conditions are different, the methods must also be different?

No: the immeasurable violence and pain of our history are the result of age-old inequalities and untold bitterness, and not a conspiracy plotted 3,000 miles from our homes [in the Soviet Union]. But many European leaders and thinkers have thought so.

The most prosperous countries of the world have succeeded in accumulating powers of destruction great enough, a hundred times over, to destroy not only all the human beings that have existed to this day but also the totality of all living beings that have ever drawn breath on this planet of misfortune. . . . Faced with this awesome reality, we the inventors of tales, who will believe anything, feel entitled to believe that it is not yet too late for people to try to create a perfect world. A world where no one will be able to decide for others how they die, where love will prove true and happiness be possible, and where the races condemned to one hundred years of solitude will have, at last and forever, a second opportunity on earth.

Nobel lecture of Gabriel García Márquez printed in *The New York Times*, February 6, 1983.

1. How do the nations of the West view Latin America, according to García Márquez?
2. What does García Márquez see as the main cause of Latin America's suffering?
3. What is García Márquez's dream for the future?

nizations to deal with specific problems. One of these organizations is the **Contadora group**. The group is named for the Panamanian island where it first met in 1983. The member nations are Colombia, Mexico, Panama, and Venezuela.

The Contadora group has sought to bring about an end to the violence in Central America. The organization has emphasized negotiation, democratic coexistence, and economic development. It has also sought to separate the regional problems of Central America from the larger conflict between East and West—between the Soviet Union and the United States. However, Contadora has been unable to gain support from the United States and its allies. And as far back as 1983, the Nicaraguan government made clear that it did not wish to participate in formal multilateral discussions (talks with many countries together). It preferred to deal with its neighbors and with the United States on a one-to-one basis. Without U.S. and Nicaraguan support, little progress has been made toward the Contadora group's goals.

Arms Control.   In 1967, the nations of Latin America signed the Treaty of Tlatelolco. This treaty established a nuclear weapon-free zone in Latin America. It prohibited the purchase and use of nuclear weapons by any nation of the region. However, disagreement has arisen about some of the treaty's provisions. Several Latin American nations interpret the treaty as prohibiting all nuclear devices. Other nations claim that, under the terms of the treaty, nuclear explosions can be conducted for peaceful purposes. By the 1980s, four Latin American nations—Argentina, Brazil, Chile, and Mexico—had developed nuclear programs for civilian purposes.

Boundary Disputes.   Over the years, relations among the nations of Latin America have frequently been marred by armed clashes. There have also been several full-scale wars. The major cause of trouble has been disputes over national boundaries.

- In 1825, Brazil and Argentina fought over the territory that is now Uruguay.

- From 1879 to 1883, Chile fought Peru and Bolivia because of an argument over mineral rights. Chile won and gained vast mineral-rich territory. But Chile and Peru continued to argue over their boundary until 1919.

- In the 1930s, Bolivia and Paraguay went to war over ownership of the Gran Chaco. After three years of fighting and three years of peace negotiations, both sides remained dissatisfied.

- Ecuador and Peru quarreled for years over the ownership of a wild, uncharted area in the Amazon basin. In 1940, Peru bombed and invaded Ecuador. Peru took most of the disputed territory. Armed conflict over the disputed region flared again in 1981. This ended only when other Latin American nations negotiated a cease-fire. Peru retained control of the area.

- Belize, formerly the colony of British Honduras, became independent in 1981. However, Guatemala claims the land of Belize and refuses to recognize the new nation.

- One Latin American territorial dispute recently had a happy ending. For 100 years, Chile and Argentina argued over ownership of three small islands in the Beagle Channel, a 150-mile-long waterway at the southern tip of South America. Finally, with the aid of Pope John Paul II, the two nations reached a compromise agreement. The resulting treaty was signed in 1985. It gave the islands to Chile but recognized Argentina's **sovereignty,** or control, over the waters to the east of a line drawn south of Cape Horn. Chile retained sovereignty over the waters to the west of the line.

In Search of Unity.   The nations of Latin America have made progress toward unity and cooperation, despite the many differences. Agreement has been reached on a number of important issues. Latin Americans have endorsed a policy of non intervention in the internal affairs of other nations. Somewhat less successfully, Latin Americans have also agreed to resolve disputes by peaceful rather than by military means.

Latin America has worked to enlarge markets and increase the standard of living in the region. However, the organizations created to achieve these goals have not survived. Efforts to make the economies of the region's republics work together have also been largely unsuccessful.

The return to civilian government that marked the region in the 1980s revived hope for Latin American unity. The region's new civilian presidents are making great efforts to communicate and to establish cordial relations among themselves. They have pledged themselves to work together to solve the Western Hemisphere's serious political and economic problems.

ROLE IN THE WORLD TODAY

Traditionally, Latin America has been most closely tied to its cultural parent, Europe, and its geographic neighbor, the United States. Following World War II, however, this began to change. Latin America tried to become less dependent on the industrialized nations. It worked with its neighbors to limit foreign investment and to encourage lower tariffs. Economic cooperation within Latin America became a goal. The region also began to seek a leadership role in the world.

The Third World.   Latin American influence began to grow in other parts of the world. Latin America had experienced tremendous industrial growth since World War II. As a result, the region was economically far more advanced than the other developing nations. These nations are mostly in Africa and Asia. Together with Latin America, they are known as the **Third World.**

Because of this economic superiority, most Latin Americans saw themselves as the natural leaders of the Third World. They called for a new and fairer economic relationship with the industrialized world. They began taking positions that did not always agree with those of the United States. At the same time, Latin America moved closer to the countries of Africa and Asia. It began to develop trade with them.

Trade.   Traditionally Latin America produced raw materials and agricultural products, such as coffee, cotton, and sugar. These were traded for manufactured goods, such as refrigerators, trucks, and radios. Following World War II, however, the demand for Latin America's exports declined drastically. Latin America was faced with a choice. The region had to learn to produce its own manufactured goods or do without them.

In the 1950s, a new policy, called **import substitution,** was developed to help solve the problem. Under this policy, the Latin American nations determined which imported goods could efficiently be produced at home. To encourage local manufacturers to produce these goods, the government provided various kinds of help. It imposed high tariffs or established quotas on the importing of similar goods.

Import substitution proved fairly successful. By the early 1960s, Latin America was producing automobiles, washing machines, and many other consumer goods. As the domestic demand for manufactured goods was filled, the larger industrial nations—Brazil, Mexico, and Argentina—began exporting their manufactured goods to other countries.

An auto factory in Mexico. Brazil, Argentina, Mexico, and several other Latin American countries have become major industrial powers. What are some of the social and economic problems they face?

Despite this progress, economic problems persisted. Latin America is the leader in world population growth. Many of the region's nations are unable to provide enough food for their people. Mexico and Venezuela, both of which have enacted extensive land reform programs, have to import wheat, corn, milk, and eggs. Bolivia imports one-half of all its food.

For the majority of Latin America's population, the availability of automobiles or washing machines is of little interest. To them, "luxury" means being able to obtain enough food to avoid hunger.

Latin America and Foreign Oil. As you have read, in the 1970s the price of world oil skyrocketed. This created economic chaos in the majority of Latin American nations, which rely on imported oil and oil-based products. The oil shortage affected all areas of the economy. Industry depends on oil to power machinery. And agriculture depends on fertilizers and pesticides made from oil.

The nations that imported oil—mainly Brazil and Chile—needed to increase exports to raise the money to pay for the oil. However, as oil prices rose, market prices for the region's principal products—coffee, bananas, cotton, and sugar—fell. Earnings from exports thus were never sufficient to cover the demand for oil.

Soon almost every nation in the region was hit by a severe economic depression. The standard of living declined. Unemployment increased.

Political unrest began to grow. To ease the desperate situation, many governments increased public spending in order to provide employment. This means they spent money on government programs such as housing, bridges, roads, public buildings, and education. However, money for such projects was short. To meet the need, these governments therefore often borrowed from foreign banks. Often these governments simply printed more paper money. This in turn led to inflation. As you remember, inflation is an economic condition marked by rising prices and a decrease in the value of money.

At first, those Latin American countries that produced oil—Mexico, Venezuela, and Ecuador—enjoyed an economic boom. They believed the boom would last forever. They too borrowed huge sums of money from foreign banks. The goal was to increase oil production. Brazil discovered more oil and developed new oil industries. The oil-rich nations also borrowed more money to expand the rest of their economies. Then, in the mid-1980s, world oil prices dropped. Export earnings nosedived. Inflation soared. There was no money to repay the foreign debt.

For Latin America's oil importers and oil exporters, the 1980s brought economic crisis. For both, it was the result of inflation and foreign debt.

Foreign Debt Crisis.   For many years, foreign loans to Latin America were seen as a way to promote the region's economic development. Foreign money enabled Latin American nations to import needed

Learning to write in a literacy class in Ecuador.

goods and to build roads and bridges. It enabled them to develop their own resources, and to encourage the growth of their industry.

At first, the loans were made by foreign governments. Many had developed aid programs to help Latin America. By the 1970s, however, commercial banks had begun to replace governments as the major source of foreign loans. Latin American nations began to increase the amount of money they borrowed as their economic problems deepened.

In 1980 to 1981, there was a sharp rise in interest rates. **Interest** is the charge made by banks or other lenders for borrowing money. Usually interest is a percentage of the amount borrowed. Even a minor increase in interest rates would have resulted in a major increase in the amount of money that the Latin American debtors had to repay. The increase in 1980-1981 was not minor, however, but major.

By 1982, eight Latin American nations had foreign debts totaling nearly $300 billion. By 1985, the figure had grown to $370 billion. By 1986, the developing world's three largest debtors were all from Latin America. Brazil was first, with $103 billion in debt. Mexico owed $97 billion. Argentina owed $50 billion.

In 1982, Mexico shocked the world by announcing that it could not afford to make the monthly payments on its foreign debt. Brazil, and then Argentina, soon followed this action. Like Mexico, they asked to postpone payments on their debt. Latin America's three largest economies were in deep trouble.

By the mid-1980s, the situation was still serious. The major debtor nations had reached agreements that made repayment easier. However, in exchange, international lenders demanded that the Latin Americans cut back drastically on spending at home. They were told to end public projects, freeze wages, and lower inflation. The debtor nations had little choice but to agree. However, people at home began to complain as decreased government spending brought worsened conditions for private citizens. In Argentina in 1985, the government took drastic steps to solve the problem. Prices and wages were frozen. The government stopped printing more money to balance its budget. These steps were taken to stop the inflation, which was over 3,000 percent per year. (In the United States, price increases of 10 percent per year are considered very high.) In addition, a new money called the austral was introduced. Government spending was cut. By 1986 all these steps, together called the austral plan, seemed to be working.

Although progress was made in the late 1980s, by 1991 the problem of Latin America's foreign debt was far from solved. Many Latin American leaders pointed out the great difficulty they were having with their

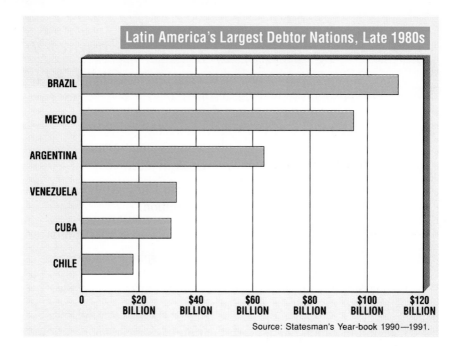

Latin America's Largest Debtor Nations, Late 1980s

	0	$20 BILLION	$40 BILLION	$60 BILLION	$80 BILLION	$100 BILLION	$120 BILLION
BRAZIL							
MEXICO							
ARGENTINA							
VENEZUELA							
CUBA							
CHILE							

Source: Statesman's Year-book 1990—1991.

debts. In 1985, for example, President Alan García of Peru announced that his nation would limit its debt repayment to 10 percent of all export earnings.

Almost all Latin American countries argued that new formulas for debt repayment needed to be worked out. Plans needed to be made that would tailor debt repayment to the debtor nations' ability to pay. Further, in order for the debtors to earn money with which to repay their debts, foreign markets for their products needed to be opened or expanded. Only when these conditions were met would Latin America begin to grow again. By the early 1990s many of these steps had been taken, and the economies of some countries—Mexico, in particular— began to improve. In other countries, such as Brazil, serious economic problems continued.

The last years of the twentieth century pose serious challenges to Latin America. By the year 2000, the region's population could swell to more than 600 million. More and more of this expanding population will live in urban areas. The foreign debt will not quickly vanish. Difficulties will remain in narrowing the gap between rich and poor.

Yet the Latin American nations are more developed and industrialized than any other Third World nations. Although the problems facing Latin America are great, the potential for change and growth is also great.

Chapter 9:
CHECKUP

REVIEWING THE CHAPTER

I. Building Your Vocabulary

In your notebook, write the numbers from 1 to 5. After each number, write the term that matches the definition.

interest   alliance   import substitution

protectorate   sovereignty   sphere of influence

1. freedom from outside control; power over an area or people
2. region that has its own ruler although it is under foreign control
3. region in which one powerful nation has special economic and political privileges
4. charge made by lenders for the money they lend
5. close relationship formed among nations to achieve a common goal

II. Understanding the Facts

In your notebook, write the numbers from 1 to 5. After each number, write the term that best completes the sentence.

the Monroe Doctrine

the Roosevelt Corollary

the Alliance for Progress

the Good Neighbor Policy

the Contadora Group Manifest Destiny

1. A regional organization created in 1983 by Mexico, Panama, Colombia, and Venezuela is _____.
2. President Kennedy's program to promote land reform and improve social conditions in Latin America was _____.
3. Since 1823, the United States has sought to keep any influence but its own out of the Western Hemisphere under _____.

4. The idea that the United States had a historic duty to expand its territory to the Pacific Ocean was called _____.

5. The idea that the United States would exercise an "international police power" to block foreign meddling in Latin America was called _____.

III. Thinking It Through

In your notebook, write the numbers from 1 to 5. After each number, write the letter of the correct ending to the sentence.

1. Latin Americans who called the United States the "Colossus of the North" were
   a. referring to the fearful size and power of the United States.
   b. praising the economic strength of the United States.
   c. admiring the military strength of the United States.
   d. referring to the combined economic power of the United States and Canada.

2. From independence to the present day, the major cause of wars between Latin American nations has been
   a. clashes over territorial borders.   b. language and cultural differences.   c. disputes over trade.   d. U.S. interference in local affairs.

3. A major cause of Latin America's economic crisis of the 1980s was
   a. grandiose building projects launched by dictators.
   b. high tariffs in industrial nations that prevented Latin Americans from selling their raw materials.
   c. sharp increases in the world price of oil and slumping economies in the industrial nations.
   d. decreased spending by Latin American governments on social projects and food subsidies.

4. A significant problem facing the OAS is
   a. a feeling by some members that the United States has too much power over the organization.
   b. the organization's inability to enforce an economic boycott against Cuba.
   c. the large number of Latin American nations that have dropped out of the organization.
   d. the organization's inability to stop border war from spreading to neighboring nations.

DEVELOPING CRITICAL THINKING SKILLS

1. Discuss reactions to the Monroe Doctrine and the Roosevelt Corollary among Latin Americans.

2. Describe the U.S. role in Latin America during the 1980s.

3. Show how the policy of import substitution was intended to improve the economies of Latin American nations.

4. Explain how Latin American countries have sought to reduce their dependence onother nations.

READING A FLOW CHART

A flow chart is a special kind of diagram. It is used to show at a glance the progress from one stage to another in a complicated sequence of events. The following flow chart shows the steps in the development of the foreign debt crisis in Latin America. Study the chart and then answer the questions.

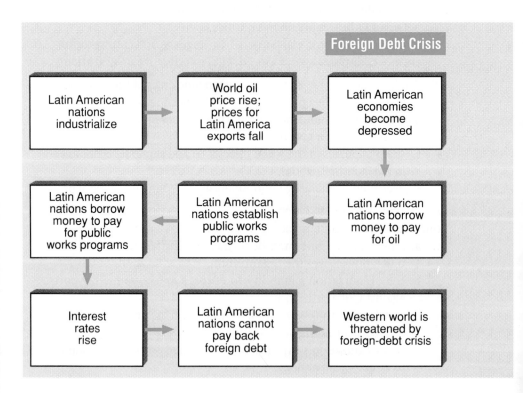

1. What world events caused Latin American economies to slump?

2. Which happened first, the borrowing of money to pay for public works programs, or the depression of Latin American economies?

3. Why did Latin American countries borrow money from foreign banks?

4. What new event was the crushing blow that made it impossiblefor Latin American nations to repay their debts?

5. Make a similar flow chart for Mexico, based on the information in Chapters 5 and 9. Mexico exports oil. The first item on the flow chart should read: "Mexico makes major new oil discoveries." The last item should read: "Mexico may not repay its foreign debt."

ENRICHMENT AND EXPLORATION

1. Choose one Latin American country. Using library resources such as encyclopedias, almanacs, and the Reader's Guide to Periodical Literature, create a time line that covers significant events in that country's relations with the United State since 1950.

2. Visit a grocery store, an auto supply store, and a variety store. Make a list of products from Latin America that are available there. Combine such information from all members of the class. Create a classroom display showing selected U.S. imports from Latin America.

3. In the 1990s, as military rule in Latin America diminished, the OAS has become more active in protecting democratically elected governments. Find out how the OAS dealt with the overthrow of Haiti's elected government in 1991 or a more recent incident. Make a written or oral report to the class.

4. A political cartoon uses drawings to express an opinion about a news event. Imagine you are a political cartoonist working for a Latin American newspaper. Create a political cartoon expressing your reaction to one of the following U.S. policies: the Monroe Doctrine, Manifest Destiny, the Roosevelt Corollary, the Good Neighbor Policy, the Alliance for Progress.

5. Consult the graph about Latin American debt on page 233. For each of the six nations, calculate how much each person in that country owes. To do this, find each country's population. Then divide the country's debt by its population. Make a new graph showing the per capita (per person) debt for each country.

Glossary

altiplano (ahl-tee-PLAH-noh): the high plateau of Bolivia and Peru

amnesty (AM-nus-tee): a general pardon of prisoners

archipelago (ahr-kuh-PEL-uh-goh): a group of islands

audiencia (ow-dee-EN-cee-ah): in the Spanish colonies, a court appointed by the king to assure that the viceroy carried out his orders

barrio (bah-REE-oh): a neighborhood, usually segregated by income level, in a Latin American city

buccaneer (buhk-uh-NEER): a pirate who raided the islands of the West Indies during the 1600s and 1700s

captain: in Brazil, a person appointed by the Portuguese king to rule a large district of land

caravel (KAIR-uh-vel): a small, light sailing ship developed by the Portuguese in the 15th century; unlike other ships of the time, it could sail against the wind

caudillo (kow-DEE-yoh): "strong man"; a Latin American dictator, usually a military leader

chinampa (chee-NAHM-pah): one of the artificial islands on which the Aztecs farmed

conquistador (kahn-KEES-tah-dohr): a Spanish adventurer who led the conquest of the Indian civilizations of the Americas

Contadora bloc (kohn-tah-DOH-rah): an association of Mexico, Venezuela, Colombia, and Panama to work for peace in Central America

contra (KOHN-trah): in the 1980s, a member of a U.S.-backed guerrilla group in Nicaragua that sought to overthrow the Sandinista government

convoy: a group of merchant ships sailing together and protected by warships

cordillera (kohr-dee-YEH-rah): a chain of volcanic mountains in Costa Rica

coup (koo): the violent overthrow of a government

criollo (kree-OH-loh): in Spain's American colonies, a person of European ancestry born in America

Cristero (kree-STEH-roh): one of a rebel band organized in Mexico in the 1920s to protest government policies toward the Roman Catholic Church

crown colony: a British colony ruled directly by the British government

devalue: to lower the value of a nation's currency

dialect: a form of language spoken in a particular region or by a particular social class, differing in vocabulary, grammar, and pronunciation from other dialects of the same language

drug cartel (kahr-TEL): a large group of independent organizations that work together to deal in illegal drugs

ejido (ay-HEE-doh): a farm owned and worked by the community, which shares its products

embargo: the prohibition of trade with a country

encomienda (en-koh-mee-EN-dah): a system under which Indians were forced to work as laborers for Spanish and Portuguese colonists; the colonists were supposed to protect and educate the Indians, but in fact treated them as slaves

estancia (es-TAHN-see-ah): a vast cattle ranch in Argentina

238

estuary: the wide mouth of a river where the current is affected by the tides of the sea

extended family: a family unit that includes several generations

extradite: to turn an arrested person over to another state or country to be tried on criminal charges

favela (fah-VEL-ah): a shantytown in Brazil

fazenda (fah-ZEN-dah): an enormous sugar planation established by the Portuguese in Brazil

fiesta (fee-ES-tah): a festival

gasohol: a mixture of gasoline and alcohol, used as a fuel

gaucho (GOW-choh): an Argentine cowboy on the pampas

Grito de Dolores (GREE-toh day doh-LOH-rays): "Cry of Dolores"; an 1810 statement demanding that Spain grant independence to Mexico

gross national product: the total value of goods and services produced in a nation each year

guerrilla (guh-RIL-uh): a member of an irregular, usually small military force, trained to move quickly and attack without warning

hacienda (hah-see-EN-dah): a large commercial farm in Latin America

ideographic writing (id-ee-oh-GRAF-ik): picture writing

illiterate (il-LIT-er-it): unable to read or write

import substitution: encouraging domestic manufacture of goods that previously were imported

infant mortality rate: the percentage of children who die before reaching the age of one year

inflation: rising prices and a corresponding decrease in the value of money

junta (HUN-tah): a small group of military leaders that rules a country after the overthrow of its previous government

land reform: distribution by the government of land among peasants

latifundia (lah-tee-FOON-dee-ah): large agricultural estates owned by a wealthy few and farmed by peasants under slavelike conditions

liberation theology: the belief held by some Latin American priests in the 1960s that the Roman Cathlic Church should play an active role in helping to eliminate poverty

life expectancy: the average number of years that people in a place live

literacy rate: the percentage of persons in a place who can read and write

llanero (yah-NEH-roh): a skilled horseback rider on the llanos

llanos (YAH-nohs): Spanish for "plains"; tropical grasslands of Venezuela and Colombia

magic realism: a technique of many Latin American writers that combines dreamlike and realistic elements

maize: corn

maquiladora (mah-keel-ah-DOH-rah): in Mexico, a factory near the U.S. border, U.S.-owned but with Mexican workers

mercantilism (MUHR-kuhn-til-iz-um): an economic policy under which colonies supply raw materials and serve as markets for colonizing countries

meseta (meh-SEH-tah): the central plateau of Costa Rica, where most of the people live

mestizo (mes-TEE-zoh): a person of mixed European and Indian ancestry

Mexican Cession: territory transferred by Mexico to the United States in 1848, including present-day California, Nevada, Utah, and parts of New Mexico, Arizona, and Colorado

milpas (MEEL-pahs): cornfields of the Maya

Monroe Doctrine: a U.S. policy, announced in 1823, warning European powers not to interfere in the Americas

mulatto (muh-LAHT-oh): a person of mixed European and African ancestry

nationalize: to transfer privately owned resources or industries to government ownership

neutral: not taking sides in a conflict

pampas: the grassy, treeless plains of central Argentina

peninsulares (peh-neen-soo-LAH-rays): in Spanish colonies, people who had been born in Spain; the small, privileged group at the top of colonial society

peonage: a system of labor under which Indians were forced by their debts to continue working for colonists

peon: a person forced to work for a colonial employer until his or debts to the employer were paid

per capita income (puhr KAP-ih-tuh): the average income of the people in a place

piñata (peen-YAH-tuh): a brightly decorated papier-maché or clay container filled with toys and candy and hung from the ceiling; children take turns hitting it with a stick until it breaks open

plaza: a town square

population density: the number of people living in a place in relation to its area; usually expressed as the number of people per square mile

pre-Columbian civilizations: civilizations that flourished in the Americas before the arrival of Christopher Columbus

protectorate (proh-TEK-tuhr-it): a region controlled by a foreign power while the native ruler remains the official head of the government

quipu (KEE-poo): bundles of knotted and colored string used by the Inca to keep records and send messages

rain shadow: an area that receives little rainfall because it is blocked by the mountains

Rastafarian (ras-tuh-FAIR-ee-un): a member of a Jamaican religious group that worships the Ethiopian Emperor Haile Selassie and believes that all people of African descent should live in Africa

reggae (REG-ay): the popular Jamaican music and dance of the Rastafarians

repartimiento (reh-par-tee-MYEN-toh): a system requiring all male Indians to work for a certain amount of time each year in colonial Spanish mines, factories, farms, or ranches

Roosevelt Corollary (KOHR-uh-lair-ee): a U.S. policy, announced in 1904, that the United States would act as an "international police power" to prevent foreign nations from interfering in the Western Hemisphere

Sandinista (sahn-dee-NEES-tah): a member of a group that overthrew the Somoza regime in Nicaragua and established a government with close ties to Cuba and the Soviet Union

subsidy (SUB-sid-ee): payment for a product at a price greater than its market value

surrealism (suhr-REE-uhl-iz-um): an artistic movement that sought to portray life as if it were a dream

tariff: a tax on imports

Third World: the developing nations of Latin America, Africa, and Asia

tierra caliente (TYEHR-ah kah-LYEN-teh): "hot land"; the hot climate zone found at low altitudes

tierra fría (TYEHR-ah FREE-ah): "cold land"; the cold climate zone, found at the highest altitudes

tierra templada (TYEHR-ah tem-PLAH-dah): "temperate land"; the temperate climate zone, found at middle altitudes

tortilla (tohr-TEE-yuh): a corn flour pancake; the basis of the Mexican diet

trade winds: winds that blow steadily toward the equator

trafficking: drug smuggling

tropics: the region between the Tropic of Cancer and the Tropic of Capricorn; the climate is generally warm to hot

vertical climate: climate that changes according to altitude; the higher the altitude, the lower the temperature

viceroy (VYS-roy): governor of a Spanish colony, appointed by the king to serve in his place

viceroyalty (vys-ROY-uhl-tee): in the Spanish colonies, the area governed by a viceroy

yerba maté (YEHR-bah mah-TAY): bitter tea grown in Paraguay

Bibliography

Chapter 1

Burno, E. Bradford. *Latin America*. Englewood Cliffs, N.J.: Prentice Hall, 1990.

Forsyth, Adrian, and Mujata, Kenneth. *Tropical Nature*. New York: Scribner, 1984.

Morrison, Marion. *Central America*. Englewood Cliffs, N.J.:Silver Burdett Press, 1989.

Chapter 2

Moctezuma, Eduardo Matos. *Treasures of the Great Temple*. La Jolla, CA: ALTI, 1990.

Sabloff, Jeremy A. *The Cities of Ancient Mexico: Reconstructing a Lost World*. New York: Thames and Hudson, 1989.

Salmoral, Manuel Lucena. *America 1492: Portrait of a Continent 500 Years Ago*. New York: Facts on File, 1990.

Schele, Linda. *A Forest of Kings: The Untold Story of the Ancient Maya*. New York: William Morrow and Company, 1990.

Chapter 3

Prescott, William H. *The Civilization of the Incas and Pizarro's Discoveries and Disasters*. Albuquerque: Institute for Economic and Political World Strategic Studies, 1988.

Chapter 4

Ford, Peter. *Around the Edge: A Journey among Pirates, Guerrillas, Former Cannibals, and Turtle Fishermen along the Miskito Coast*. New York: Viking Penguin, 1991.

Gross, Susan H., and Bingham, Marjorie W. *Women in Latin America: From Pre- Columbian Times to the Twentieth Century Vol. I*. Saint Louis Park, MN: Glenhurst Publications, 1985.

Gross, Susan H., and Bingham, Marjorie W. *Women in Latin America: The Twentieth Century Vol. II*. Saint Louis Park, MN: Glenhurst Publications, 1985.

Chapter 5

Machado, Manuel A. *Centaur of the North: Francisco Villa, the Mexican Revolution and Northern Mexico*. Austin, TX: Eakin Press, 1989.

Oster, Patrick. *The Mexicans: A Personal Portrait of a People*. New York: William Morrow and Company, 1989.

Rummel, Jack. *Mexico*. New York: Chelsea House, 1990.

Chapter 6

Delano, Jack. *Puerto Rico Mio: Four Decades of Change*. Washington, D.C.: Smithsonian Institution, 1990.

Chapter 7

Biesanz, Richard *et al*. *Costa Ricans*. Prospect Heights, IL: Waveland Press, 1988.

Burgos-Debray, Elisabeth. *I, Rigoberta Menchu: An Indian Woman in Guatemala*. London: Verson, 1984.

Gelman, Rita Golden. *Inside Nicaragua: Young People's Dreams and Fears*. New York: Franklin Watts, 1988.

Krauss, Clifford. *Inside Central America: Its People, Politics, and History*. New York: Smith Books, 1991.

Perez-Brignoli, Hector. *A Brief History of Central America*. Berkeley, CA: University of California Press, 1989.

Wekesser, Carol, ed. *Central America: Opposing Viewpoints*. San Diego, CA: Greenhaven Press, 1990.

Chapter 8

Editors of Time-Life Books. *Brazil*. Amsterdam: Time-Life Books, 1986.

Freyre, Gilberto. *The Mansions and Shanties of Modern Brazil*. Berkeley: University of California Press, 1986.

Guillermopietro, Alma. "Letter from Medellín," *The New Yorker*, April 22, 1991.

Martz, John D. "Colombia at the Crossroads," *Current History*, February, 1991.

Meiselas, Susan, ed. *Chile: Seen from Within*. New York: W. W. Norton, 1990.

Chapter 9

Blasier, Cole. *The Giant's Rival: The USSR and Latin America*. Pittsburgh, PA: University of Pittsburgh Press, 1983.

Information Aids, Inc. *Latin America and the United States*. Plano, TX: Information Aids, Inc., 1987.

Nuñez, Emilio, and Taylor, William. *Crisis in Latin America*. Chicago: Moody Press, 1989.

Index